The International Relations of Middle-earth

The
International Relations
of
Middle-earth

LEARNING FROM
The Lord of the Rings

Abigail E. Ruane *&*
Patrick James

The University of Michigan Press · *Ann Arbor*

Published in the United States of America by
The University of Michigan Press
Manufactured in the United States of America
⊗ Printed on acid-free paper.

2015 2014 2013 2012   4 3 2 1

A CIP catalog record for this book is available from the British Library.

Library of Congress Cataloging-in-Publication Data

Ruane, Abigail E.
    The international relations of Middle-Earth : learning from The lord of the rings / Abigail E. Ruane and Patrick James.
        p. cm.
    Includes bibliographical references and index.
        ISBN 978-0-472-07182-1 (cloth : alk. paper) — ISBN 978-0-472-05182-3 (pbk. : alk. paper) — ISBN 978-0-472-02859-7 (e-book)
        1. International relations—Philosophy. 2. Feminist theory. 3. Tolkien, J. R. R. (John Ronald Reuel), 1892–1973. Lord of the rings. 4. Middle Earth (Imaginary place) 5. International relations in literature. I. James, Patrick, 1957– II. Title.

JZ1242.R83   2012
327.101—dc23
                                                        2012005035

Acknowledgments

Our collaboration has been characterized by the best kind of egalitarianism and professional conduct. Each of us has contributed equally to this project. We are grateful to each other for making the journey of developing this book just as refreshing as the subject matter. Furthermore, we are encouraged about the outlook for engagement between scholars with ties to more critical and more problem-solving approaches because of our own engagement and dialogue.

Colleagues have commented constructively on this project throughout its development. For reactions to work at early stages, we are indebted to the anonymous reviewers from *International Studies Perspectives*, the journal that published our initial study. We also thank Christina Gray, Stuart J. Kaufman, Angela McCracken, V. Spike Peterson, Jennifer Sterling-Folker, Ann Tickner, and especially the late Hayward Alker Jr. for thoughtful comments on previous drafts of the article. We are particularly grateful to have benefited from Hayward's attentive and extensive critique before his passing and will miss his excellent colleagueship.

Some have read this manuscript in full or in part and offered helpful commentary. We are grateful to the referees, along with Catia C. Confortini, Cynthia Enloe, and Angela McCracken. Carolyn C. James read multiple drafts of our manuscript and offered extensive commentary. She also used the manuscript in her International Relations of Middle-earth classes at Pepperdine University; the students helped this project by providing reactions to earlier drafts. Both of us are also grateful to the Center for International Studies and School of International Relations at the University of Southern California for supporting this project.

Abigail Ruane would also like to thank the Josephine De Kármán Fellowship Trust for financial assistance, and her family (Alex, Aidan, and Kiana Ruane) for their encouragement and support during this time. Finally, we thank Jennifer Barrios, Ki Evelyne Kim, and Daniel J. Smith, who provided excellent assistance with the preparation of this manuscript.

We are very grateful to our outstanding editor, Melody Herr, who provided valuable advice and guidance at all stages of this project. We also appreciate the fine work of Susan Cronin in the handling of our manuscript.

Contents

Introduction: Middle-earth, *The Lord of the Rings*, and International Relations

After disputed Iranian elections in which President Mahmoud Ah-madinejad claimed victory over his rival, Mir-Hossein Mousavi, Iranian government central television put a marathon showing of *The Lord of the Rings* (*LOTR*) on Channel Two to help keep the peace. The government normally treated its citizens to just a couple of Western films per week. However, widespread unrest in June 2009 followed election results that the public perceived to be illegitimate. This response instigated an extra effort by the government to quell riots through entertainment-related incentives, as well as the arrest and slaughter of protesters.

According to one resident of Tehran, the government intended this three-movie marathon to convey a message "Don't worry, be happy." However, for many Iranians, the TV movie "bribe" encouraged resistance: the audience read political meaning into the films. Viewers detected similarities between various characters and Iranian political opponents and religious leaders, even interpreting each part of the trilogy's ending ("*In edame dare.* This will be continued") as a "hesitant slogan, our words of reassurance" ("A Time Reporter in Tehran," *Time*, 2009). In doing so, they used fictional *LOTR* characters to clarify the hero/villain story that they saw in their own world and were inspired by what they saw to persist in opposing Ahmadinejad's regime. Although watching *LOTR* certainly cannot be credited with singlehandedly sustaining Iranian political opposition, it did connect effectively with citizens on issues and questions important to them in a politically charged environment. In this instance, *LOTR* became part of a broader struggle for the "hearts and minds" of people, not just a military battle for their bodies. Thus the tactic of using *LOTR* to distract the public backfired on the government. Instead of staying home and being entertained, many disenfranchised Iranian citizens strengthened their resolve to oppose the regime, at least in part because they interpreted the films as suggesting that *their* battle would continue and current setbacks should be seen as only temporary.

Just as *LOTR* helped people interpret their political environment and draw inspiration in Iran during a time of political turmoil, we hope this book will enable students of International Relations (IR) to clarify their understanding of existing interpretations of world politics and to suggest alternative meanings. This volume seeks to complement efforts to introduce the field of IR systematically through textbooks while retaining a connection with long-standing issues and current events. What makes this book unique is its use of the imaginary world from *LOTR* to obtain insights about the one we live in today. The journey begins with tentative answers to two sets of queries.

1. What are the lasting questions about international affairs that we as citizens of the world want to see answered? Which contemporary issues are most important to address?
2. Can we enhance learning about global politics in our world through study of an imaginary world? If that is possible, why should J. R. R. Tolkien's "Middle-earth" be chosen? In what way is Tolkien's story of the Ring of Power, told in *LOTR*, especially worthy of attention?

Before considering these questions, however, it may be helpful to look over appendix A, which overviews the story of the Ring of Power as it takes place in the imaginary world of Middle-earth up to its climax. This material is essential for those who have neither read the books nor seen the film versions and can refresh the memories of those already familiar with Middle-earth. The ending of *LOTR* also appears in appendix B, to be introduced later in this book.

MAJOR QUESTIONS AND ISSUES

Have you ever heard the story of the blind men and the elephant? In this Indian story, a group of blind men touch an elephant to find out what it is like. However, because each man touches a different part of the elephant (e.g., forehead, leg, ear), none of them can agree on what it is they are touching (a breast? a pillar? a fan?) (Sharma 2000, 52–53). In the version of this story taken from the philosophy of Jainism (time honored in India), a wise man resolves the conflict by pointing out that all the men are right: the elephant has all of those parts but is one elephant.

Like the people in this story, IR scholars tell stories about international conflict and cooperation in our world. These stories can be understood as myths that IR as a discipline draws on to address various major aspects of world politics. Such stories or myths are ways of making sense of the things we deal with in our experience. However, as the story of the blind men and the elephant suggests, different stories focus on different parts of the world as understood from different perspectives. Understanding different IR perspectives as myths can help us both organize our understanding of international politics and see the benefits and limits of understanding international politics in these ways. This book is meant to introduce students to IR perspectives in that way and to demonstrate how these perspectives have been applied to international politics on the ground.

To begin with, what are some key questions in IR scholarship? Across history, two questions have guided pretty much any specific point of interest about IR.

1. How can the world be made a *more stable* place?
2. How can the world be made a *more fair* place?

These queries can be applied across a broad range of issue areas, including:

a. Weapons of Mass Destruction (WMDs), conventional war, and terrorism
b. Human rights and security
c. Globalization, states, and people
d. Inequality and development
e. Environmental degradation
f. Population and global health

These major questions have been asked for thousands of years. While the specific issues listed are topical now, none fits the description of a "fad." All command the attention of policymakers and academics and remain both pressing and unresolved. Although specific issue areas often are discussed more in terms of one question (e.g., stability or order) than another (e.g., fairness or justice), both sets of questions are relevant to all issue areas.

Several key issues in today's world particularly bring to mind the first question: How can the world be made a more stable place? Responses to this first issue usually focus on what can broadly be understood as "Order." *Order* usually refers to a stable and predictable status quo that tends to support common goals such as freedom from violence, enforcement of promises, and reduction of chaos (Bull 2002: 4). As such, some kind of Order is a precondition of safety.

Many things threaten the international society of states that orders our world today. Great danger is posed by WMDs. Nuclear arsenals in Iran, North Korea, and Pakistan, to cite today's principal instances, give pause to people everywhere. Recent confrontations, along with the closed nature of the regimes in question, create a sense of danger. While less overwhelming than conflict involving WMDs, conventional war continues to plague the world. Interstate wars in Afghanistan and Iraq have turned into lingering, destructive civil strife. Recent events in North Africa include the overturning of long-lived autocracies in Tunisia and Egypt, along with revolution in Libya; while encouraging in many ways, these events—most notably those in Tripoli—create the possibility that major violence will ensue throughout the region. Al-Qaeda and other terrorist organizations, mostly but not exclusively associated with radical Islam, continue to pose a menace while raising questions about the underlying reasons behind their origins and persistence.

In addition to these threats to states or the state system, there are threats to individual security. Violations of human rights both reduce individual security and increase opportunities for interstate and other intergroup disorder and conflict. Human rights rhetoric contrasts bleakly with human wrongs practiced in so many places; people are neither totally safe nor secure in most places in the world. The silencing of critics by China's government, notably against the backdrop of the Beijing Olympics of 2008, and Iran's questionable election and associated violence in 2009 are just two examples among many.

Matters beyond human survival and safety are particularly brought to mind by the second general question: How can the world be made a more fair place? Answers to this query are linked to the greater concept of Justice. Globalization is an ongoing source of controversy. Is the expanding interdependence of the world a good thing for its people? Its effects certainly are not uniform. The overall issue then becomes one of whether gains in some areas or for some people are worth losses in others or for other people. What about the staggering gap in wealth between rich and poor states, generally referred to in IR as the North and the South because of their usual locations in the respective hemispheres? Can anything be done to close the development gap without making everyone worse off as a result? This query leads into the issue of the environment. As more countries industrialize, especially huge ones like China and India, the world must be ready to pursue collective action to avert serious environmental degradation. The South is industrializing and pursuing a standard of living closer to that of the North, but only limited good will result from that process if development is not environmentally sustainable. Other issues, such as the world's growing population and concerns about global health, also require significant attention and are linked to development and the environment. Along with shortages of water and other basic needs, the risk of pandemics threatens global health in a sustained and pressing way.

Thinking about how to manage or resolve increasingly global challenges must start somewhere. We organize our discussion with these perennial questions about the stability that makes survival possible on the one hand (Order) and the fairness that makes life worthwhile on the other (Justice). While at first glance different issues are linked to different questions, Order and Justice are always intertwined. This will become more apparent as you read through this book. One example of this is the condition of the environment: Burning fossil fuels at unsustainable rates increases risks of extreme weather such as heat waves and hurricanes, which can destabilize societies (an issue of Order). The current Order of society is highly dependent on fossil fuels, which prioritizes the interests of oil and coal companies today at the expense of both future generations and vulnerable populations right now, which bear the brunt of the costs of environmental degradation (an issue of Justice). Another example of this linkage is human security: investment in militarized state security may contain the aggression of other states, promoting the current international Order. However, militarization may also increase human insecurity, especially for women and certain men for whom it normalizes a continuum of violence from the personal to the international—an issue of Justice. Thus, categorizing issues in terms of either Order or Justice should not be regarded as mutually exclusive, exhaustive, or permanent.

The issues we have raised have staying power among what dominates the headlines of today. The general questions, in some form or another, have been asked by IR scholars across human history and are very unlikely to be answered once and for all time. This volume is intended to facilitate thinking about the overarching concepts of Order and Justice as informed by history, contemporary experience, and the imaginary world of Middle-earth. As such, it is meant to help students think about the subject of world politics, and about how the stories IR scholars tell about it help our understanding of world politics in some ways and limit it in others. Students are encouraged to follow current events and ask themselves about what questions have not been asked that should be, and what current priorities should be rearranged.

IMAGINARY WORLDS: MIDDLE-EARTH
AND THE RING OF POWER

We build on a newly emerging dialogue that addresses the intersection of popular culture and IR. A leading feminist scholar calls for accessing the arts to obtain insights about IR not otherwise available (Sylvester 2002b: 316, 317). The case also is made specifically for utopian and dystopian feminist science fiction as a means of gaining new insights into world politics (Crawford 2006: 198, 199). We also see a similar call for "poetic inspiration" in search of "multiple worlds" in IR (Athangelou 2004: 21, 22). Our work builds on the insights of such scholars, who emphasize how drawing on multiple media and a wide range of perspectives can avert cognitive closure.[1]

We propose that light waves are a useful analogy for understanding how to think about the relationships between different perspectives on global politics. As Isaac Newton discovered, white light is made up of a rainbow of visible light. This becomes clear by playing with prisms: if you shine white light through a prism, it separates into a rainbow of colors;

---

1. See also Boyer et al. 2002; Dougherty 2002; Kuzma and Haney 2001; Morgan 2006; Nexon and Neumann 2006; Rowley 2007; Tierney 2007;Waalkes 2003; Weber 2001, 2005; Webber 2005; and Weldes 2003.

and if you shine this rainbow through another prism, it combines those colors back into white light. So, too, each perspective provides a particular lens that sheds a certain kind of light on the world. All focus on certain colors or patterns over others in order to organize the complexity of our changing world. For some, things look red, for others blue. No single color provides unfiltered light, and no single perspective has all of the answers. White light is made up of rainbows. With this in mind, we think it is important to recognize that the strongest understanding of global politics requires diverse perspectives.

Our volume seeks to connect systematically with popular culture in two ways: (1) to *illustrate* the stories IR scholars tell about world politics, and (2) to *critique* those stories and suggest what might be missing. Nexon and Neumann (2006: 11–12) describe this as being both a *light* and a *mirror* for academic study.

First, as a light, popular culture can illustrate and explore political theory and historical events. For example, the Iranian citizens discussed earlier drew comparisons between the apparently defeated presidential candidate Mir-Hossein Mousavi in Iran and the character Boromir in *LOTR* as both being "imperfect warrior[s] ready to die to defend humanity" ("A Time Reporter in Tehran," *Time*, 26 June 2009). In another example, a review of the movie version of *The Two Towers* compares the Fellowship's mission to the West's struggle against radical Islam, noting that Saruman looks "eerily" like Osama bin Laden (*"The Lord of the Rings: The Two Towers," Time*, 23 December 2002). In these cases, Iranians and Americans drew on fictional *LOTR* characters to clarify the stories about heroes, villains, and the many people in between in their own world.

Of course, analogies are never perfect: they highlight certain similarities and minimize other differences. In the cases just noted, *LOTR* characters are used to highlight characteristics that reinforce stories about "good guys" and "bad guys." However, in this text, we will use *LOTR* characters to illustrate different ways of seeing and engaging with the world. In doing so, we do *not* mean that scholars who advocate a particular theory should be associated with the vices or virtues of related characters from *LOTR;* instead, we mean that certain characters may be *explained* most effectively by one theory or another. Although our world and Middle-earth are clearly different in many ways, as a light *LOTR* still can clarify our understandings of politics by providing illustrations we relate to in order to clarify different IR perspectives on politics.

Second, as a mirror, popular culture can help us to be more critical and move away from our a priori beliefs and open up to new points of view (Nexon and Neumann 2006: 12). For example the Iranian citizens discussed earlier continued their opposition despite official propaganda saying that the political battle was "over"—in part because of inspiration such as from *LOTR* credits saying in Farsi and then English: "*In edame dare.* This will be continued" ("A Time Reporter in Tehran," *Time*, 26 June 2009). In this case, rather than clarifying or illustrating existing perspectives, *LOTR* provides its own unique form of inspiration. So, too, *LOTR* can help us see how politics in our world continues beyond the traditional stories IR scholars tell about it and keep an eye out for political struggles that are hidden (in the credits or elsewhere) rather than being center stage.

Popular culture can do both of these things because it includes stories of its own that help make our world more meaningful. These stories are instructive because we recognize them *as stories,* rather than any complete or impartial truth. Because of this, popular culture can help us see how other stories we tell (especially in IR) also create meaning but are influenced by perspective. We believe it is important to engage with *LOTR* to both illustrate (as a light) and critique (as a mirror) so that students can learn from political theories without losing their ability to think critically and creatively about the world on their own terms.

A clear combination, therefore, exists for *LOTR* as mythology and IR as curriculum to engage students more effectively with abstract concepts. As Webber (2005: 389) argues, those of us alive today, perhaps more than people at any other time, live in a world of fantasy: vastly greater exposure to all manner and variety of fictional entertainment is the norm, at least in the developed world. Delving into a fantasy world and linking it to reality, therefore, is an idea whose time has come, whether the desire is to communicate ideas about IR or other fields or to critique those ideas. Thus, by connecting with popular culture, film can help students look forward to IR courses (Tierney 2007), get excited about politics (Dougherty 2002), and engage more because of increased stimulation, concretized abstractions, and affective learning (Kuzma and Haney 2001; Boyer et al. 2002).[2] By incorporating storytelling into the study of

---

2. *The Lord of the Rings* is available in both narrative and film, and as such it allows us to engage with it in both a more dictated way (as film) and a more imaginative way (as novel). The exposition that follows focuses primarily on the novel rather than the film version, but it is understood that the latter creates the more immediate opportunity to connect with

IR, we will take advantage of this proven technique to illuminate prominent theories.

As one particular story within popular culture, Tolkien's (1993, 1994) epic literary trilogy, a renowned work of literature set in a fictional world known as Middle-earth, is a potential gift to pedagogy and self-awareness in IR for both experienced scholars and students. Written over half a century ago, this classic tale of adventure returned to prominence with the release of three very successful movies in the last decade, each corresponding to one book in the trilogy: *LOTR* includes *The Fellowship of the Ring*, *The Two Towers* and *The Return of the King*. It is an excellent resource for us because of its prominence, familiarity, and depth.

Since *LOTR*'s publication in 1954–55, its story has achieved a degree of prominence rivaled by very few told in history—a cultural phenomenon, as described by Shippey (2001) in *J. R. R. Tolkien: Author of the Century*. Tolkien's trilogy is estimated to have sold over fifty million copies. Middle-earth is credible because many things in it are recognizable (Kocher 2004). Few worlds created ever have been so intricate as to inspire their own multivolume history spanning thousands of pages (Tolkien 2002a, 2002b, 2002c). Middle-earth also includes fourteen invented languages (Chance 2001: 3). Appendixes to *The Return of the King* (III: 1009–1112) incorporate specifics about calendars and geography, along with a sweeping historical summary that appears at greater length in the multivolume history noted earlier. Tolkien's meticulous creation of Middle-earth even includes references to phases of the moon that are consistent across the full story. Other manifestations of Middle-earth's complexity are publication of *The Tolkien Companion* (a guidebook and encyclopedia) and *The Atlas of Middle-earth* (containing many maps), both by authors other than Tolkien himself (Tyler 1976; Fonstad [1979] 1991).

Tolkien's work is as visible as ever in academe as well: "Master's theses and doctoral dissertations continue to appear; handbooks and concordances that aid the scholarly reading of Tolkien have been added to the bookshelf" (Chance 2001: 17). Consider also the Tolkien Society, founded in 1969 "for those who would wander with friends in Middle-

---

students because of the vastly popular movies from the turn of the millennium. For that reason, references to the novel mention the three volumes (I, II, and III) that correspond to the movies rather than the six books that collectively make up the three volumes in which the novel frequently is published. It should be noted that Tolkien scholars normally cite the six books within a single-volume edition of *LOTR*.

earth." The society holds an annual gathering in September, usually at Oxford University, where Tolkien held a professorship for a long time, and it also sponsors more limited events throughout the year (http://www.tolkiensociety.eu/index.html).

With regard to popular culture, bumper stickers that proclaim "Frodo Lives" and substantial acclaim for all three movies about the trilogy (appearing in 2001, 2002, and 2003, they all received Best Picture nominations and stand sixteenth, ninth, and second, respectively, in world box office receipts [http://www.imdb.com/boxoffice/alltime gross?region=world-wide]), among other manifestations, make the staying power of *LOTR* quite obvious. *The Return of the King* won eleven Academy Awards, including Best Picture. References to *LOTR* story lines and characters pervade popular culture. For example, in an article in *Sports Illustrated* on the Los Angeles Lakers, the team's near-legendary coach, Phil Jackson, is described as "Gandalf." " 'He's a mysterious dude,' [Shannon] Brown says, but the mystery is part of the magic" (Jenkins 2010: 44). As this reference suggests, *LOTR* characters are well known enough to convey a relatively complex set of ideas to a broad audience.

The chapters that follow expand on how students and teachers alike can benefit from examining intersections of IR with Tolkien's *LOTR* and popular culture more broadly. Tolkien's Middle-earth clearly is a priority for this kind of intellectual venture: its depth facilitates comparison with real world events, its popularity makes it highly familiar, and its characters also interestingly show a limited understanding of their world—something that is helpful in learning about foreign policy decision making in particular and IR in general. This is a good point at which to recognize that Tolkien emphatically rejected attempts to discern allegory in *LOTR* (Wright 2003) and did not intend for readers to link specific characters and events to world history *in real time* (I: xiv–xv). Despite this, we believe that Middle-earth can help teach lessons about world politics that Tolkien himself did not intend, and that it is useful in understanding events that occurred both during his time (e.g., World War I) and afterward (e.g., the War in Iraq).

A summary of *LOTR* is provided in appendix A, with the ending held back until appendix B. Everything essential to understanding references to *LOTR* in the chapters that follow appears in appendix A. Details about the story are added sequentially and as relevant from this point onward. For those who are curious immediately, the movies by Peter Jackson convey the three books in approximately nine hours. (The extended versions of the movies are significantly longer.) The novels are a greater investment of time—but very worthwhile. Many interesting characters and story lines are not even mentioned in the brief summary provided in the appendixes.

SUMMING UP: RATIONALE AND PLAN OF THE BOOK

The overall goal of this book is to join forces with textbooks on IR and to use *LOTR* to make their contents more enlightening about the world around us. To minimize the tendency of IR theory, once encountered, to enhance sophistication on the one hand but also possibly limit imagination on the other, this introduction has focused on broad questions of Order and Justice as applied to our real world, complemented with the "basics" regarding the imaginary world of Middle-earth. Like the "Common Speech" used in Middle-earth, which enables characters from different races or regions to communicate directly, this chapter deliberately stays away from the language of IR theory and intends to set the book's agenda in words that all can understand. Future chapters will delve more deeply into particular IR approaches and issue areas using Tolkien's Middle-earth as a basis for clarification and critique.

This volume can be used either individually or in tandem with a standard textbook on IR. Such works will as a matter of course begin by introducing a theoretical perspective of some kind. Here, however, we start off with two other components—Middle-earth and basic questions about IR—and then make connections with the curriculum. An online appendix lists the textbooks that are referenced from this point onward. In this text, we relate the questions of Order and Justice as addressed by different theoretical perspectives to *LOTR*. Figure 1 illustrates how these different views of the world are brought together in this volume. It lists the peoples of Middle-earth (see appendix A), broad approaches to IR scholarship, and the general questions and issues introduced at the outset of the chapter. Each triangle corresponds to a different lens or window on the world. The IR approaches listed highlight how scholarship tends to be portrayed as taking place between scholars who tend to take the world as it *is* and search for explanations of what goes on in it (i.e., problem solving) or focus on what *ought* to be and how things might be changed (i.e., critical theory) (Cox 1981). These themes will be developed in more detail in subsequent chapters as we work through various characters and story lines from Middle-earth. The question mark in the

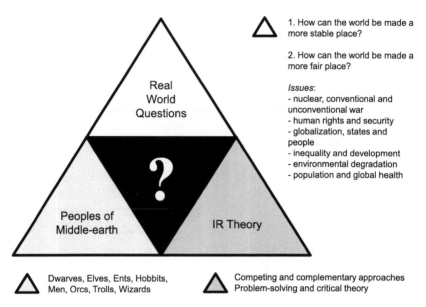

1. How can the world be made a more stable place?

2. How can the world be made a more fair place?

Issues:
- nuclear, conventional and unconventional war
- human rights and security
- globalization, states and people
- inequality and development
- environmental degradation
- population and global health

Dwarves, Elves, Ents, Hobbits, Men, Orcs, Trolls, Wizards

Competing and complementary approaches Problem-solving and critical theory

Fig. 1. Triangulating International Relations

center of the figure represents what will happen when light from all three of the components of this figure is combined. You will be the judge of how that turns out. We hope that, like shining a rainbow of colors through a prism to form white light, combining perspectives on each of these areas will provide a brighter, stronger way of understanding global politics. By the end of the book, this collision of worlds is aimed at helping students take a fresh look at both world politics, and IR as a discipline, thereby developing a stronger, more critical understanding of both.

This book unfolds in eight additional chapters. Chapter 1 uses *LOTR* to encourage a critical eye (using *LOTR* as a mirror). We evaluate Order and Justice in Middle-earth at the time of Frodo's quest. Chapters 2–6 then apply *LOTR* to illustrate IR scholarship (as a light). Chapter 2 focuses on how one might think about IR at a theoretical level, while chapter 3 illustrates contemporary IR through the historical context of the three "Great Debates" of the twentieth century. We use characters and story lines from *LOTR* to illuminate IR's development as a discipline through these exchanges about human nature, methods, and the ways in which knowledge is acquired, respectively. Chapter 4 illuminates a central problem for IR theory: the causes of war. We apply levels of analysis, perhaps the most pervasive concept within problem-solving IR theory, to facilitate a comparison of three wars: World War I, the War in Iraq, and the War of the Ring from Middle-earth. Chapter 5 introduces one kind of critical theory, feminist theory. The chapter explores different kinds of feminist theory from the initial liberal wave onward. Chapter 6 applies a "gender-sensitive lens"—a key concept within feminist IR theory—to the same three wars from Chapter 4: World War I, the War in Iraq, and the War of the Ring in Middle-earth. Chapter 7 revisits *LOTR* as a source of critique (as a mirror); we evaluate potential lessons for IR to be learned from its characters and images. The "Conclusion" reviews the book's contributions and assesses *LOTR*'s ability to help us engage more effectively in IR debates and global politics.

CHAPTER 1

Order, Justice, and Middle-earth

J. R. R. Tolkien's *The Lord of the Rings* is an epic tale that chronicles the quest of Frodo Baggins, along with both expected and unexpected allies, to destroy the Ring of Power and save Middle-earth from evil Sauron. This chapter explores how Tolkien addresses ideas of Order and Justice. We use a technique drawn from literary analysis, tracing a theme (of Order and Justice), to achieve that goal. As part of this enterprise, we compare and contrast images of Mordor, the Shire, and Rivendell in terms of the degree of Justice apparent in their societies and then highlight concerns about how to pursue Justice.

Of course, although we make inferences based on his work, it is important to reiterate that Tolkien wrote *LOTR* as a grand exercise in storytelling. He did not in any way put forward the tale to communicate a particular kind of Justice and Order. Instead, with a lifelong interest in languages and mythology, telling tales about the imaginary world of Middle-earth that would enthrall readers served a purpose for Tolkien in and of itself. Despite this character, Tolkien's story still usefully allows us to address these concepts within the world of Middle-earth.

We set the context for evaluation of Order and Justice in Middle-earth with the Council of Elrond. This meeting determines the strategy of the Free Peoples regarding the Enemy's Ring. It shapes the entire story to come. Attending the Council are representatives of all the Free

Peoples: Wizards, Elves, Dwarves, Hobbits, and Men. The key questions to be answered are:

- What will be done with the Ring?
- Who will do it?

The world at the time of this crisis decision making, in the eyes of those at the Council, is utterly black and white. Sauron is the essence of evil and must be stopped, at all costs, from regaining the Ring. This creates a stark choice regarding strategy. Since it becomes quite clear that the Ring cannot be hidden, the only options left are to use or destroy it.

We will return to the decision made by the Council at a later point in this chapter. For now, we explore relative levels of Order and Justice in three of the domains central to the story of the Ring: the Shire and Rivendell, where Hobbits and Elves live; and Mordor, the home of Sauron. This review provides context, first for understanding how the Council decides what actions to take and, second, for assessing how the Council pursues certain kinds of Justice and Order but also allows other injustices within Middle-earth to continue.

JUST AND UNJUST ORDERS

Tolkien's story develops the concepts of Order and Justice in Middle-earth by conceiving a variety of societies, some of which clearly are more just than others. This becomes evident when we examine the imagery *LOTR* uses to describe different places within Middle-earth. At one extreme, Mordor represents a corrupt and unjust Order, while at the other, the Shire and Rivendell represent examples of relatively more functional and just Order. Each of these places is ordered or organized in more democratic or dictatorial ways, entails different kinds of relatively stable and predictable status quos, and supports more or less common goals. As a result, each location provides different levels of safety and quality of life for different groups of its inhabitants. And overall each place is also—whether implicitly or explicitly—evaluated as constituting a status quo with more or less Justice.

Within the societies of Middle-earth it is clear that Justice is not completely relative and that some orderings of society are more just than others. Despite this, Justice is usually imperfect, and certain segments of society bear more of the brunt of the cost of maintaining the status quo than others. Consequently, what "the best" society looks like depends on one's position and experiences within it. This point was crystalized by Kenneth Arrow, who won the Nobel Prize in Economics in 1972. Among his principal accomplishments is the Arrow Impossibility Theorem. While the theorem can be expressed mathematically, for our purposes its substantive conclusions are sufficient. In particular, it indicates that with three or more options, no method of voting can honor a small number of very innocuous conditions, such as nondictatorship, and produce an unambiguous choice that represents the preferences of group members. In other words, it is impossible to obtain a straightforward conclusion about collective as opposed to individual preferences. This means that it is never clear what is "best" regarding Order for a given society. It requires asking what is best *for whom.*

Mordor

Mordor under Sauron's dictatorship is the antithesis of Justice. It is described as an expansionist, militarized dictatorship ruled by Sauron and used as a stronghold from which to expand his power and desire for world domination (see Barnett 1969; Lloyd 1976; Davidson 2003: 100). When Gandalf first tells Frodo about the Ring, before the beginning of the quest, he says that Sauron's aim is to "beat down all resistance, break the last defenses, and cover all the lands in a second darkness" (I: 51). This darkness would make the "free" lands of the West resemble the land of Mordor. If realized, it would be a devastating change: Mordor is described ominously as "barren and ruinous," a "land of fear," and a "place of dread" edged with "gloomy" mountains around "mournful plains" and a "bitter inland sea" (I: 238; II: 623, 635). It is full of "evil things" (I: 238), including the Ringwraiths, whose "power is terror" (I: 171). The Orcs encountered by Frodo and based there are organized in military units and appear to have the sole purpose of combat bent on conquest. Mordor's "darkness" would enslave the rest of the free world under the domination of evil Sauron.

Dictatorial domination is evident in that even the evil things in Mordor are coerced to stay: Gandalf observes that Mordor "draws all wicked things, and the Dark Power was bending all its will to gather them there" (I: 57). When Merry and Pippin are abducted by the Uruk-hai, even the Orcs show that they are afraid of the Ringwraiths: the Orc Grishnákh responds to a reference to the Ringwraiths by "shivering and licking his lips, as if the word had a foul taste that he savoured painfully" (II: 441). And when Frodo, Sam, and Gollum watch day begin over the black gates before they enter, they see the Orcs begin to work, and Tolkien writes, "Another dreadful day of fear and toil had come to Mordor" (II: 623). This fearful servitude is developed in *The Silmarillion* (Tolkien 1977), which chronicles how certain Elves were imprisoned by Sauron's predecessor and superior, Melkor (also known as Morgoth). He bred Orcs in "envy and mockery" of the Elves, toward whom he had absolute hatred, and these wretched creatures served Melkor out of fear while loathing him as well—a life of absolute misery (I: 50).[1] As such, Mordor is built to support Sauron's interests and goals in pursuing world domination at the expense of all others—even his own army.

Narrow and dictatorial interest embodied in Mordor is further developed in the conversation between Gandalf and Saruman at the Tower of Orthanc when Saruman tries to convince Gandalf to join the dark side. Gandalf later tells the Council of Elrond how Saruman tried to persuade him by saying:

> We must have power, power to order all things as we will, for that good which only the Wise can see. . . . We can bide our time, we can keep our thoughts in our hearts, deploring maybe evils done by the way, but approving the high and ultimate purpose: Knowledge, Rule, Order; all the things that we have so far striven in vain to accomplish, hindered rather than helped by our weak or idle friends. There need not be, there would not be, any real change in our designs, only in our means. (I: 253)

Saruman is basically arguing that because only the Wise (perhaps only he and Gandalf) know how to order things for the "good," these positive ends justify the evil means of temporarily allying with Sauron (see Davidson 2003, 106). However, it becomes clear that a dictator of any kind—even one with possibly good intentions—cannot truly promote Justice.

When Gandalf remains unconvinced, Saruman continues, "The Ruling Ring? If we could command that, then the Power would pass to *us*." Gandalf responds, "Saruman, only one hand at a time can wield the One" (I: 253). Here Saruman tells Gandalf, in essence, that he would

---

1. This is the most popular version of the origins of Orcs, although Tolkien appears to have changed his mind about their beginnings and gave varying inferences about this over time. Regardless of details concerning their origin, however, all versions of Orc creation share the idea that these creatures represent absolute evil.

have the power to define (his idea of) a "good" Order (he repeats this argument later in II: 567). Gandalf, however, calls his bluff. The Ring only answers to one master; consequently, the power to define a good Order could only be Sauron's (or, if Saruman took it, Saruman's). Not only would this be a very narrow basis for defining interests, but, given the description of Mordor, those interests are not shared by Gandalf or the overwhelming majority of the Free Peoples of Middle-earth.

Overall, Mordor is described as being a dark, evil, and fearful place, from its geography and landscape to its emotional impact and organizational structure. It is maintained for the sole purpose of Sauron's militant world domination, and whatever means necessary are used to defend its military stronghold and offensively expand beyond it. This purpose is defined dictatorially and at the expense of most others, even Sauron's own Orcs. It is structured to uphold an all-encompassing, exclusive belief system: adherence to Sauron's power. As such, Mordor would be a tragic and unjust exemplar for the rest of the world to be modeled after, and it provides the clearest example of an unjust Order evident in *LOTR*.

The Shire

Toward the other end of the spectrum, the Shire is described in stark contrast to Mordor: where Mordor is dictatorial, dark, militarized, and fearful, the Shire is collaborative, light, peaceful, and joyful. It is the relatively pacific, populist, and agrarian home of Hobbits, who desire to live simply and well, with little bother to their neighbors (Barnett 1969). In the prologue of *LOTR*, Tolkien notes that Hobbits "love peace and quiet and good tilled earth: a well-ordered and well-farmed countryside was their favorite haunt" (I: 1). They were "a merry folk" and "fond of simple jests at all times, and of six meals a day (when they could get them)" (I: 2); they were "hospitable and delighted in parties and in presents, which they gave away freely and eagerly accepted" (I: 2); and they also "came to think that peace and plenty were the rule in Middle-earth and the right of all sensible folk" (I: 5). The Shire itself is described as "a district of well-ordered business" that was "rich and kindly," full of "well-tilled" earth and able to support "many farms, cornlands, vinyards, and woods" (I: 5). The Hobbits who originally settled the Shire "fell in love with" it (I: 4), and Frodo thinks of it as "safe and comfortable" (I: 61). At earlier times in his life, Frodo has gotten tired of its calm—he has "felt that an earthquake or an invasion of dragons might be good" for the Hobbits of the Shire (I: 61)—but on his quest it becomes a "firm foothold" on which he can look back (I: 61). Overall, the Shire is described as a pacific place in which life is relatively ideal.

Order in the Shire was closer to a clanlike existence than to either democracy or anarchy. Tolkien notes, "The Shire at this time had hardly any 'government.' Families for the most part managed their own affairs. Growing food and eating it occupied most of their time" (I: 9). However, "family management" stood as a strong organizing principle, as the Shire was divided into four quarters, each of which "still bore the names of some of the old leading families," with the Took family preeminent for some centuries. Family management was complemented by minimal government positions: the major government posts were those of the tradition of the King (though no king existed anymore), of Thain (a "nominal dignity" carried by the Took family for some centuries), and of the Mayor (in charge of presiding over banquets and managing the two Shire services of mail and border patrol/animal control) (I: 9–10). Despite the virtually nonexistent bureaucratic infrastructure, Tolkien writes that Hobbits usually "kept the laws of free will, because they were The Rules (as they said), both ancient and just." Tolkien suggests that the Shire relied on family management in a way that supported (with democratic impact if not formal structure) the interests of most Hobbits, who were interested in eating well, exchanging gifts, and participating in community life.

Ultimately, the Shire depended on a global hierarchy to maintain its day-to-day existence. Tolkien emphasizes this much more extensively than the Shire's internal class structure: a repeating theme in *LOTR* is that Hobbits in the Shire are largely unaware of the outside world—such as the rise of evil in the South, or Gondor's sacrifices to keep them safe. In the prologue, Tolkien writes that Hobbits "forgot or ignored what little they had ever known of the Guardians, and of the labours of those that made possible the long peace of the Shire. They were, in fact, sheltered, but they had ceased to remember it" (I: 5). As Boromir points out at the Council of Elrond, the safety of the Hobbits (as well as that of the other Free Peoples) is paid for largely by the people of Gondor (see I: 239–41). Toward the end of the story, when the Shire is overrun with intruders led by Saruman (then known as Sharkey), Hobbits also come to understand the impact of the Rangers' vigilance in their protection, which becomes clearer when the Rangers (led by Aragorn, known then as Strider) are forced to leave so as to support Gondor in its defense against Mordor. Relevant in both regards, Boromir's point at the Council of Elrond implicitly judges an unjust status quo: it is unfair for Rangers and the people of Gondor to pay in blood and treasure for the safety of all of the lands of the West. Why should the burden be distributed so unequally while the benefits are distributed so much more equally? It is unjust. As this suggests, although the Shire is a relatively pacific and just place, it is not perfect, in part because it depends on Gondor and the Rangers to remain in that state.

Rivendell

Like the Shire, Rivendell is described in contrast to Mordor: where Mordor is headed by a malignant dictatorship, Rivendell is headed by a benign lordship; where Mordor is decaying, Rivendell is rejuvenating; where Mordor is dark and evil, Rivendell is light and good. Rivendell is characterized as a safe haven for the Elves, managed by Lord Elrond and used to protect and preserve lore and defend against the Enemy. *The Silmarillion* notes that Rivendell (or Imladris) was founded by Elrond as a "stronghold and refuge" (Tolkien 1977: 288) and used as a base for the Last Alliance against Sauron in earlier times (291). In *LOTR*, Rivendell is again used as a base by what becomes the Fellowship of the Ring in preparation for its quest against Sauron. Gandalf even calls it a "fortress" (I: 221).

Rivendell, however, is a refuge as well as a stronghold: Tolkien describes it as a verdant "green vale" (I: 233) and notes, "Merely to be there was a cure for weariness, fear, and sadness" (I: 219). Pippin says about Rivendell that "it seems impossible, somehow, to feel gloomy or depressed in this place. I feel like I could sing, if I knew the right song for the occasion" (I: 220). In *The Silmarillion,* Tolkien (1977) notes that "the house of Elrond was a refuge for the weary and oppressed, and a treasury of good counsel and wise lore," including records of the ancestry of the Dúnedain (i.e., Aragorn's people) (298); with Lothlórien, it was one of two domains in which "the bliss and beauty of the Elves remained still undiminished while that Age endured" (298).

Taken together, the traits of Rivendell establish it as both a treasury and refuge and a stronghold used to defend against the expansive domination of Sauron. It is characterized in heavenly and idyllic language as a "green vale" (I: 274) full of glimmering and twinkling light (I: 233) and a place of "peace" (I: 65); it was the home of Elves, whom Pippin earlier had described as so beautiful that it was as if he existed "in a waking dream" (I: 81); according to Bilbo, Elrond's home was "a perfect house, whether you like food or sleep or story-telling or singing, or just sitting and thinking best, or a pleasant mixture of them all" (I: 219). Admiration is the basic reaction across the board from other Free Peoples when they encounter Rivendell.

Rivendell is able to be a "stronghold and refuge" because of its power. This power can be understood as rooted in Elrond's wielding of Vilya, the Elven Ring of Air, which enables him to "ward off the decays of time and postpone the weariness of the world" (Tolkien 1977: 288). In *LOTR*, Gandalf hints at this when he tells Frodo before the Council of Elrond that "there is a power in Rivendell to withstand the might of Mordor, for a while" (I: 217). And at his Council, Elrond says of the Elven Rings that "they were not made as weapons of war or conquest: that is not their power. Those who made them did not desire strength or domination or hoarded wealth, but understanding, making, and healing, to preserve all things unstained" (I: 262). This power is manifested when Frodo crosses the ford into Rivendell and the flood stops his Ringwraith pursuers from reaching him. Afterward, Gandalf explains to him that Elrond commanded the flood: "The river of this valley is under his power, and it will rise in anger when he has great need to bar the Ford" (I: 218).

However, the power also is limited: it is meant to preserve rather than be used militarily, and even its healing power is not total. At the Council of Elrond, the Elf Galor asks Elrond about the extent to which they can rely on the power of those who bear the Elven Rings (Elrond, Galadriel, and at one point Círdan): "What power remains lies with us, here in Imladris, or with Círdan at the Havens, or in Lórien. But have they the strength, have we here the strength to withstand the Enemy, the coming of Sauron at the last, when all else is overthrown?" Elrond responds, "I have not the strength . . . neither have they" (I: 259). As such, the power in Rivendell is a limited one, which enables Elrond to preserve lore and provide a refuge to gird efforts against the Enemy. However, it is not strong enough to withstand a direct attack by Sauron in full force.

The preservative rather than dominating power of the Elven Rings suggests that the organization of Elvish society is similarly collaborative rather than dominating. Tolkien's references to Elves generally support this inference. The internal structure of Rivendell is little discussed in *LOTR*, which makes it difficult to determine, one way or another. Only Elrond's position as an overall leader is clear. In *LOTR*, Elves are characterized as highly collaborative rather than dominating—so much so, that it is difficult to have them direct others, even if asked. At their first encounter with Elves on the way out of the Shire, Frodo notes that "it is also said. . . . Go not to the Elves for counsel, for they will say both no and yes," and the Elf Gildor responds, "You have not told me all concerning yourself; and how then shall I choose better than you?" (I: 83). Similarly, in Lothlórien, when Frodo asks if Galadriel advises him to look into her mirror, she responds, "I do not counsel you one way or another. . . . Do as you will!" (I: 354). And in Rivendell, Elrond affirms each individual's decision to be there: "That is the purpose for which you are called hither. Called, I say, though I have not called you to me, strangers from distant lands" (I: 236). Despite this collaborative style, Elves are ordered through Lordships: for example, Elrond is the Lord of Rivendell, and other Elven Lords exist as well. In both *The Silmarillion* and *LOTR*, these hierarchies tend to be patriarchal, with male Elves leading groups, although female Elves (such as Galadriel) can also take this position of leadership. Overall, Tolkien refers to both Rivendell and the Elves in idyllic language and says little in *LOTR* to suggest that their organization is anything other than essentially perfect.

THE COUNCIL OF ELROND, ORDER, AND JUSTICE

Now consider the Council of Elrond as an entity. Its representation appears to be just because each of the Free Peoples has representatives there, although most members are relatively elite. The participants are riveted on the overwhelming issue of what is to be done with the Ring. Order is paramount in a world threatened with domination by the ultimate evil of Sauron. With this priority, however, comes neglect of Justice in full measure. If the members of the Council had been able to look at issues of Order and Justice from the perspective of those on the "bottom rungs" in each society, they would have been better able to notice the many injustices that remained. Certainly, the Shire and Rivendell are more Just than Mordor—but the picture is more complicated. Failing to recognize this creates a missed opportunity for a more creative and comprehensive interpretation of the quest for Just Order in Middle-earth.

The Shire, Revisited

Despite their contrasts, Mordor and the Shire do share a limited degree of similarity. Although it is nowhere to the same degree, both are characterized particularly by certain degrees of social hierarchy: This is most clearly made evident by the internal class structure of the Shire, which Tolkien refers to but does little to critique. Even in the "days of their peace and prosperity," a gap between rich and poor Hobbits resulted in significantly different quality of life outcomes. Tolkien notes, "The poorest went on living in burrows of the most primitive kind, mere holes indeed, with only one window or none; while the well-to-do [like Bilbo and Frodo] constructed more luxurious versions of the simple diggings of old" (I: 6). Tolkien tends to refer to this informal economic class structure in relatively positive terms, noting that Hobbits "were, as a rule, generous and not greedy, but contented and moderate, so that estates, arms, workshops, and small trades tended to remain unchanged for generations" (I: 9).

This description, however, suggests that rich Hobbits remained rich, and poor Hobbits remained poor, with little opportunity for changing the social structure. That family social class tended to extend from one generation to another is also evident in particular cases. For rich Hobbits, Tolkien notes that the Took family had been "pre-eminent" for some centuries and "remained both numerous and exceedingly wealthy, and was liable to produce in every generation strong characters of particular habits and even adventurous temperaments . . . [which] were now tolerated (in the rich) rather than generally approved" (I: 9). For working-class Hobbits, upward mobility appears limited: Tolkien notes that the servant-master relationship between the Gamgee family as gardeners and Bilbo's family as employers had lasted for three generations: the job had passed from Holman Greenhand (Ham Gamgee's cousin) to Ham Gamgee to his youngest son Sam Gamgee (I: 22–23). Both Ham and Sam Gamgee were "on very friendly terms with Bilbo and Frodo" (I: 22), although the relationship in each instance was certainly economically disparate.

While the Justice of the Shire is significantly limited by its hierarchical class structure, it still is clearly a more Just social Order than Mordor. First, the Shire's class system can be seen as more benign in terms of *degree*. Aristocracy does exist, but it is limited. Consider, for example, income distribution. Bag End, the home of Bilbo and Frodo, is superior to accommodations available to Sam Gamgee and others. However, Bag End is not a gated community; in fact, it is next to Bagshot Row, where Hobbits from the lower income strata live. Socializing at the local pub includes both rich and poor Hobbits at the same tables. Note also that Frodo, who is rich, is attired quite similarly to Sam, who is working class. Extravagance in lifestyle is also not evident in the Shire: for example, Bilbo is rumored to be rich beyond belief, but his daily life does not include conspicuous displays of wealth.

Second, the Shire's class system is more informally regulated than the formal, rigid hierarchy of Mordor. This can be illustrated by considering the character of Sam Gamgee. On one hand, although Sam, just like Frodo, is part of the Fellowship on the quest until the very end, he remains distinctly in a separate class from the others throughout it (Hooker 2004). This is evident from introductions where Frodo introduces everyone as "Mr." except for Sam (I: 150) to Gandalf's (unilateral) decision to send Sam on the quest with Frodo as "punishment" for eavesdropping (I: 63) and Pippin's requests that Sam get the breakfast ready and bathwater hot in the morning (I: 71) (see also Hooker 2004). These vignettes fit with the stagnant internal class structure of the Shire, where economic standing is perpetuated over time. Different social standards are applied to members of different classes.

On the other hand, Sam is clearly instrumental to the completion of the quest, and his second-class status certainly evolves over time. After the quest, Sam is elected mayor of the Shire for seven consecutive seven-year terms, a position that indicates he is both popular and respected, as the mayor is the only real official in the Shire (III: appendix B: 1071–72; I: 10).

Third, and finally, the Shire's dependency on Gondor and others for protection is not coerced to anywhere near the same degree as would occur for slaves dependent on Sauron. Like the internal hierarchy of the Shire, the international hierarchy of Middle-earth is largely enforced through the soft power of social expectations rather than the hard power of militant coercion. In fact, the Hobbits of the Shire are complicit in their own dependency: they do little to empower themselves—whether through strengthening their efforts at multilateralism, increasing their military might, or engaging with the outside world in other ways—and instead mostly free ride on the efforts of others. As Frodo's quest suggests, however, this is not because they are *unable* to take action. In fact, the Hobbits' experience in isolating themselves also provides them with a source of strength: unlike many members of other races, who would be tempted to wield the power of the Ring, Frodo shows remarkable resilience to its seductions. Similarly, the self-imposed isolation of Hobbits, which encourages others to underestimate them, may also hide a strength in leadership or diplomacy that could, if drawn on, significantly impact relations among peoples in Middle-earth. Despite this possibility, the international hierarchy of Middle-earth remains, even though the Hobbits' complicity in their dependency suggests that there may at least be some opportunity for change. In comparison, Hobbits and other Free People would have little choice in being slaves if Sauron gained lordship over Middle-earth and would have fewer sources of strength in such a rigidly restrictive setting. Overall, even the global hierarchy on which the Shire is dependent in Middle-earth appears to be far less militantly coercive than what would be imposed under world domination by Sauron.

Rivendell, Revisited

Although the Shire and Rivendell clearly contrast with Mordor in terms of life, light, and good intentions, they share the existence of social hierarchy. This is most clearly evident in the historical gender relations among male and female Elves. To illustrate, consider an ancient love story of the Man Beren and the Elf Lúthien referred to in *LOTR* (for Aragorn's summary, see I: 187–89) but told in full in *The Silmarillion*. In the story, a mortal Man, Beren, falls in love with Lúthien, who is "the fairest of all the Children of the World" (Tolkien 1977: 166) and daughter of the Elf King Thingol and his wife Melian, who is a Maia (angelic being of the same order as Sauron, though uncorrupted). Lúthien loves Beren, too, but when her father finds out about their love, he is furious. King Thingol gives Beren the apparent death sentence of retrieving a glorious jewel (a Silmaril) from the crown of Evil Morgoth (noted already as Sauron's predecessor and superior). Thingol tells Beren that if he does this Thingol will allow Lúthien to choose Beren, and "[t]hen you shall have my jewel" (167). Beren responds, "For little price . . . do Elven-kings sell their daughters" (168) and decides to accomplish the task. The rest of the story tells of how Beren tries to accomplish the seemingly impossible. He is aided again and again when hope seems lost by Lúthien, even though her father, Thingol, locks her up to prevent her from supporting Beren and other Elf Lords abduct her. Furthermore, even Beren himself repeatedly tries to leave her behind for her own protection. Eventually, they together take the Silmaril from Sauron's crown, and Beren gives it to King Thingol. However, it is at great cost.

As this tale suggests, despite its major differences with Mordor, Rivendell shares with the dark empire a reliance on social hierarchy: in this case, a gendered social hierarchy. This tale of Beren and Lúthien is referenced repeatedly in *LOTR* as one of the great love stories of all time. However, it highlights the clear injustices that Elven women can face both within their societies and within their own families. Here, although Thingol supposedly loves Lúthien "above all things" (Tolkien 1977: 166), he treats her like a commodity that can be traded; she has no say in her marital decisions, and Thingol does not deem it unreasonable to lock her up against her will to stop her from aiding Beren. Similarly, the Elf Lords who abduct Lúthien apparently believe that their action is justified, despite it being against her will, because they believe that marrying her would "advance their power" (173). Even Beren, who is a mere Man with relatively little power, ignores Lúthien's powerful heritage, and even after Lúthien saves him from death, Beren still tries to "protect" her by leaving her behind and trying to complete his quest alone.

This tale implies that the Order maintained by Elves is characterized by less than full Justice. Lúthien's value as a person is minimized and her opportunities restricted, while at the same time she is upheld as a beauty without compare; this is accomplished through the belittling of her interests, concerns, and abilities by the men in her life, whether out of concern for her "protection" or the simple decision that her interests are secondary to theirs. As such, this story suggests that, although Elves may not dominate the decisions of others, this standard may not always apply within their own families or groups. Furthermore, it suggests that even the apparently benign (usually patriarchal) governance of the Elves can be restrictive and harmful, particularly when the interests of those in charge (the men) are different from the interests of those subordinated (the women). Consequently, although the Elves in Rivendell may provide an alternative, relatively just exemplar in Middle-earth, it is imperfect because it is not structured to provide protection from internal abuses, particularly those suffered by women in Elven families.

While the Justice of Rivendell is significantly limited by its hierarchical gender relations, it still is clearly a more Just social Order than Mordor's. First, although Thingol's behavior in trading his daughter for a jewel demeans and restricts her, his intention is certainly to promote *his interpretation* of her best interests. Thingol states, "I sell not to Elves or Men those whom I love and cherish above all treasure. And if there were hope or fear that Beren should come back ever to Menegroth, he should not have looked again upon the light of heaven, although I had sworn it" (Tolkien 1977: 168). In other words, Thingol assessed Beren's errand as hopeless, and, even if somehow Beren came back, he had no intention of honoring any sort of "deal" for Lúthien. This is a major contrast to Mordor, where Sauron looks after his own interests and does not even attempt to pursue (even his interpretation of) the best interests of those under his domination.

Second, the constraints imposed on Lúthien do not stop her from taking an active, rather than passive and victimized, role in pursuing her goals. Although Lúthien's goal of being with Beren is blocked repeatedly by her father and lover (for her "protection") and the Elf Lords who abduct her (in their own power-seeking interests), these obstacles cannot stop her from asserting and pursuing her goals.

Consider in that context more general observations about dependency in our world. Social theorists point out that people who are made dependent on others often can be assumed to be passive victims who are unable to contribute in a valuable way. However, it is frequently their position of dependency, rather than any of their inherent qualities, that limit them.

For example, feminists have argued that women (especially minority women) are often made dependent, whether on men or state welfare programs, through unjust political, economic, and cultural institutions. It is these institutions, rather than any deficiencies of women themselves, that primarily restrict women's participation and opportunities in political, economic, social, and other areas of their lives. As a result, women around the world are most likely to be poor and are also more likely to face a variety of forms of violence (such as domestic violence, bride burning, and sexual slavery). Despite this, treating women as passive victims and handing down some kind of "silver bullet" to fix these problems from on high are frequently ineffective. Instead, more effective efforts treat women as active agents and give them the resources they need to take charge of, define, and implement relevant and meaningful change on their own terms.

Lúthien takes the initiative to defy efforts to confine her and more than once escapes and aids Beren. She uses special powers in order to make good her escape—"arts of enchantment" (Tolkien 1977: 172)—

counteracting any assumptions by Beren or others that she is weak or dependent. Furthermore, the great wolfhound Huan understands the urgency of her quest and by implication respects Lúthien's efforts to work together with Beren—perhaps even to save his life. Because of this Huan allows her to ride him—a rare to nonexistent privilege otherwise. All of these points suggest that the gendered hierarchy of the Elves is not perfectly restrictive, and Elven women still are able to actively influence their lives, even within their constraints. Overall, the gendered hierarchy of the Elves is less coercive than that which would have been imposed under world domination by Sauron.

Rethinking Mordor, the Shire, and Rivendell

We have compared Order and Justice in more nuanced ways, over and beyond the single issue on the agenda for the Council of Elrond. What, then, does the Council do with the Ring? After significant debate, Bilbo intervenes by announcing, Hobbit style, that he is in great need of a meal. The debate concludes in favor of destroying the Ring, with Frodo to be its bearer. Frodo does this as part of a Fellowship of the Ring, which includes leading figures from among the other Free Peoples and the Hobbit companions with whom he had departed from the Shire. Thus Frodo's quest is launched. Its success will preserve Middle-earth from the horrors of Sauron. However, defining the decision as being one of choosing between *either* the status quo *or* a nightmare perpetuates, rather than transforms, many inequalities—especially those based on class, gender, and a global position of dependency. As such, even though the opportunity to work toward a more just form of Order at Elrond's Council is pursued in many ways admirably, it remains restricted in creativity and scope.

Does Changing the World Make It a "Better" Place?

When Frodo takes up the quest to destroy the Ring of Power, he pursues a world that is characterized by a more just form of Order. Rather than a world modeled after Mordor, where Sauron enslaves all people so that he can accomplish his interest in world domination, the quest pursues a world that looks more like Rivendell or the Shire, where the broader interest in decent and worthwhile lives would be possible. In this alternative world, a long lost king descended from the Dúnedain would be able to take up his rightful place; he would heal the hurts of Sauron, and make peace in the land. Rather than the dark, evil and fearful land of Mordor, the world would become full of light, peace, and joy. The end of the story shows what happens with this pursuit.

A world modeled after the Shire or Rivendell would be a dramatic improvement over one modeled after Mordor: it certainly would be a more just form of Order that would result in both more fair and safer lives for most inhabitants, relative to what would be possible under the iron rule of Sauron. Yet the profile of Order and Justice even in these societies is open to debate. The world that Frodo pursues is not a perfect one. Its imagination is limited by the models of just Order that exist in Middle-earth before it. As discussed earlier, the model of a just Order embodied by the Shire is limited at least by internal class structure and dependence on Gondor (and the Elves and Rangers) for protection, while the one embodied by Rivendell is limited at least by a patriarchal family structure.

In the new world, some of these limitations could be resolved. Particularly, if Sauron is destroyed, Gondor and the Elves will no longer have to bear the burden in blood and treasure of protecting the free world from him. This means that some worldwide structural injustices will be resolved. Despite this, other injustices seem likely to remain. Particularly, Sauron's destruction would appear to do little to change the existing class structure of the Shire, or the patriarchal hierarchy within families of Elves or other races. Consequently, although the lives of servants and women in the new world would probably be better than they would be under Sauron, they probably would remain unjustly restricted because of social organizations based in gender and class. This said, it is undoubtable that the new world would be a better one than whatever would be possible under Sauron. What remains a question is whether more inclusive and creative involvement of people on "the bottom rungs" could make it even better than what Tolkien envisions.

"Justice" Defined by Some Does Not Mean Justice for All

The pursuit of this kind of limited just Order in Middle-earth is linked to the kind of council of the decision makers involved. Although Boromir was at the Council of Elrond and highlighted the problem of the unequal burden of protection at that meeting, similar advocates who could highlight problems of gender and class had no place: the most likely advocate would have been Sam, and he was not invited to the Council's discussion where the decision was made of what to do with the Ring (I: 264). (Bilbo and Frodo attended by invitation, but while they are Hobbits, each would be identified more with the aristocracy of the Shire.) Even though Sam attended anyway, he did so without the legitimization of invitation and did not speak up until after the Ring Bearer offered to pursue the quest. As this suggests, having just one or a small number of representatives for "minority" viewpoints is not enough to challenge the dominant assumptions of the rest of the group.

In this case, dominant concerns reflected an elite male viewpoint: although the participants at Elrond's Council were drawn from all the Free Peoples of the earth, they were lords, wizards, stewards, princes of royal lines, or persons of affluent background, and the members of the Fellowship appear to be unmarried as well. Learning from more diverse experience was unlikely because of the similarities among the elites present and because conditions of secrecy and time pressure meant that consultation beyond this elite group would have been inadvisable, impossible, or both. As such, the breadth of experience drawn on in the Council of Elrond was informed narrowly by concerns such as gender and class, even though concerns informed by race and geographic location were more broadly included.

CONCLUSION

Certain social orders entail more Justice than others, but they often remain limited by various forms of injustice. On one hand, it is clear that Frodo's quest promotes an Order with more Justice in society than would be possible without it. The quest stops the evil Sauron from subduing and enslaving the Free Peoples of Middle-earth. On the other hand, this accomplishment is tempered by the many forms of unjust domination that remain. The quest does not change the existing unjust class structure within the Shire, eliminate the restrictions on women's political participation evident among Elves or other races, or alter other forms of inequality such as the rule of hereditary monarchy among Men. Despite these limitations, the net effect of Frodo's quest is clearly (though imperfectly) positive. The hierarchies of both the Shire and Rivendell are less coercive than those of Mordor, the intentions of their leaders are good, and descriptions of these places are light and joyful. Furthermore, it is evident that the Free Peoples are restricted by internal gender and class hierarchies, yet they still are able to actively influence their circumstances and may even benefit in certain limited ways—even if they are also restricted in other ways—by hierarchical social structures. Thus, *LOTR* suggests that unlikely heroes can enable more just forms of societal Order, but also that injustices not prioritized in this process will continue to limit the extent to which a world that is more fair can be achieved.

Although both the Shire and Rivendell are clearly more Just than Mordor, making this kind of generalization is not enough: We want to know more. Applying a higher standard of Justice demonstrates that certain groups within the Free Peoples have only limited freedom and would be better off if their society were more just. Particularly, the status quo in these societies allows for relative safety and a relatively good life for many. However, this Order comes at the expense of certain interests—such as upward social mobility, dependency, or personal autonomy and security—which particularly impact certain groups. How, then, can Justice be pursued? We will come back to this difficult question as we continue through the book. We hope you will keep this question in mind as you develop your own ideas about pursuing stability and fairness in your world.

CHAPTER 2

Thinking about
International Relations
and Middle-earth

THE LIGHT OF EÄRENDIL AND IR THEORY

When the Fellowship left Lothlórien, Lady Galadriel gave each of its members a gift to aid them along a road fraught with danger. To Frodo she gave a phial that contained the rare light of Eärendil, most precious among the Elves. This light aided him when he confronted the gigantic spider, Shelob, in her dark and frightening cave. While hardly frightening in the same way as a monstrous spider, the arcane terms of debates in IR theory can be intellectually challenging and off-putting to those new to the field. So this chapter seeks, like the light of Eärendil, to brighten our thinking about IR.

This chapter discusses how people with different perspectives draw on various paradigms and analytical frameworks to evaluate global politics. Each perspective can be understood as looking through a different kind of lens or window on our world: some may view the world through rose-colored classes, while others see blue or gray. Each perspective makes sense of the world by focusing on certain patterns and paying less attention to others. Because interests and goals influence the development of knowledge, scholars prioritizing Order tend to develop different kinds of knowledge—and draw on different methods and ways of thinking—than scholars who prioritize Justice. Of course, these concepts and approaches also overlap. Different approaches, however, can be thought of as what Max Weber described as "ideal types"—simplified, abstract versions of phenomena that highlight their characteristic features, even while the particular phenomena involved always are manifested in more historically varying ways. As such, scholars focusing on Order (e.g., "problem-solving") and Justice (e.g., "critical"), as well as particular schools of thought within each approach (e.g., "realist" or "feminist"), can be discussed in terms of their ideal type. Discussion of "ideal typical" positions within debates allows us to highlight major differences while also recognizing the important point that, historically, scholars within any such type did not take these exact positions and were always engaged in discussion and debate. We introduce a schematic to outline how such perspectives influence ways people think about IR.

THINKING ABOUT IR

Figure 2 provides a sense of how one might think about IR. Adapted from Nau (2009), the figure shows how perspectives influence the paradigms and analytical frameworks that people use to understand and explain global politics and how these paradigms and frameworks then also influence those perspectives. Note that the arrows connecting boxes in the figure form a cycle. While the discussion that follows will work from left to right for ease of exposition, bear in mind that thinking about IR includes feedback effects, and that relationships are interactive and dialectical (i.e., a dialogue of alternatives leading to synthesis). Some components of the figure are addressed in the context of *LOTR* later in this chapter, while other aspects fit more naturally elsewhere. Overall, this figure highlights how scholars analyze world politics by applying different paradigms or analytical frameworks (such as "levels of analysis" or "gender-sensitive lenses") to the world—either our own or Middle-earth—using different methods to analyze the world and drawing on experience and perspective to make interpretations and reach conclusions.

Paradigms: Problem-Solving and Critical

The far left of the figure depicts how "paradigms" and "analytical frameworks" organize thinking in IR. *Paradigm* is a word derived from the Greek language that means "an example, model, or essential pattern" (Kegley with Blanton 2010: 578). On one hand, paradigms involve assumptions about the nature or Order of the world and how knowledge is

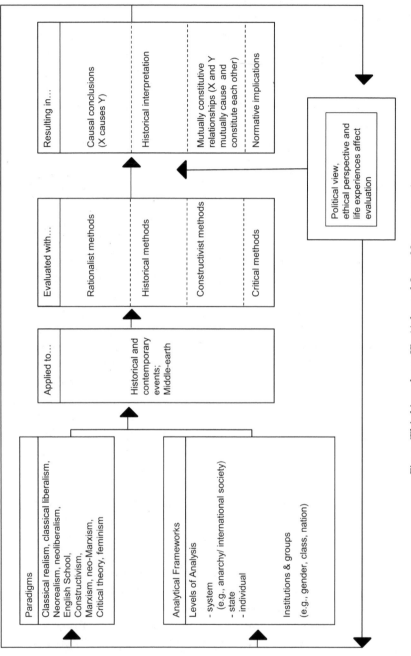

Fig. 2. Thinking about IR. (Adapted from Nau 2009, 5.)

obtained about it. On the other hand, paradigms also involve assumptions about what the world should be or its Justice. In IR scholarship from the twentieth century and beyond, this divergence between focuses on Justice and Order has been described by Cox (1981) as a fundamental division between "critical" and "problem-solving" paradigms. Problem-solving paradigms, which focus on Order, tend to be dominant in IR scholarship within the United States. Critical paradigms, which focus on Justice, tend to be more popular in Europe, Latin America, and elsewhere outside the United States.

On one hand, problem-solving approaches accept the existing social order as it is (e.g., as normal or acceptable) and seek to fix specific problems within that world. Problem-solving paradigms include classical realism, neorealism, and neoliberalism (presented in detail in chapter 3) and frequently focus on describing, explaining, and predicting conflict and cooperation between states and international security (or the security of states). For example, the realist tradition focuses on trying to solve the problem of war, assuming ceteris paribus conditions, or all else being equal. On the other hand, critical approaches ask how the (unjust) structural conditions of the existing social order came about (overturning ceteris paribus assumptions) and seek transformative structural change to empower people and reform or transform governments. Critical approaches, also presented in chapter 3, include classical liberalism, Marxism, neo-Marxism (such as Frankfurt School Critical Theory), and feminism; such approaches frequently interpret and critique relationships among people(s), groups, and institutions in terms of their impact on the freedom and security of people. For example, feminist theory, reviewed in chapters 5 and 6, explores how dominating and militarized masculinity supports various forms of violence and investigates how alternative forms of citizenship might promote greater opportunities for positive peace.

Differences between problem-solving and critical paradigms also can be related to what Habermas (1971) describes as different "knowledge interests" (see, e.g., Alker 1996b, 2005; Diez and Steans 2005: 131). Habermas argues that different kinds of interests generate different forms of knowledge: interest in prediction or control generates explanatory, causal knowledge; interest in understanding generates contextual, interpretive knowledge; and interest in human emancipation generates emancipatory, reflective knowledge (Tinning 1992; Alker 1996a: 383). As such, problem-solving theories are characterized primarily by (a) technical interest in managing the existing Order more effectively and (b) use of empirical-analytic methods, which refer to observation of the world guided by scientific principles. Critical theories, by contrast, are characterized primarily by (a) interest in emancipation from injustices of the existing order and (b) use of reflective or interpretive methods, which recognize the influence of power and perspective on research.

Categorizing IR scholarship in terms of problem-solving or critical ideal types usefully highlights different relative areas of focus. However, it is important to recognize that there is no clear division here. For one thing, it is certainly the case that problem-solving approaches highlight the mechanics of existing social systems and minimize discussions of their levels of (In)Justice. However, they also entail a normative commitment because accepting the status quo reinforces and legitimates existing levels of social Justice. For another, it is also the case that critical approaches critique the Justice of existing social orders and promote transformative change. However, such critiques also involve analysis of existing and potential alternative social orders. As such, it is a matter of relative emphasis that distinguishes these approaches from each other.

Although critical and problem-solving approaches to IR involve different perspectives and relative influences on debate, we believe that they share some important and underrecognized common ground. We suggest that commonly accepted understandings about foreign policy decision making within the problem-solving tradition support critical concerns about the influence of standpoint on perspective and discussion, and also create the opportunity for mutual discussion. Particularly, scholars in the foreign policy analysis tradition have recognized that, at least for the decision makers they study, "where you stand depends on where you sit" (Miles 1978; see also Allison 1971: 176). Known as Miles' Law, this assertion resonates with critical scholars, who suggest that all knowledge is situated in experience and "objective" truth is a questionable concept (see Habermas 1971; and Price and Reus-Smit 1998: 261). Although members of the problem-solving traditions rarely apply Miles' Law to themselves or the scholarly institutions they are part of (for a critique here, see, e.g., Tickner, 1997), we believe this assertion serves as one starting point for a bridge between problem-solving and critical IR. While problem-solving studies of foreign policy have tended to focus on the impact of context on "real world" politics, Miles' Law would recommend a step beyond such measures: it suggests not only that the position of policymakers depends on their role but also that the position taken by academic theorists depends on their own personal and institutional background. As such, this creates at least some common ground for problem-solving and critical scholars in recognizing that the ways people understand and explain the world are rooted in their different perspectives and experiences.

Consider the Council of Elrond as conveyed via Miles' Law. For Elrond, speaking on behalf of Elves, a clear priority is to communicate the impossibility of the Ring staying in Rivendell. Dwarves, meanwhile, are determined to prevent the Elves from somehow obtaining the Ring— even though they do not want it! Suspicion of Elves is communicated emphatically by Gimli in the movie version of *The Fellowship of the Ring*. For the Men of Gondor, the agenda is to obtain relief from the burden of being the long-standing front line of defense for the Free Peoples; this explains Boromir's determination to see the Ring used against Sauron. In short, all of the Free Peoples formally represented at the Council have a common goal in opposing Sauron, but each shows parochial interests as well.

Analytical Frameworks: Levels of Analysis to Gender-Sensitive Lenses

Different paradigms in IR draw on different analytical frameworks. Analytical frameworks organize the world in different ways: they highlight particular features of the world as important and minimize other elements as less important. Because problem-solving approaches in IR (which focus on Order) and critical approaches in IR (which focus on Justice) make different assumptions about the world, they tend to also draw on a variety of analytical frameworks to tell different stories about different actors in world politics.

On one hand, problem-solving approaches draw most prevalently on "levels of analysis," which will be covered at length in chapter 4. This framework is particularly useful for problem-solving approaches such as neorealism and neoliberalism, which focus on states and their individual foreign policymakers within an anarchic system. Three levels of analysis are conventional within this analytical framework and are commonly used in the field. The first and most aggregated is the international system. The second, seen as the principal units of world politics, are states. Finally, the third, which is also the most variegated, includes individual decision makers. Problem-solving paradigms argue that breaking things down into these three levels is a useful way of understanding international conflict and cooperation.

Consider a few examples from within levels of analysis as might be applied by problem-solving IR to the study of Middle-earth. At the system level, it is striking to note the lack of integration among the political entities of Middle-earth. Various story lines reveal that, in some instances, one group may regard another as more rumor than fact; this point comes across when Treebeard first encounters the Hobbits. At the state level, problem-solving IR might characterize Middle-earth as more medieval than modern vis-à-vis political actors. While Gondor and Rohan are recognizable as monarchies, and Mordor and Isengard look like totalitarian states, what is one to make of the Shire, the Wild Men, and others who participate in the story? They clearly do not resemble states in any meaningful way and stimulate memories of the medieval world, with its anything but uniform assortment of political actors.

On the other hand, critical approaches frequently focus on institutions and groups that overlap with multiple "levels," such as gender, class, and nation, or instead focus on the stories that are told about such institutions and groups in discourse. These frameworks are particularly useful for critical approaches such as Marxism and neo-Marxism, which highlight institutionalized class conflict, and feminism, which highlights institutionalized gendered relationships (i.e., role expectations). This is in part because they better capture the multilayered and dynamic understandings of these areas of focus and also because they highlight how politics is not about hard or objective actors (e.g., states) as much as it is about changing "constructions" of politics—the stories we tell about some actors and the silence we perpetuate about others. Chapter 5 covers a "gender-sensitive lens" as one example of a critical analytical framework. Gender-sensitive lenses highlight how dominating relationships in a variety of areas are based in unequal assumptions about masculinity and femininity. Although dominant problem-solving paradigms frequently ignore these kinds of processes, feminists argue that this does not make them any less prevalent or influential on global political processes. From a critical perspective in general and a feminist outlook in particular, one might note the relative dearth of female characters in *LOTR*. Even those present, with a few exceptions, are in subordinate positions. Moreover, role-based expectations are troubling even to an elite character such as Éowyn, who is all but prevented from going to battle in defense of Rohan despite her commitment to life as a shieldmaiden.

Depending on which paradigm and analytical framework you use, different methods of evaluation tend to be seen as appropriate. All approaches can be informed by historical and contemporary events in our world, as well as the fantasy world of Middle-earth.

On one hand, problem-solving approaches tend to use "rationalist" or scientific methods, including comparative case studies and statistical compilations of large-scale quantitative analysis, to assess a given proposition. Great emphasis is placed on the replication of results. In particular, findings confirmed with multiple methods and data sources by a range of scholars are regarded as strongly representing objective reality. From this perspective, even if someone might have a particularized view of historical or contemporary events, other scholars can replicate their research and effectively triangulate results. Furthermore, because a major interest here is in prediction, the wider the scope of application for ideas the better. Rationalist methods of testing produce causal conclusions; either X is now more likely a cause of Y or it is not.

For example, is anarchy (X) the ultimate cause of war (Y)? It certainly exists in all three ages of Middle-earth. As will become apparent in the next chapter, anarchy plays a role as a background condition in bringing on the War of the Ring, with other more proximate factors proving significant as well.

On the other hand, critical approaches tend to use interpretive methods, including narrative analysis, interviews, hermeneutic analysis (i.e., identifying text meanings and suppositions) and narrative or discourse analysis, to evaluate structural relationships of power and opportunities for their transformation. Because "facts" are seen as dependent on interpretation, findings are regarded as useful for particular purposes (not "objective" conclusions). From this perspective, replicating research does not make it any less influenced by individual and institutional perspectives, experience, values, and interpretation. Furthermore, efforts to do so can create the illusion of objectivity while promoting scholarship favorable to certain people and purposes. Consequently, some such scholars argue that acknowledging a researcher's standpoint and pursuing research that draws on a diversity of viewpoints and experiences is a more transparent way of promoting stronger research. Critical methods frequently produce normative evaluations: defining X in terms of Y in certain ways assumes particular dominating relationships, so redefining those relationships in alternative ways creates the opportunity for emancipatory change. For example, how does defining anarchy as a risky and fearful arena of individualistic and unconnected states rely on assumptions about masculinity and femininity that restrict cooperation and promote conflict?

Consider Denethor through the eyes of critical IR. His character can be interpreted as ironic and pitiful. Denethor, as Steward of Gondor, occupies a very high-level position by right of birth. Given the social system that exists, he is thrust into a position that he is ill-suited to have and makes one mistake after another when subjected to the intense pressures of crisis decision making. Thus, from a critical standpoint, is Denethor a villain or at least in part a victim of circumstance? Instead of focusing strictly on what he does, we might look at Denethor as the unfortunate product of a dynastic system that tends to mismatch people with their best capacities. What if, for instance, someone with the character of Éowyn had been Steward of Gondor instead? The question virtually answers itself and urges us to think further, from a critical point of view, about the wider context of action for both characters in Middle-earth and leaders in our own world.

Some theorizing, such as that of the English School and constructivism, includes scholarship that draws on a combination of problem-solving and critical approaches. First, the English School focuses on a "society of states" that it argues exists despite conditions of anarchy. For example, the postal system worldwide continues to operate regardless of crises and wars. It suggests that this international society creates conditions for cooperation that are greater, or more hopeful, than assumed by classical realists but lesser, or more pessimistic, than assumed by classical liberals. The English School draws on historical or "pluralist" (multiple positivist, historical, and critical) methods to assess how and to what extent states cooperate internationally over such issues as humanitarian intervention and human rights.

Second, constructivism focuses on the role of ideas in shaping events; it draws on multiple methods but especially interpretive and hermeneutical methods, which involve reading or interpreting texts in historical context (e.g., discourse analysis, case studies). In doing so, authors in this tradition seek to contextualize data to assess and evaluate reality that is "socially constructed" or made meaningful by interpretation. Constructivist methods frequently produce constitutive evaluations: X and Y define each other or make each other possible and meaningful. (For example, do perceptions of systemic anarchy and threatened behavior by states make each other possible, or coconstitute each other, because states act *as if* they are part of a threatening anarchic system rather than, for example, within an international *society*?) Both the English School and constructivism highlight the importance of perceptions in global politics and include efforts to address concerns of Order as well as Justice.

Consider, from a constructivist or English School point of view, the presence of Sauron in Middle-earth. His ongoing efforts at world domination ensure that international society will exist in at best a rudimentary form. Prospects for building a world of trust and resultant cooperation will remain poor as long as Mordor in its current form persists.

How "Objective" Is Reality?

As the intervening upward arrow in figure 2 points out, evaluation of results is influenced by political point of view. This box at lower right reflects the presence of Miles' Law as a key element in our frame of reference, that is, where you stand depends on where you sit: Like different colored glasses, ethical perspectives and life experiences influence the stories people tell about data. Note that the box has *two* borders (i.e., there is an outer, shaded area and an inner, unshaded, area). This box highlights how problem-solving scholars assume that perspective plays less of a role in evaluation than critical scholars do. Critical scholars, who see a much greater degree of individual and institutional interpretation in the research process, assume the larger version (including the outer area), while problem-solving scholars, who believe that objective research is possible, assume the smaller version of this box (excluding the outer area). Constructivist and English School scholarship, which includes both problem-solving and critically oriented strands, would occupy varying points *within* the outer area depending on their respective commitments. In other words, the size of the box corresponding to political view distinguishes critical (maximum size of box), problem-solving (minimum) and intermediate approaches vis-à-vis the degree to which they understand interpretation and perspective to shape their analysis of the world.

Looking once again at figure 2, it becomes clear that there are many feedback effects. Research evaluations influence paradigms and levels of analysis. Certain paradigms, such as those that scholars see as being successful in their goals and value as generating worthwhile results, can attract more attention. Attention in one area can encourage related work in other areas. Double-headed arrows connect paradigms and analytical frameworks with political view. These double-headed arrows, which wrap around the exterior of the figure, reveal a dialectical relationship between paradigms and levels of analysis on the one hand and political views on the other: these ideas continuously influence each other with varying degrees of intensity. For example, a highly anomalous research finding may shock adherents of a given paradigm and produce efforts to refute it while also creating doubt among those anchored to an associated political point of view. A stunning instance of that is the collapse of the Soviet Union, which was almost entirely unanticipated by any IR paradigm. Overall, figure 2 illustrates how the discipline of IR includes a "big tent" of vastly different research projects and suggests how this tent has created the opportunity for major debates.

MOVING ON TO THE DEBATES

This chapter introduces a frame of reference for thinking about IR. Regardless of what kinds of glasses are chosen—what paradigm or theory within it might be selected—the process of understanding and explaining IR moves from the mind to the world and back again. In other words, both individual and institutional glasses exist, and each influences the other. Paradigms, analytical frameworks, real and imagined events, methods, and conclusions—with the final stage mediated by political point of view—constitute the basic apparatus of IR theory and its assessment. The next chapter will look at paradigmatic waves in IR in connection to *LOTR*.

CHAPTER 3

Middle-earth and Three Great Debates in International Relations

This chapter uses *LOTR* characters to illustrate ideal typical perspectives of major approaches within the three "Great Debates" of twentieth-century IR, all of which influence discussion today. It is important to note here that, although in this book we use the giant spider Shelob to illustrate one "prowoman" approach and the Orcs to illustrate one realist approach, feminists are *not* blood-sucking monsters, and realists are *not* genocidal maniacs! As discussed in the introduction, our use of *LOTR* characters is meant to illustrate different ways of seeing the world, not to malign scholars of different perspectives. Each involves its own kind of colored glasses. Although our world and Middle-earth are clearly different in many ways, *LOTR* can still provide illustrations to which we can relate. Thus Middle-earth can clarify different IR perspectives on politics. We conclude by setting the stage for the next chapter, which focuses on the long-standing problem of war.

GREAT DEBATES IN IR THEORY: CLASHING PARADIGMS

The discipline of IR often has been mythologized by IR scholars as being defined by three Great Debates. Telling a story about the history of IR in this way can be useful because it focuses on abstract versions of more historically diverse dialogues in order to highlight differences and create abstract ideal types. However, it becomes problematic if such ideal types are understood as being what "really" happened—especially since, as Woodrow Wilson noted, it is often the case that "history is written by the victors."

In the mythology of IR, each of the Great Debates features a different point of contention: over visions of the future in the 1920s and 1930s, the means of obtaining knowledge (referred to as "method" in short form) in the 1950s through the 1980s, and what counts as knowledge in the 1980s and 1990s (Lapid 1989).[1] In the new millennium debate continues over worldviews, methods, and how to learn about IR but with less of a firm sense of a main axis of conflict. Examining IR's stories about the major dialogues of the past, which provide a sense of the field's evolution, is a good way to move toward grasping where IR is now and how it can inform the world around us.

Table 1 displays approaches to IR in terms of these three Great Debates of the twentieth century in the context of races and characters from *LOTR*. The first column lists the debate, its focus, and its time period; the second column names the major approaches included in the debate; the third column notes the race of beings we use to illustrate this approach in *LOTR;* and the fourth column names the specific male character who best illustrates this worldview. Of course, neither table 1 nor the others in this volume convey exhaustive sets of categories but instead are simply "cuts" at using *LOTR* to inform IR.[2]

---

1. Those who know the field of IR well will recognize that the dates assigned to respective Great Debates do not match those in Lapid's (1989) highly informative exposition. The reason is the present volume's emphasis on the second Great Debate as a very extended referendum on instrumental rationality. (*Instrumental rationality* refers to assessment of the expected value of a policy based on information available at the time of a decision, allowing for the cost of obtaining additional knowledge about the situation; a highly accessible presentation of this perspective appears in Bueno de Mesquita 2009: 15–18.) Hence the range of dates is longer than the span over which scholars in IR and throughout the social disciplines argued over the merits of behavioral—generally meaning quantitative (i.e., statistical)—methods.

2. For example, the rational choice tradition is included as a main heading in the summary of the second Great Debate, with the rationalist neorealist and neoliberal institutionalist approaches that competed with each other appearing as subheadings. In addition, although the approaches listed under the Third Debate are more critical leaning, they can be considered with respect to the dominant neorealist-neoliberal debate (but see also Waever 1996) as exemplified by the neorealists and neoliberalists listed under the second Great Debate row. Problems with mythologizing history in this manner are further discussed later in the volume. For purposes of clarity in introducing paradigms, the table also does not elaborate on the various subsets of the neo-Marxist paradigm that have proliferated in recent years.

Although use of male characters does not mean IR insights apply only to men, it does highlight how most IR theory today is rooted in men's lives and experiences: it uses glasses made by and for men. For example, even today, most political leaders are men. Chapters 5–6 highlight feminist IR scholarship, which builds on the question "Where are the women?" This chapter, however, focuses on IR scholarship more generally, which tends to zero in on other kinds of questions.

THE FIRST GREAT DEBATE: ELVES, ORCS, AND HUORNS

The IR Myth

Within the first Great Debate, IR mythology defines the major ideological competition as being between classical liberalism (the Kantian tradition) and classical realism (the Machiavellian tradition). According

TABLE 1. Approaches to International Relations from World War I Onward and Illustrative Characters from *LOTR*

Great Debate	IR Theory	Race	Character
1. Vision of future (pessimistic/hopeful): 1920s/1930s	Classical realism	Orc	Uglúk, led by Saruman
	Classical liberalism	Elf	Elrond
	Marxism	Huorns	Old Man Willow
2. Method (history/science): 1950s/1980s	Rational choice	Wizard	
	• bounded		Gandalf
	• unbounded		Saruman
	Neorealism	Men	
	• defensive		Boromir
	• offensive		Ringwraith leader
	Neoliberal institutionalism	Dwarf	Gimli
	English School (international society theory)	Elf	Legolas
	World Systems Theory	Wild Men	Ghân-buri-Ghân
	Postcolonialism	Hobbit	Sméagol/Gollum
3. Knowledge (positivism/postpositivism): 1980s/1990s	Positivism (see Rational choice, above)		
	Constructivism	Hobbit	Frodo Baggins
	Frankfurt School Critical Theory	Ent	Treebeard
	Postmodernism	Wizard	Saruman

to this story, classical liberalism is the opposite of classical realism, with realism focusing on the "hard facts" of international conflict and liberalism focusing idealistically and unrealistically on world peace. Between these two, the story goes, classical realism "won" over classical liberalism.

In this story, liberal arguments in favor of cooperative conflict management are frequently discounted by drawing on historical instances such as the failure of the League of Nations (see, e.g., Baylis, Smith, and Owens 2008) or the conduct of World War II, where conciliatory policies were discredited by rapaciously self-interested dictatorships bent on conquest. Although this historical context did have important cautions for some classical liberal arguments, such an impact has become overblown in IR's mythologized historical account.

As part of this, the mythologized story of realism winning over liberalism is often bolstered by language denigrating a weak version of liberalism, such as that labeling classical liberalism as "utopianism" or "idealism" (see Baylis, Smith, and Owens 2008; and Mansbach and Rafferty 2008). It has also been reinforced by many IR textbooks, which use such language, and in doing so associate "idealists" or "utopians" with *un*realistic ideas (Mansbach and Rafferty 2008: 581–82). Despite the persistence of this caricature, it would be more accurate to say that no idealist paradigm existed and, instead, a more diverse set of authors, especially within the classical liberal tradition, debated the classical realists (Ashworth 2006). Like with idealism or utopianism in history, discussion of "radicalism" today is oversimplified. However, discussion of both schools of thought would be more fair and empirically accurate if it avoided denigrating and lumping together nondominant approaches in broad brushstrokes and instead referred to particular approaches associated with terms by name, such as classical liberalism, neo-Marxism, feminism, and so on.

Victor's history is also apparent in the IR myth's minimization of the existence and importance of class-oriented (i.e., Marxist) contributions to discussion both during this time and through critical scholarship today. Unlike dominant discourses, which take problem-solving approaches to address a world of states, Marxism takes a critical approach to pursue Justice for people of different classes. In part because of this focus, which in some contexts might be labeled subversive, Marxist contributions are minimized in dominant discourse today.

Consider, in that context, the classical distinction made by Martin Wight related to problem solving and critical theory. Wight (1992) argued that three basic approaches are available to IR: realism, rationalism, and revolutionism. Realist approaches assume the status quo will be maintained and work within it; Revolutionists work to transform the status quo into a new, emancipatory social order; and Rationalists exist between the two, holding the belief that states exist in a society rather than anarchy and that reform can bring about beneficial developments without requiring revolutionary change. Early in the century, realism took realist approaches, classical liberalism and Marxism took revolutionist approaches, and the English School took a rationalist "via media" approach in between these two.

Overall, the IR myth frequently treats classical liberal and Marxist arguments as "straw men." It creates the illusion that classical liberalism was refuted by misrepresenting diverse arguments as unrealistic and impossible dreams for world peace. It also creates the illusion that Marxism was hardly even part of the discussion by misrepresenting the impact of its arguments on discussion both then and now.

Classical Realism

Classical realism can be illustrated with the Orcs from *LOTR* and their fallen but powerful Wizard leader Saruman. Orcs are fallen Elves, corrupted by Morgoth (former master of Sauron, from the First Age of Middle-earth) and are depicted as an utterly inhuman, evil presence throughout the story. The most powerful Orcs, hybrids bred by Sauron and then Saruman and known as the Uruk-hai, are exemplified by their captain, Uglúk. The latter engages in a rampage of violence intended to maximize the power of Saruman, his master, by destroying the Wizard's enemies.

Table 2 provides a definition of classical realism, which focuses on human nature. Classical realism assumes that people—like the Orcs and their master Saruman—are inherently aggressive (Rourke and Boyer 2010; Viotti and Kauppi 2009). Consequently, it pessimistically expects one power struggle after another—the more things change, the more they stay the same (Mansbach and Rafferty 2008; Kegley with Blanton 2010). Because people are inherently flawed and war cannot be averted, classical realism assumes that political actors will pursue the most self-serving ends with whatever means are available. In that sense they are designated as *Machiavellian*, that is, amoral toward the global community in their pursuit of what they perceive to be in the national interest (but

TABLE 2. International Relations: A Rainbow of Theoretical Approaches

Theoretical Approach	Definition
Classical realism	Classical realism is an approach to International Relations that holds that interstate conflict is rooted in (bad) human nature.
Classical liberalism	Classical liberalism is an approach to International Relations that holds that international cooperation is possible if (good) human nature is effectively harnessed by international institutions.
Marxism	Marxism is an approach to International Relations that holds that class conflict is rooted in capitalist economic relations.
Rational choice	Rational choice is an approach to International Relations that holds that international relations involve rational actors. For the unbounded rationality approach, this means that actors attempt to achieve their preferred outcome, choose the best of all possible options, and believe that others think the same way. For the bounded rationality approach, actors are regarded as seeking their preferred outcomes but make the best choice that they can under constraints such as limited information and thus accept that they may not be fully aware of how and why choices are being made by others.
Neorealism	Neorealism is an approach to International Relations that holds that interstate conflict is rooted in conditions of international anarchy, or lack of overarching world government.
Neoliberal institutionalism	Neoliberal institutionalism is an approach to International Relations that holds that international cooperation is possible despite conditions of international anarchy through international institutions.
English School	The English School, or international society school, is an approach to International Relations that holds that international cooperation is possible because we live in an international society of states that recognizes community through dialogue and consent.
World Systems Theory	World Systems Theory is a neo-Marxist approach to International Relations that holds that capitalist global economic relations in the current world system as a whole create a division of labor that benefits states in the core at the expense of states in the periphery and semi-periphery.
Postcolonialism	Postcolonialism is an approach to International Relations that holds that colonialism and neocolonialism are supported by cultural chauvinism and the construction of racial, gender, and class differences.
Constructivism	Constructivism is an approach to International Relations that holds that opportunities for international conflict and cooperation depend on how relationships between and among participants in global politics are interpreted or "constructed" rather than any totally "objective" measures.
Frankfurt School Critical Theory	Frankfurt School Critical Theory is an approach to International Relations that investigates the social conditions that enable social justice and societal self-determination and explores alternatives to dominant instrumental rationality.
Postmodernism	Postmodernism analyzes language to uncover how power imbues truth; it highlights how political action involves being incredulous of—rather than taking for granted—the progressive stories of modernity.

see De Grazia 1994 for another view of Machiavelli). Of course, realist scholars certainly do not advocate that we conduct our lives in this kind of manipulative way; they simply argue that realism provides the best description of *political processes:* it is the political *actors* they study, not the scholars themselves, who are assumed to behave in such a Machiavellian manner.

Saruman, for example, takes a very Machiavellian standpoint throughout *LOTR* (Davidson 2003: 106). At one point, Gandalf, seeking to prevent the dominion of evil (and serving as de facto strategist for the Free Peoples), meets with Saruman at Isengard in his Tower of Orthanc and is taken hostage. Before resorting to force in a confrontation with Gandalf, Saruman asks him to join with Sauron because his "victory is at hand." Saruman claims that the Wizards can "bide [their] time" and, while "deploring evils done by the way," ultimately come to exert control (I: 253). Thus, for Saruman, the ends justify the means. The reason for going along with Sauron, obviously, is expediency. After all, if he cannot be stopped, why engage in futile resistance? Why not, instead, seek to make gains, even at others' expense?

Saruman's leadership of the Orcs illustrates Machiavellian assumptions about both the flawed nature of individuals and power-oriented behavior. It becomes obvious that Saruman, in spite of the claims just enumerated, has no intention of cooperating with Gandalf and merely attempts to deceive him. This devious approach forms part of an effort to obtain the Ring for Saruman's own purposes. Thus Saruman sends Uglúk and his troop of Uruk-hai on a mission to take the Ring by whatever means necessary. This action occurs in tandem with Saruman's wanton destruction of the Forest of Fangorn, which he cuts down and burns to accelerate the building of his army. The objective is to deploy this huge army against the isolated and troubled Kingdom of Rohan, a potentially valuable force on behalf of the Free Peoples—an action obviously planned well before Gandalf's arrival at Isengard. Saruman and Uglúk, in sum, represent the unconstrained exercise of force. Their self-aggrandizement is not tempered in any way.

In terms of IR mythology, the Orcs also illustrate how classical realist arguments may be useful but are not the whole story. For example, although it is certainly the case that Orcs as a group are depicted as evil and bent on conquest, this existence of conflict does not eliminate cooperation among the Free Peoples (as in the Fellowship among members of a variety of different races) or even among the Orcs, who must cooperate among themselves to function as efficient military teams. Understanding the social and other institutions that facilitate such cooperation, whether ultimately for peace or war, or for Order or Justice, are aims on which IR traditions beyond realism, including classical liberalism and Marxism, can shed light.

Classical Liberalism

Classical liberalism posits that human nature is good and thus cooperation is feasible. It can be connected with the Elf Elrond from *LOTR*, who is both ancient and wise. Elrond is depicted as someone who is essentially good and whose ability to learn from the past helps him restrict tendencies toward war. He is described in angelic terms as noble, wise, and virtuous, and like Elves in general, he is characterized by an "eagerness for knowledge" (I: 236).

Table 2 provides a definition of classical liberalism, which also focuses on human nature but from a different point of departure. In contrast to classical realism, the Kantian tradition of classical liberalism assumes that people are inherently good—as Elrond and the Elves appear to be in *LOTR*. Consequently, it is hopeful that international conflict can be reduced through social learning and that world peace is possible. Because people are basically good and war is not inevitable, classical liberalism assumes that the ends (or goals) that political actors pursue depend on what they have learned as socially conscious members of their communities (see especially Viotti and Kauppi 2009; and Baylis, Smith, and Owens 2008). As with realist scholars, the behavior of liberal scholars is not necessarily in accord with classical liberal norms; they simply argue that liberalism provides the best description of *political processes*.

Elrond illustrates a Kantian (or classical liberal) standpoint throughout *LOTR* in his social learning, facilitation of collaboration, and support of relatively democratic problem solving. There are at least three different contexts in which Elrond illustrates how social learning can facilitate cooperation.

First, Elrond safeguards one of the three Elven Rings of Power, which had been made for "understanding, making and healing, to preserve all things unstained" (I: 262). This power protected Rivendell from the evil spreading in Middle-earth (at least for a time) and shows how social learning among good people can promote peace.

Second, it is Elrond's commitment to learning that enables him to be a skilled healer. Without this ability, he would not have been able to save Frodo from dying (due to a wound inflicted by a Wraith before he arrived at Rivendell) and the Hobbit never would have had the chance to succeed in the quest to destroy Sauron's evil Ring (I: 215–16).

Third, and finally, it is Elrond's understanding of the history of the evil Ring that is the key to its undoing: In the past, Elrond and Círdan, another prominent Elf, had tried to persuade Isildur to destroy the Ring. Because they were unsuccessful, evil was postponed for a time but eventually returned, in the form of the conflicts highlighted by the Fellowship's quest. Having learned from the experience of the Elves that cooperation was critical to defeating evil when it arose, Elrond facilitated his Council and the Fellowship that was created there. Elrond's Council can be understood as a quasi institution, formed under adverse circumstances in pursuit of a positive outcome for the Free Peoples of Middle-earth. This secret and crucial gathering of representatives from the Free Peoples of Middle-earth (I: 236–58) forms a plan that eventually defeats Sauron by building on Elrond's examination of this history of the Ring at his Council and relying on "the helpful exchanges of the many" in order to "work logically through all the possibilities to the one solution that Sauron will never imagine [i.e., destroying the Ring]" (Chance 2001: 50). With support from others, notably Aragorn, Gandalf, and Legolas (all of whom end up in the Fellowship), Elrond persuades the Council to destroy the Ring rather than engage in a hopeless effort to wield its inevitably corrupting force. Creation of the Fellowship is an example of cooperation among generally "good" people aimed at promoting more peaceful and just orderings of Middle-earth societies. This part of the story highlights the importance both of social learning and of drawing on a community of good people to solve problems effectively (see Blount 2003: 95).

Overall, Elrond illustrates the classical liberal argument that people are not doomed to repeat the errors of the past: the Ring was not predestined to survive, as Isildur permitted it to long ago, with horrendous consequences. Instead, Elrond illustrates the view that progress beyond the "recurrence and repetition" of war is possible and that social learning can promote peace.

In terms of IR mythology, Elrond also illustrates how classical liberal arguments are often thoughtful rather than unrealistic and should not be dismissed offhand. For one example, as with characterizations of the classical liberal perspective (Mansbach and Rafferty 2008), Elrond seems anything but naive and foolish. Instead he wisely learns from experience and in doing so can help the Free Peoples who, while good, are not without weakness and proneness to error. For another, classical liberalism, as Elrond's conduct reveals, does not accord with stereotypes about a lack of willingness to consider active resistance to tyranny. Elrond confronts the evil of the Ring pragmatically; his rejection of its direct *use*, along with the holding of a meeting to consider strategy and tactics, follows from principles of classical liberalism.

Marxism

Marxism can be illustrated with Huorns, or Ents gone tree-ish (II: 551), which exist as a classless society in *LOTR*. They resist fiercely, as Marxist theory would advocate, perceived efforts to exploit them. After the battle of Helm's Deep, the extended film version of *The Two Towers* shows the remaining Uruk-hai attempting to escape the forces of Rohan by running into Fangorn Forest. A great disturbance takes place in the forest right away; it is clear that the Uruk-hai are being destroyed by the Huorns. In essence, the Huorns are taking revenge on Saruman for the destruction of trees. Here trees of Fangorn forest had been destroyed to facilitate military industry carried out under authoritarian hierarchy, with Saruman at the top and a range of subordinates under him. Class warfare, with the exploited rising up against the exploiters, subsequently ensues.

Table 2 provides a definition of Marxism, a perspective based on class analysis. Derived from work by Karl Marx and Friedrich Engels, from the mid–nineteenth century onward, this approach concentrates on conflict among different economic classes of people rather than focusing on interstate conflict and cooperation (as realism and liberalism do). It argues that economic inequalities are foundational to other inequalities and that capitalist economies enable a minority to exploit the majority, particularly that capitalism enables the owners of the means of production, known as the bourgeoisie, to exploit the working class, known as the proletariat. Because of this ongoing pernicious relationship, Marxism argues in favor of a social revolution. It becomes essential to replace capitalism with collective ownership to achieve a classless society, which, in turn, eliminates the exploitative system of capitalism and promotes greater equality in all areas of life.

No Huorn is singled out as a character, which in a way works quite well with the idea of a classless society. Here it might make sense to "borrow" a character from elsewhere in the story who is described as though he could be a Huorn, although this identification is never made explicit: Old Man Willow is described as a sentient tree who lives in the Old Forest where the Hobbits Frodo, Sam, Merry, and Pippin meet Tom Bombadil (an extraordinary creature mentioned briefly at the Council of Elrond but not otherwise involved in the main story line) at an early part of the quest. Old Man Willow is quite hostile to the four Hobbits and ends up entrapping Merry and Pippin, who eventually are rescued by Tom Bombadil but not before Sam tries to use fire to set them free (I: 115–16). Old Man Willow's point of view is not difficult to infer; intruders, such as the Hobbits, are dangerous and likely to engage in acts such as chopping wood and starting fires. Thus the attack on the Hobbits is motivated, within a Marxist context, as resistance to potential exploitation.

In terms of IR mythology, this also illustrates how Marxist approaches that—like Huorns—have minimal roles in the main stories (or *LOTR* or IR mythology) make important contributions and are not unimportant or worthy of dismissal. For example, after the battle of Helm's Deep, the Huorns play an important role in destroying the Uruk-hai, who otherwise could have escaped to fight another day. Although Huorns otherwise are marginal in the *LOTR* story, without the collaboration of all members of the allies in battle—including the Huorns—a very different outcome could have ensued. Similarly, Marxist theory, which does not receive much recognition in IR mythology for either its existence or its contributions, has provided a rich basis for scholarship addressing class conflict in a variety of forms.

THE SECOND GREAT DEBATE: WIZARDS, HUMANS, ELVES, AND DWARVES

The IR Myth

Within the second Great Debate,[3] IR mythology defines the primary contention as being between scholars who adopted assumptions of individ-

---

3. As hinted at earlier, the Second Debate included a rather extensive conflict over the value of qualitative versus quantitative methods. In operational terms, this came down to a major difference of opinion over case studies as opposed to statistical analysis in research methods. Many years later, after the intense arguments at the time of the Behavioral (i.e., quantitatively oriented) Revolution in the social sciences during the 1960s, each side moved toward greater acceptance of the methods pursued within problem-solving IR. Agreement centered around a commitment to valid scientific inference regardless of the type of data-gathering and processing techniques that are used.

ual rationality and scholars with a historical approach. According to this story, rationalist approaches largely "won" over historical approaches.· Here arguments in favor of historical contextualization are frequently assumed to be less important than arguments relying on assumptions about self-interest. In this case, the victory of rationalism over historicism appears less extreme than in the previous debate, given that both approaches continue to coexist. However, rationalism still appears victorious in dominant IR scholarship's prioritization of assumptions regarding action based on self-interest and its confinement of historicist contributions to more marginal discussion. It also is evident today in discussion that focuses on debates *within* rationalist methods (such as game theory) rather than between historical and rationalist contributions. Beyond this, the IR myth also continues to minimize neo-Marxist contributions such as World Systems Theory, which focus on nonstate, rather than state, actors.

Rational Choice

Wizards from *LOTR* can illustrate different possibilities created by the rational choice tradition, which borrows from the discipline of economics and emphasizes optimal decision making under constraint. Gandalf can illustrate bounded rationality, while Saruman (and his eventual master, Sauron) can illustrate unbounded rationality. Rationality is bounded by self-awareness and the understanding that not everyone necessarily wants the same things as oneself. On one hand, Saruman and Sauron are greedy for the dominating power of the Ring and cannot imagine that others either might not have that desire or might wish to destroy such an important thing. On the other hand, Gandalf does not desire power over others and recognizes that Sauron's interest (in possessing the Ring) is different from the Fellowship's (in destroying it). As such, both Saruman and Gandalf pursue their interests, but Saruman does not recognize that the interests of those in the Fellowship are different because they are informed differently than his own.

Table 2 provides a definition of rational choice. Unbounded rationality assumes actors perfectly maximize their interests, along with the belief that others think the same way and have corresponding goals. In other words, they choose the best of their alternatives based on benefits versus costs (Mansbach and Rafferty 2008: 10). Bounded rationality, by contrast, allows for certain constraints on decision making in terms of time and energy. As will become apparent, unbounded rationality is not an accurate description in general of either Middle-earth or the real world, in which bias and error form a significant part of the story. Despite this, it provides the framework for other rational choice approaches, which address some of these criticisms such as bounded rational decision-making models. As Gandalf indicates to the Council of Elrond, the Enemy "is very wise, and weighs all things to a nicety in the scales of his malice" (I: 262). The "scales," however, do not balance all that they should. Sauron's tactics are optimal but only if he correctly comprehends what the Free Peoples of Middle-earth intend to do with the Ring. He is in error because the Dark Lord cannot "think outside the box" and see that goals other than world domination motivate his adversaries. As the Wizards in *LOTR* will illustrate, assumptions about decision-maker preferences make a big difference in what decision makers are expected to do and, in turn, how accurate predictions are about projected outcomes.

To begin, consider Gandalf's further observation regarding Sauron: "*But the only measure that he knows is desire, desire for power, and so he judges all hearts.* Into his heart the thought will not enter that any will refuse it, that having the Ring we may seek to destroy it. If we seek this, we shall put him out of reckoning" (I: 262, emphasis added). Later Gandalf revisits this limitation: "That we should try to destroy the Ring itself has not yet entered his darkest dream. . . . So the forces he has long been preparing he is now setting in motion, sooner than he intended. Wise fool" (II: 485–86; see also Chance 2001: 64). The perfectly calculating minds of Sauron and Saruman might have triumphed if the Fellowship had similar preferences (i.e., the preferred ordering of possible states of the world) to theirs—but all but one of its members did not think that way. This is in spite of the diversity of Free Peoples—Elves (Legolas), Men (Aragorn, Boromir), Hobbits (Frodo, Sam, Pippin, Merry), Wizards (Gandalf), and Dwarves (Gimli)—included. Consequently, the Enemy's lack of imagination disadvantaged him (see Lloyd 1976: 5). Sauron could not conceive of anyone seeking Justice rather than Order based on the aggrandizement of personal power.

Similarly, rational choice can be an effective conceptualization of decision making for certain purposes; however, its traditionally material or economistic comprehension of preference formation needs to be elaborated in various contexts. For example, experience in recent decades points out that religious beliefs significantly shape action, some of which is transnational and aggressively committed to transforming the world. This includes radical "Islamists," who have garnered extensive media attention by conspiring to commit acts of violence against many people, but it also includes lesser-known social movements based on particular interpretations of Christian and other religious beliefs (e.g., the Spanish Inquisition or modern efforts to limit women's rights in the name of fundamentalist versions of various religions). Rational choice can be aided in its contribution by factoring nonmaterial interests of participants into respective calculations about what people can be expected to do.

Gandalf the Wizard can illustrate the bounded rationality tradition. which attempts to overcome these limitations by starting with more inclusive assumptions. As Aragorn (a Man of hidden nobility and closely allied with Gandalf) notes, this Wizard holds preferences different from those of Sauron and Saruman: "The Counsel of Gandalf was not founded on foreknowledge of safety" (II: 430). He recognizes how Sauron and Saruman's interests are different from the Fellowship's, so Gandalf can better understand how the Enemy will behave and what the best strategy for the Fellowship should be (Lloyd 1976: 5). In *LOTR*, Gandalf is like IR theorists who question how "interests" are defined or consider the psychological maximization of self-interest: he complicates the picture, but consequently can improve his strategy and understanding of the situation.

Sauron's calculation of probability, in the language of rational choice, is rigid and even *ir*rational in the sense that he does not update his beliefs on the basis of information readily available: "Sauron, being so mighty and evil, cannot conceive of other beings who think differently from himself, whose attitudes toward power could be different. This lack of imagination on his part proves fatal" (Levetin 1969: 12). Sauron tracks the Ring but fails to consider the lack of correspondence between its movements and the presumed goal of wielding it against him. The Ring is traced to the Shire, but Frodo and his companions leave just in time to elude the Black Riders sent by Sauron to retrieve it. From Sauron's point of view, the most obvious destination for the Ring would be Minas Tirith, stronghold of Gondor, the most powerful realm among those in opposition to him. As depicted quite dramatically in the movie version of *The Return of the King,* Sauron does not consider destruction of the Ring to be an option even when he becomes aware that Hobbits, one of whom may be the Ring Bearer, are within Mordor itself. This should be even more puzzling to him in light of the absence of any sort of accompanying protection for the Ring via Gondor's army. No matter what happens, Sauron, as rational choice would put it, assigns a probability of zero to the goal of destroying the Ring. Sauron's failure to guard the entry to Mount Doom arguably is the single most important error made by any character in *LOTR*.

From the movie version of *The Fellowship of the Ring* can be gleaned a helpful example of how Gandalf's calculations are informed by self-awareness. After departing from Rivendell, the Fellowship is blocked by a snowfall caused by Saruman. They must choose between once again trying the mountain pass of Caradhras or giving up and seeking passage through the Mines of Moria. Gandalf suffers from a sense of dread at the prospect of going to the Mines; Saruman is depicted in a vision as reminding Gandalf that to go that way may be his undoing. Given the need for legitimacy in decision making under such difficult conditions, along with his own doubts, Gandalf passes the decision on to the Ring Bearer. Frodo, with a clearer mind on the subject, realizes that the Mines, while dangerous, represent the best hope for the company as a whole. In spite of great reluctance among the Fellowship, aside from Gimli, a Dwarf with much experience in caves and mines and thus a disposition toward Moria, the decision is accepted.

As this discussion suggests, it is clear that rational choice can offer one integrated approach to decision making, but with qualifications. The bounded or *instrumental* version of the rationality postulate better captures decision-making outcomes. Gandalf's ability to see other ways of looking at the world, in the end, plays a decisive role in the ultimate victory of the Free Peoples over Sauron, who cannot imagine the existence of any goal other than world domination.

One ready example from our world is the unfortunate misunderstanding of George W. Bush by Saddam Hussein and vice versa. It is hard to imagine two leaders who misread each other's preferences as thoroughly as these two did in the lead-up to the Iraq War of 2003. In the aftermath of the 9/11 attack, Bush and his advisers saw Saddam Hussein as a likely user of Weapons of Mass Destruction who also might pass along such capabilities to terrorists. The Bush administration tended to see hostile forces in the world aligned with al-Qaeda, the perpetrator of the 9/11 attack, in particular. We now know, however, that Saddam's fiery rhetoric and behavior, which suggested possession of such weapons, instead covered up weakness. He feared being overthrown and hoped to convey strength, even invulnerability, through WMDs. The Iraqi dictator hoped to deter US action against him, given the superficial evidence that he had WMDs, and these capabilities therefore would be available for use against any would-be invader. Saddam's efforts to elude United Nations weapons inspectors simply reinforced the false impression concerning WMDs and contributed greatly to Bush's sense that (a) Iraq had WMDs and (b) might use them against the United States. Instead, the Iraqi dictator had worries of his own and also hoped to intimidate any potential usurper of power from within.

In terms of IR mythology, Gandalf and Saruman also illustrate how rationalist arguments are particular approaches to politics that are helpful with certain things but are not the whole story. Just having two Wizards illustrate two kinds of (bounded and unbounded) rationalism highlights how neither approach is necessarily the "last word" on politics. As discussed earlier, Sauron would be right to assume that someone like Boromir would have similar preferences but wrong to infer that the rest of the Fellowship would. So, too, rationalist approaches (like other approaches) are useful for certain purposes but not all: depicting people as rational actors who maximize their preferences may be a fast shorthand for decision making, but its abstractions based on "economic man" do not capture all of the psychological or social processes through which decisions are made. Furthermore, because of this, rationalist assumptions can miss important factors that might, at least under certain conditions, change the projected outcome.

Neorealism

Neorealism emphasizes the immanent effects of international anarchy. Its offensive and defensive variants can be connected with the Man Boromir and the Ringwraith leader, the Witch King of Angmar. Both of these characters pursue perceived self-interest in military security for their respective lands. However, Boromir seeks only to secure Gondor defensively against encroachment by Mordor, while the Ringwraith leader and his lord Sauron seek military expansion and domination of Middle-earth.

Table 2 provides a definition of neorealism, which focuses on anarchy as the reason for interstate conflict and the prime mover of IR. Neorealism conceives of states as rational actors and argues that interstate conflict—like that between Gondor and Mordor during the Third Age in *LOTR*—is inevitable because of the anarchic structure of the international system. Particularly, neorealist scholars argue that under anarchy the lack of overarching power or government puts states into a security dilemma, which perpetuates a cycle of conflict because each state is concerned with its position vis-à-vis the others and can maximize security only if it becomes a hegemon (i.e., an overwhelming power). As such, neorealism follows a rationalist path in emphasizing the structure of the international system and the distribution of state military capabilities as a causal variable as opposed to philosophizing about human nature and drawing conclusions about behavior in that way (Kegley with Blanton 2010; Mingst 2008; Viotti and Kauppi 2009; Rourke and Boyer 2010). The neorealist tradition includes both defensive neorealists (who argue that states only seek to expand under certain conditions) and offensive neorealists (who argue that states seek to maximize their power to maximize their security).

Most prominent among neorealist propositions is the expectation that a system with two great powers (bipolarity) will be less prone to war than one with three or more great powers (multipolarity). The rationale comes from the relative simplicity of bipolarity. Absent the gyrations of great power alliances, the international system should be simpler to manage even allowing for some degree of confrontation. Neorealists cite the Cold War, which produced no major shooting war directly between the United States and the Soviet Union, as their principal evidence in favor of bipolarity. They play down the significance of the "proxy wars" that the great powers perpetuated during the Cold War, such as those in Afghanistan, Angola, Korea, Vietnam, the Middle East, and Latin America.

In *LOTR*, the Man Boromir can be explained by defensive neorealism, while the Ringwraith leader, the Witch King of Angmar, greatest of the nine Nazgûl and the right hand of Sauron, connects easily with offensive neorealism. Boromir and other Men, such as those of Gondor (Boromir's people) and Rohan (King Théoden's people), are uncertain of their security and alliances and seek to retain autonomy and sovereignty over their own domains without necessarily expanding their land or power. For example, Éomer (nephew of Théoden and leader of the kingdom's cavalry) states when he first meets Aragorn, Gimli, and Legolas that "wanderers in the Riddermark would be wise to be less haughty in these days of doubt" (II: 422–23). This air of suspicion is the norm in Middle-earth. The bands of Men in *LOTR* usually are not actively trying to expand their sovereignty but are influenced by their fear of others trying to take over their land.

Boromir, from the race of Men, acts in a manner consistent with defensive realism. A member of the Fellowship, Boromir is also heir to the Stewardship of Gondor, a domain contiguous to the rival and evil Sauron's land of Mordor. Boromir believes the Ring of Power should be used in Gondor for defense against the Dark Lord and eventually tries to seize the Ring from Frodo. As such, he seeks power for defensive purposes, just as defensive realists argue occurs in our world among states. (Note that, at least with respect to the preferences of Men, Sauron generally calculates accurately regarding the Ring.)

The Ringwraith leader, a "corrupted" Man (I: 50), can be accounted for by offensive realism. Unlike other Men, Wraiths are not content with maintaining their sovereign space in Mordor, but are tools of Sauron's desire to hegemonically dominate all of Middle-earth (see Lloyd 1976: 10; and Davidson 2003: 100). This is consistent with offensive realism's position that great powers maximize power. Because relative gains are what count, no state can be totally secure unless it dominates all others. The impact of this approach is evident in that, although the Free Peoples of Middle-earth are not expansionist before Sauron's move to take over the world, once he tried to do so, even they pursue total destruction of the Enemy (and therefore their own domination, at least over the former adversary) as the only way to go.

Overall, Boromir and the Ringwraith leader both illustrate rational pursuit of military security, with Boromir seeking defensive security against border encroachment and the Ringwraith leader engaging in aggrandizing world domination. As part of this quest, Boromir's fixation on obtaining more power for Gondor to enhance security against Mordor makes him ignore potentially harmful consequences of his preferred action. This parallels a famous criticism of realism in general: the practice of power politics is associated with an outcome of war rather than peace (Vasquez 1999).

Neoliberalism

Neoliberal institutionalism in *LOTR* can be connected with the Dwarf Gimli, whose people avidly pursue gold and treasure. Gimli demonstrates the importance of absolute rather than relative gains by never expressing envy toward the wealth of others but cherishing lasting works of great value on their own merit, such as the spectacular Mines of Moria. Gimli's people also illustrate interdependence. In Middle-earth, examples include the trade networks and allies that Dwarves maintain because of their pursuit of gold, mithril (i.e., silver-steel, the most valued among all commodities in Middle-earth), and other precious metals (see III: appendix A, 1046 in section III on Dwarves). In our world, related examples include the World Trade Organization (WTO), North Atlantic Treaty Organization (NATO), and Association of Southeast Asian Nations (ASEAN).

Table 2 provides a definition of neoliberal institutionalism, which focuses on the possibility of achieving cooperation under anarchy. Neoliberalism assumes that, regardless of whether human nature is "good" or "bad," international institutions can overcome barriers to cooperation and enable collaborative problem solving (D'Anieri 2010; Bueno de Mesquita 2010; Mingst 2008; Nau 2009; Russett, Starr, and Kinsella 2010). This is because states focus on absolute rather than relative gains: consequently, conflict can be reduced by increasing institutions that reduce cheating and promote collectively valuable rule-constrained behavior. *Cheating* refers to making an agreement and then deliberately seeking ways around it. An example of cheating would be efforts by members of the Organization of Petroleum Exporting Countries (OPEC) to get around quotas assigned to them in order to produce more oil and increase short-term revenues. Collectively valuable rule-constrained behavior refers to compliance by individuals that rebounds to the advantage of all members of the group. To continue with the same example, when members of OPEC stay within the limits set for production, this helps to keep the price of oil higher, which in turn maximizes the collective profit margin.

Gimli's friendship with Legolas (the Elf in the Fellowship) and admiration for the Elf Lady Galadriel provides an example of nonmilitary societal connections and becomes the basis for renewed good relations between Dwarves and Elves (see I: 346, 363, 367). These relationships between and among Dwarves, Elves, and Men provide a foundation on which to build and ally against Sauron and illustrate how complex interdependence can reduce perceptions of insecurity and create opportunities for cooperation rather than conflict.

Nuances of neoliberalism with regard to the effects of interdependence emerge through the "fabled feud" of the Dwarves and Elves. They once engaged in significant trade but came to loathe each other out of "cultural difference: for Dwarves were quite unable to perceive any particular merit in trees, in skies and in hunting under the stars; while the very contemplation of dwelling underground filled Elves with abhorrence" (Tyler 1976: 119). Thus contact through trade and investment can create the possibility for conflict, as well as providing a foundation for increasing levels of cooperation. Fought long before *LOTR*, the war between Elves and Dwarves may have come about because of a lack of institutionalization. Consider problems such as the reported greediness of the Dwarves or the haughtiness of the Elves. (These problems might have been more perceived than real, but that does not matter in conditioning responses.) War, the by-product of ongoing tensions, might have been ameliorated, and a positive relationship sustained, if institutional mechanisms for conflict management had existed. Without such means, high levels of contact through trade can generate friction. In our world, the League of Nations, which failed to rein in aggression and prevent World War II, is an example of a neoliberal idea good in principle but flawed in application. For instance, the United States eschewed membership in the League, which significantly reduced the new organization's capabilities for conflict management. Neoliberals urge us to improve existing institutions in order to work out problems without resort to arms and to pursue additional linkages as technology creates new areas of conflict. It is fair to say that, collectively speaking, today's institutions perform better than the League of Nations did in its time. Examples include the International Criminal Court and WTO at the global level, along with regional mechanisms for cooperation such as the European Union and African Union. While imperfect, these entities provide opportunities to build cooperation between and among states that might otherwise resolve their differences through unilateral, even violent, means.

The English School

The English School can be connected with the Elf Legolas in *LOTR*. Legolas engages both with the Elves and with the Dwarves—first as an Elf himself and second as a friend of the Dwarf Gimli, as well as other members of the Fellowship. This occurs despite the obstacle that Gimli is a Dwarf—a member of a race with which the Elves once went to war. Legolas is also involved in the dialogue and consent at the Council of Elrond at which the Fellowship is created. He agrees to be part of the Fellowship; in the movie version of *The Fellowship of the Ring*, Legolas offers his bow to Frodo for protection and implicitly commits his life to the quest. By these actions, Legolas also recognizes his and his people's common interest in maintaining the Fellowship. While other Fellowship members also fit these categories in varying degrees, Legolas is the one who represents the Elven tradition of diplomacy, initiated by Galadriel and Elrond.

Table 2 provides a definition of the English School, which emphasizes the possibility of cooperation through an international society. Like realism and liberalism, the English School focuses on states within a system of (technical) anarchy. However, unlike realism and liberalism, the English School focuses on an "international society" of states: "a group of states (or, more generally, a group of independent political communities) which not merely form a system, in the sense that the behavior of each is a necessary factor in the calculations of the others, but also have established by dialogue and consent common rules and institutions for the conduct of their relations, and recognize their common interest in maintaining these arrangements" (Bull and Watson 1984: 1). English School theorists argue that an international society creates greater opportunity for cooperation than realists recognize, although such cooperation may be more limited than classical liberals hope for. As such, the English School defines itself as a bridge between classical realism and liberalism that entails a guardedly hopeful vision of the future and stresses the feasibility of reform without revolution. It builds on the classical realism and liberalism of the interwar period with a pluralist approach that focuses on interpretive, historical, and legal methods. It also provides an alternative to the rationalist neoliberal and neorealist approaches by interpreting data in historical context rather than assuming self-interest across the board.

Legolas builds a relationship with Gimli that illustrates how the English School relies on dialogue and common consent to institute rules of conduct and recognize mutual interest. The development of this relationship for the Elf and Dwarf is rocky; they have to overcome ancient quarrels in which both of their families participated. Similar obstacles to cooperation exist in international relations. However, the Dwarf and Elf are able to overcome these barriers and become strong friends because they come to recognize that their common interests, such as destruction of the Ring, are more important than anything that still divides them. Legolas and Gimli also are able to accept common standards of behavior, most notably, working together within the Fellowship. The evolution of their relationship illustrates how institutionalization can reduce conflict even in the face of historical doubt and result in enduring cross-border relationships—the building of international society—a central focus of the English School. In terms of IR mythology, Legolas also illustrates how multiple contributions to collaborations can be important, whether they are seen as major (such as realist and liberal approaches) or less so (such as the English School). Although Elrond convened the Fellowship and without him the Quest would not have continued, Legolas was a practical contributor to it by supporting Frodo on the ground as he pursued his burdensome Quest, and this practical involvement was another important contribution. So too, the English School contributes practically to discussion of IR by addressing questions about Order and Justice, conflict and cooperation, and balance.

World Systems Theory

World Systems Theory can be illustrated by the Wild Men of the Woods. These people are peripheral to the story of the Quest and are seen by neighboring free peoples as a class of subhuman creatures. Consequently, they are hunted down by those we otherwise see in positive terms as adversaries of the Dark Lord.

Table 2 provides a definition of World Systems Theory, a class-oriented approach that focuses on what is viewed as a division of tasks at the global level that is badly in need of change. This approach, which developed along with its predecessor Dependency Theory, argues that the capitalist global economy creates an exploitative international division of labor between states at the "core" (which are wealthy and powerful), and states at the "periphery" (which are poor and weak), as well as those in the "semiperiphery" in between; this structure reinforces core dominance at the expense of the periphery. With other neo-Marxists, World Systems theorists share a common focus on class conflict as influenced by changes in (dominant and dominating) ideas and culture, as well as economic institutions (on which Marxism focused).

The Wild Men play an important role in reconnaissance for the Men of Rohan on their perilous journey to aid in the defense of Minas Tirith (II: 813–17). A subject of legend more than knowledge among other Free Peoples, the Wild Men can be seen as representing the periphery of international relations in Middle-earth. They are described as "woodcrafty beyond compare" (II: 813). Their spokesman, Ghân-buri-Ghân, urges Éomer to kill the Orcs, who are known to be destructive and exploitative, but also to "leave the Wild Men alone in the woods and do not hunt them like beasts any more" (II: 815). This highlights how even the

Free Peoples in *LOTR* (who we assume are the "good guys") can have destructive and exploitative relationships with people around them (even if they are not "evil" like Sauron and his allies). Echoes of core-periphery relations can be heard in the positions put forward by Ghân-buri-Ghân. He offers help to the Men of Rohan and Gondor, in effect, as clearly the lesser of two evils in the great battle to come. The basic interest of the Wild Men is to preserve their lives and culture against a wide range of dangers coming from more militarily powerful entities (including not being hunted "like beasts"). Similarly, revolutionary theorizing by neo-Marxist scholars aims at transforming the status quo. It also strives to create worlds where people can live under more just and fair conditions rather than continuing to be exploited under the current social and economic system.

In terms of IR mythology, the Wild Men also illustrate how key players, whether in the quest (e.g., Frodo) or IR theory (e.g., neorealism or neoliberalism), prioritize their own perspectives in telling their stories, and how drawing on alternative perspectives (such as those of the Wild Men) shows them to be stories rather than totally objective truth. For example, it is the ostensible purpose of the Fellowship to pursue a better and more just world in Middle-earth, as Frodo and Sam's rejection of the nightmare they saw in Galadriel's pool indicates. However, this Justice is limited in his mind (at least explicitly) to those he cares about—especially Hobbits, and certainly *not* the Wild Men, with whom he is not familiar. It is only when the Men of Rohan interpret the Wild Men as valuable allies that they become willing to treat the Wild Men with respect instead of hunting them down like beasts. So, too, drawing on the perspective of marginalized groups as valuable highlights how dominant stories can support dominant interests, rather than the interests of all.

Postcolonialism

Postcolonialism can be connected to Sméagol, the creature who becomes known as Gollum. Gollum is a warped character who possesses the One Ring for over five hundred years while hiding under the Misty Mountains, then loses it to Bilbo Baggins, and finally becomes instrumental in its destruction after he journeys to recover it once more. Sméagol is Gollum's given name and in *LOTR* has two references: first to the creature before he happens on the Ring of Power, when he is still a normal member of the River-folk (a people related to Hobbits); and second to the "good" one of the two (split) personalities that Gollum has after he becomes warped by his possession of the Ring into a different kind of creature altogether. The split personality of Sméagol/Gollum illustrates the central postcolonial argument that construction of the (e.g., superior, Western) Self depends on construction of the (e.g., inferior, oriental) Other.

Table 2 provides a definition of postcolonialism, which emphasizes multiple aspects of domination by one group over another in the world left behind by the colonial powers. Postcolonialism analyzes and resists colonialism and neocolonialism—the domination by territorial, economic, military, or other means of one people over another. It does so by addressing how colonial and neocolonial relationships of power and subordination are perpetuated through the construction of difference, whether due to race, gender, and class or otherwise, and by supporting active resistance (not just critique) to unequal power relations (Baylis, Smith and Owens 2008: 187–89). For example, it highlights how constructing the (Western) Self as rational and progressive depends on constructing the (Oriental) Other as irrational and backward and how such narratives justify beliefs that Western countries or cultures are meant to rule the world.

In *LOTR*, the split personality of Sméagol/Gollum is apparent in a number of ways. When he guides Sam and Frodo into Mordor, Sam refers to the good personality as "Slinker" and the bad one as "Stinker" (II: 624). Sam creates this distinction in his mind after noticing a conversation that Gollum holds with himself (II: 618–19), during which a "pale light and a green light alternated in his eyes" as he took different parts of the conversation (II: 618). Sam also notices that, although Gollum normally refers to himself as "we" rather than "I" (suggesting a reference to Sméagol and Gollum), when he does refer to himself as "I" it means that "some remnants of old truth and sincerity were for the moment on top" (II: 629)—suggesting the voice is that of Sméagol.

This split personality illustrates the postcolonial argument that that constructing on or telling a story about (e.g., superior, Western) Self depends on differentiating it from an assumed different (e.g., inferior, Oriental) Other who is everything the Self is not. With Sméagol/Gollum, the original character of Sméagol almost completely disappears under the Gollum character, the name others call him in disgust after he begins using the Ring to steal and learn secrets while invisible, since it is then that he develops the swallowing habit where he says "Gollum, gollum" in his throat. It is not a name he calls himself. It also describes the despised side of the creature, the side that kills his friend Deagol to get the Ring, and becomes worse and worse over time, rather than his relatively positive, original self. However, the two are interlinked: Gollum is that much darker because he contrasts with the original Sméagol, and Sméagol (as a largely hidden personality) is that much more pitiful because he contrasts with the eventually dominant Gollum.

As the postcolonial argument suggests, constructing Sméagol as good, wholesome, and free depends on constructing Gollum as evil, dirty, and constrained by the Ring. This kind of construction supports Gollum's destruction. Frodo suggests as much when he says, "What a pity that Bilbo did not stab that vile creature, when he had a chance!" (I: 58). However, as Gandalf suggests early on and the end of the story confirms, such an action would have made everyone worse off. As Gandalf responds to Frodo, "[H]e has some part to play, yet" (I: 58). This eventually comes to pass with Gollum's pivotal importance in completing the quest. So, too, postcolonialism suggests that pursuing narratives that exalt the West over the Orient to their logical conclusion by supporting international, racial, gender, and class power differences is both unjust and shortsighted.

In terms of IR mythology, Sméagol/Gollum again illustrates how perspectives that are assumed to be irrelevant can be pivotal to international politics: Mainstream IR scholarship has only recently begun to recognize postcolonial scholarship as valuable, but it remains minimized and frequently excluded from introductory textbooks. This is like Sméagol/Gollum, who is assumed to be little more than an annoyance in *LOTR* but is really central to the whole story, from his violent acquistion of the Ring at the beginning to his guidance of Frodo and Sam through Mordor and his pivotal intervention at the end, which makes the positive outcome of the quest possible. So, too, postcolonialism is one approach that, though minimized in mainstream discourse, addresses issues of colonialism and neocolonialism, which, for many, are centrally important problems of global politics.

THE THIRD GREAT DEBATE: HOBBITS AND ENTS

Within the third Great Debate, still under way, IR mythology defines the primary source of conflict as between scholars who adopted positivist epistemologies or assumptions of what knowledge is and postpositivist scholars, with alternative assumptions of what knowledge is: Here, positivist approaches, such as neoliberalism and neorealism, adopt what the IR myth defines as a *scientific* assumption that there is a distinction between objective facts and subjective values. Meanwhile, postpositivist approaches, such as postmodern and some critical and constructivist approaches, assume that "facts" are made meaningful by values and therefore that objectivity is a questionable goal. In this story, positivism focuses practically on real world politics while postpositivism's concern with the interrelationship among language, truth, and power render it impractical for engaging actively with the world.

As with previous debates, this IR myth tends to turn postpositivist arguments into "straw men." For one thing, claiming the scientific high ground defines positivist approaches in language that claims superiority and strength. However, postpositivist approaches are also inspired by science (as well as sociology and history)—but in different ways; for example, postpositivism draws on quantum mechanics and the chaos theory postulate of indeterminacy, which suggests that "where you stand can influence what you see" (Fischer 1998). Such science, as well as history and sociology, suggests that the world is not a fixed thing out there but must be understood as something that is influenced by perspective. For another, IR mythology that discounts postpositivist contributions as being "impractical" disregards how postpositivist efforts to redefine *politics* can be highly practical in both their direct and indirect impact. For example, analyzing the politics of language involved in the "battle for hearts and minds" is an extension of the politics of the battlefield.

As positivist scholars have been discussed with reference to the neoliberal-neorealist debate, this treatment will focus on postpositivist and "middle-ground" approaches of constructivism, Frankfurt School Critical Theory, and postmodernism. Of these, postmodernism is strongly postpositivist, constructivism includes both positivist and postpositivist elements, and Frankfurt School Critical Theory includes elements of both.

Constructivism

Constructivism can be connected with Hobbits, as exemplified by Frodo Baggins within *LOTR*. Hobbit society is frequently described as thickly laden with a variety of strong social norms, which importantly influence Hobbit behavior. These norms range from the social acceptance of eating at least seven meals a day (breakfast, second breakfast, elevenses, luncheon, afternoon tea, dinner, and supper) to a general tendency not to be warlike or even fight much among themselves.

Table 2 provides a definition of constructivism, which focuses on how reality is created through social interactions as opposed to existing in some kind of fully objective way. Constructivism assumes that people—like Hobbits—create "reality" by attaching meaning to "facts" rather than processing any "objective" facts that are "out there." This approach emphasizes the role of socially constructed ideas in shaping IR. Constructivists vary in how much they emphasize Justice relative to Order in their investigations.[4] However, as a whole, constructivism suggests that conflict and insecurity are induced by how people meaningfully construct their ideas of the world rather than any completely objective, conflict-prone reality. From this perspective, seven meals a day are not necessarily objective necessities for Hobbits (e.g., because of their biological makeup or otherwise). However, they have been interpreted (as informed by biology as well as cultural traditions) as being necessary by Hobbit society. This norm then strongly influences behavior, despite being a "socially constructed" (rather than "objective") constraint. Constructivism recognizes that all rules can be broken, or redefined, and are done so in certain circumstances by members of societies.

Consider the norm of nonaggression among Hobbits: Hobbits live by peaceful agrarianism in the Shire but end up being crucial to achieving ultimate victory over evil. Unlike other races, Tolkien writes, "At no time had Hobbits of any kind been warlike, and they had never fought among themselves" (I: 5), although they could protect themselves when necessary. This tendency against warlike behavior is evident even though the Shire "at this time had hardly any 'government'" (I: 9). Tolkien further notes that the Hobbits "kept the laws of free will, because they were The Rules (as they said), both ancient and just" (I: 9). In the language of constructivist IR theory, Hobbits live in virtual anarchy but make a world of peaceful cooperation out of it. Constructivism would argue that Hobbits eschew fighting because they do not perceive threats among each other and follow the law because they make their world one in which law is the norm. This illustrates how it is not so much the objective constraints on behavior that matter, but the constructed ones that do.

---

4. These range from critical to conventional variants, for example, Zehfuss 2002. See also Kratochwil 1989; Onuf 1989; Ruggie 1998; Wendt 1999; and Finnemore and Sikkink 2001.

Despite this, limits to the Hobbit norm of nonaggression also highlight the constructivist point that norms, while constraining, are constantly reinterpreted and can be broken. Despite their peaceful tendencies, in the past Hobbits had not been immune to strife. For example, the Sackville-Bagginses, relatives of Bilbo with whom he did not get along, envied his possessions. Patrons of the Green Dragon pub in Hobbiton suspected the motives of outsiders, and Hobbit bullies working for "Sharkey" (an alias for Saruman, who terrorized the Shire after escaping the Ents) wreaked havoc on the local population while the rest of the world went to war. Gollum, from a people related to Hobbits, murdered his friend to win the Ring. It is clear, however, that Tolkien intends these actions to be surprising because they go against the central tendency of Hobbit behavior throughout the story of Middle-earth. Frodo, for example, observes that no Hobbit in the Shire had ever killed another on purpose (III: 983). The one Hobbit glorified for prowess in battle, Bandobras "Bullroarer" Took, had defeated an invasion of Orcs centuries earlier (Tyler 1976: 38), but that did not translate into a martial legacy for the Shire.

Frodo, the Ring Bearer in the Fellowship sent out from the Council of Elrond, further illustrates the constructivist argument that norms are constraining but not perfectly so. A "peculiar" or "odd" Hobbit like Bilbo, Frodo breaks many Hobbit norms both in the Shire and as the hero of an adventure story. However, he is repeatedly described (frequently by Gandalf) as having good Hobbit sense, amazing Hobbit durability, and other sorts of normal Hobbit characteristics. Frodo shows how it is possible to reconstruct the world for the better, believing the Ring can be destroyed, not only used against Sauron. However, he also shows that constructivism is not a panacea: The Ring gradually gains a dangerous influence over Frodo as he approaches Mount Doom. So, too, even constructed worlds can strongly constrain behavior in international politics.

Frankfurt School Critical Theory

Frankfurt School Critical Theory can be connected in *LOTR* with Ents, tree-sized shepherds of the forest who willingly take responsibility for the trees that live there, which no one else spends much time thinking or worrying about. Treebeard, the ancient Ent spokesperson, tells Merry and Pippin, "I am not altogether on anybody's side, because nobody is altogether on my side . . . nobody cares for the woods as I care for them, not even the Elves nowadays" (II: 461). Likewise, Frankfurt School Critical theorists frequently ask different questions and have different goals than mainstream theorists, and as such "are not altogether on anybody's side." Treebeard also tells Merry and Pippin that Saruman cut down trees that were his friends, and that "He has a mind of metal and wheels; and he does not care for growing things, except as far as they serve him for the moment" (II: 462). Similarly, Frankfurt School Critical theorists argue that normative concerns should be included in IR discussions rather than side-stepping the concept of Justice and focusing only on Order.

Table 2 provides a definition of Frankfurt School Critical Theory, which emphasizes the quest for Justice and even social transformation and eschews instrumental rationality. Originating in the interwar period in Germany, Frankfurt School Critical Theory is rooted in revolutionary thought, including that of Karl Marx and Immanuel Kant. It has been guided by an intertwined dual focus on (normatively) seeking greater Justice and (social scientifically) explaining social transformations. Over time, it has evolved from focusing on using qualitative methods to expose belief systems producing pathological behavior (under the intellectual directorship of Max Horkheimer and Theodor Adorno, 1920s–1960s) to exploring communicative reason as the basis for social progress (under Jürgen Habermas, 1960s–1990s) to exploring social groups as agents of transformation for greater human flourishing (under Axel Honneth, 1990s–2000s) (Anderson 2000). As such, Frankfurt School Critical Theory rejects rationalist assumptions and the statecentric framework. It instead focuses on alternative issues (e.g, human flourishing and security instead of state security) and alternative, marginalized, populations (see Price and Reus-Smit 1998; and Roach 2007). Frankfurt School Critical Theory can be understood as one kind of "critical theory" in IR in that it is not a problem-solving approach and shares with other critical approaches in IR an explicit commitment to pursuing Justice. However, it is only one of a multiplicity of such approaches, so it should be recognized that "Frankfurt School Critical Theory" is not interchangeable with "critical theory."

Shared by Frankfurt School theorists, as well as other critical IR theorists, the importance of the critical argument is that Justice, as well as Order, should be addressed. This point is brought out emphatically by considering how the quest to destroy the Ring influences Middle-earth. For one example, Saruman's military power in Isengard either ignores or reduces "human" security by slaughtering trees and destroying their environment and strengthening a force of Orcs and other dark creatures aimed at causing even further destruction. So, too, critical theorists point out that rationalist approaches that focus on national security can ignore or even reduce human security. Here Saruman's exploitation of the trees also parallels the subject matter emphasized by neo-Marxists, who argue that there is important class conflict between an exploitative elite core and an exploited periphery around the world, in this case between trees and Saruman. Overall, just as Ents are focused directly on the marginalized trees and forests of Middle-earth, rather than the world war of good versus evil, critical theorists often are concerned about marginalized populations (e.g., due to race, class, gender, or postcolonial position) and question assumptions and stories that explain and at least implicitly justify the status quo.

Whether Frankfurt School or, more broadly, critical theorists frequently do not mesh with more orthodox IR because of their divergent concerns and assumptions (like Ents, who are not on anyone's side), they can and do contribute to more mainstream theory. For example, Frankfurt School Critical theorists investigate how injustice leads to disorder, with implications for nonstate sources of insecurity such as domestic violence, terrorism, or ethnonational conflict. This broadens but overlaps with more orthodox concerns. Similarly, in *LOTR*, when a shared interest in fighting the Orcs arises, the Huorns (Ents gone "treeish") assist the Free Peoples in the aftermath of the crucial battle of Helm's Deep, where Saruman's forces are destroyed. Suspicious of all outsiders, the Huorns annihilate the remaining Uruk-hai, who have taken flight from the battle into Fangorn Forest. Meanwhile, the Ents attack Saruman's stronghold at Isengard, destroying the contraptions he had used to burn trees and ultimately trapping him in the Tower of Orthanc. However, the primary focus of the Ents is protecting the trees from everyday threats to security: being chopped down by Dwarves or Saruman's army.

In terms of IR mythology, the Ents also illustrate how perspective influences the stories people tell to make sense of politics: Treebeard tells the Hobbits Merry and Pippin that in his language names are like stories—they tell the story of the things they belong to. It is a language that recognizes the connections between things and consequently makes conversations using it take a long time (three full days for the Entmoot in which Ents decided to intervene with Saruman's destruction of the trees at Isengard!). In comparison, Treebeard sees the Hobbits as "hasty" for telling him their names right away and speeding through their stories. Just as the stories that Treebeard and Merry and Pippin tell are influenced by their language and perspective in Middle-earth, so, too, are different approaches to IR influenced by perspectives in our world. Because of this, Ents highlight how drawing on the perspectives of marginalized groups can broaden the basis for interpreting interests from elite to nonelite members of society.

Postmodernism

Postmodern IR can be used to generate a different interpretation of Sauron, one that focuses on how his "silver tongue" gives him power using language. After the victorious battle at Isengard, Gandalf bids Merry and Pippin to beware of his voice (II: 563). However, even with that warning, no one around who hears it is able to easily shake the feeling that Saruman's arguments are reasonable, inevitable, and right. Saruman uses his voice to try to cast a spell over those who hear him in order to maintain his position of power. For example, he tries to have Gandalf come up to him on his terms, rather than descending alone to the group of victorious allies at the bottom of his tower awaiting him. Although many below begin to be swayed by his words, Gandalf sees through them and eventually breaks his staff and banishes Saruman, breaking the spell and bringing people to their senses enough to remember the treachery and incompatibility of his honeyed words with his monstrous actions in and leading up to battle.

Table 2 provides a definition of postmodernism, which asserts the centrality of language in defining power. Just as Saruman tells a particular story at Isengard, so, too, postmodernism sees the world as being interpreted by stories or narratives, such as the modernist metanarrative that human progress occurs through human reason. Postmodernism argues that such narratives dismiss the chaos and diversity in the world and are supported by relationships and institutions of power. Consequently, all narratives are suspect and should be critically evaluated to see how they obscure a more complicated picture and are supported by structural inequalities.

Saruman's voice at Isengard illustrates this approach in a number of ways. First, it shows how simply telling a story can be a powerful way of organizing reality. Even though the Free Peoples awaiting Saruman below had just finished beating him in a full-scale battle, when Saruman welcomes them as if he wishes to see and help them, his voice is so powerful and reasonable sounding that the Riders of Rohan begin to doubt their collaboration with Gandalf and are enticed by Saruman. It takes the Dwarf Gimli pointing out the Orwellian and backward nature of these words to open the possibility of questioning his story. And eventually, his power of words is broken only after multiple dissenting voices (those of Gimli, Théoden of Rohan, and Gandalf) provide alternative interpretations of the situation. So, too, postmodernism argues that being skeptical of the dominant narratives (e.g., particular IR paradigms), just as Gimli, Théoden, and Gandalf are skeptical of Saruman, is important to analyzing global politics accurately.

In terms of IR mythology, this interpretation of Saruman also illustrates how even approaches that redefine politics—such as postmodernism, which focuses on the politics of language—still have useful contributions to make to IR, even though they are frequently framed in the IR myth as being incapacitated and impractical by their skepticism. In this case, it is because Gandalf's group is skeptical of Saruman's narrative that they are able to demonstrate how empty it is, to remove him from his position of power, and to act on alternative interpretations of the situation that benefit a broader group of people. So, too, postmodern IR contributions cannot simply be reduced to "navel gazing" but instead can enable a broader basis for understanding and acting on the world by investigating how injustices are perpetuated by dominant Orders.

WHERE IS IR THEORY NOW?

The discipline of IR mythologizes the Great Debates of the twentieth century as broadly addressing human nature, methods, and whether knowledge is factual or theory laden. In this story, realism and liberalism vie with each other in different rounds, first focusing on human nature (classical realism and classical liberalism) and then assuming rational state actors (neorealism and neoliberalism). Their competition in explaining cooperation and conflict in the international system contributes to problem-solving IR on an ongoing basis. However, minimized in dominant discourse within the United States are significant contributions of World Systems Theory, postcolonialism, Frankfurt School Critical Theory, and postmodernism, which focus on nonstate actors and emphasize issues of Justice. What people want is not a given, as argued by more critical perspectives, and dominant IR therefore should broaden its problem solving to an agenda that includes a critical consideration of Justice and emancipation and a reevaluation of constructed actor identities (individual, groups, and institutions, as well as states). These issues will be taken up more extensively in chapters 5 and 6.

Chapter 4 will move on from the paradigmatic conflict reviewed here to zero in on levels of analysis, the most pervasive concept in problem-solving IR. Levels of analysis will be applied to war and its causes, the preeminent problem to be solved. Wars in human history will be compared to *LOTR*'s War of the Ring in search of greater insight about this scourge of humanity.

Middle-earth,
Levels of Analysis,
and War

> War's stupid. Nobody wins. You might as well talk first.
> You have to talk last, anyway.
>
> —*Henry Allingham in an interview with the BBC*

THE PROBLEM OF WAR

When Henry Allingham died on 19 July 2009, at the age of 113, the world lost its oldest man. In the context of this volume's focus on IR, we also lost one of just three known surviving British veterans of World War I. Along with Allingham and millions of others, Tolkien experienced the horrors of trench warfare: artillery barrages, machine-gun fire, poison gas, and dreadful living conditions. The Oxford scholar and later great author had to be removed from battle after four months of service because of trench fever. Millions of others did not come home at all or returned from the war with lifetime disabilities.

Allingham's observation about war in the epigraph to this chapter is profound: Aside from rare instances of genocide, combatants still have to share the postwar world. Some kind of settlement, which by definition could have been obtained without war, must be reached.

Despite its pernicious nature, war continues to plague humanity. Accounting for the causes of war, along with its other characteristics and consequences, stands as a sustained priority across generations of scholarship. War animated problem-solving research in the academic discipline of IR long before other ideas.

In the mythology of IR, the traditional focus on accounting for war is framed as unproblematic. There is an implicit argument that understanding war's destructiveness should be a top priority because it so dramatically influences people and states. This is framed as unsurprising because the field of IR is portrayed as seeking relevance to the human condition. However, because it is assumed rather than explicitly addressed, this story minimizes other sources of human insecurity and discussion of relative priorities (e.g., on explicit war rather than a broader spectrum of violence). The stories that end up getting told minimize discussion of how cultures of war can *perpetuate* human insecurity (rather than protecting against it) and *limit* opportunities for human flourishing (rather than enabling them). Feminist scholarship is introduced in the next chapter as one kind of critical approach in IR that problematizes these kinds of assumptions and consequently prioritizes other things as important. While perspectives in IR are widening the range of subject matter quite steadily, war as traditionally understood remains a major issue of concern in both political practice and theory.

This chapter delves more deeply into the causes of war as a good faith effort to convey the record of dominant IR research so far. While exceptions exist, the field of IR generally tends to take a problem-solving approach that focuses on interstate war rather than individually oriented issues such as human security. This tendency also reflects a value system based on the priorities of states, that is, statecentrism. The centrality of studying the causes of war in IR is overdetermined: dominated by US scholarship, the field generally has followed the lead of one variant of realism or another for decades, and even neoliberal rivals of the power politics approach tend to be statecentric in perspective. Such scholarship focuses on preserving Order by heading off war, as opposed to emphasizing Justice, which would seek a world significantly better than one that merely escapes violent conflict (e.g., to which critical and peace studies scholars give more attention).

The mythology of IR categorizes problem-solving approaches as objective rather than taking a moral stance. However, the sustained presence of war at the top of the problem-solving agenda demonstrates that even a superficially amoral paradigm such as realism contains a normative dimension. One way of thinking about it is to see realists as being ethical within a national framework: they are trying to do what they think is best by their own state's citizens. Their ethical framework is based on their understanding of *their* state, not other peoples' states.

How, then, does the primarily state-oriented discipline of IR put together its ideas about war? Recall the major theoretical components at the outset of figure 2, which outlines how people might think about IR in terms of paradigms and levels of analysis. Covered in chapter 2, paradigms are sources of ideas, including those about the causes of war. Levels of analysis, the main focus of this chapter, is the field's standard way of organizing assessments of cause and effect. In other words, levels of analysis serves as a common tool in much IR investigation.

Among all theoretical constructs, none appears more consistently in IR textbooks than levels of analysis, a "means to organize systematic thinking about world politics" (Viotti and Kauppi 2009: 84). A general consensus exists among problem-solving scholars that three levels can best be used for analysis: individual, state, and system. This analytical framework is based in understandings by classical political theorists of the causes of war (Waltz 1959). Many ideas are already covered thoroughly in IR textbooks, so we will not seek to "reinvent the wheel." Instead, we apply ideas from respective levels to *LOTR*'s War of the Ring in comparison with two other wars: World War I and the War in Iraq, the latter of which continues as large-scale civil strife at this time of writing. This focus complements many IR textbooks (see online appendix), which address these wars, respectively, as the most frequently analyzed among past and present cases.

We start with an overview of factors from each level commonly identified in IR textbooks (see especially Viotti and Kauppi 2009: 86; Ray and Kaarbo 2008; Russett, Starr, and Kinsella 2010; and Rourke and Boyer 2010). A factor is discussed only if it applies to at least one of the three wars at issue here. Figure 3 displays the standard organization of causal factors in problem-solving IR: system, state, and individual. Factors from realism predominate, as already noted, because of that approach's position as either predominant or at least coequal with others for many decades. Causal analysis begins at the system level because these factors provide the ultimate framework for action; put differently, analysis begins with the structural and moves up to the immediate. The state level is next and makes the picture more complex. Finally, individual decision makers and decision-making groups provide the most immediate impact on action. The pyramid of influence exerted by respec-

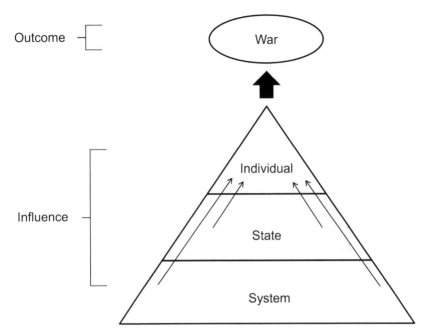

Fig. 3. Levels of analysis and the causes of war. (Adapted from Kegley and Blanton 2010, 16.)

tive causal factors reaches a peak and points upward toward accounting for war as an outcome.

Once variables are identified, a wide range of options exists in terms of research designs that fall within problem-solving IR. These designs vary in complexity; this chapter stays within a relatively simple narrative analysis that considers the possible effect of each variable, in turn, on the potential for war. It should be noted that the incremental, additive model of assessing the possible impact of causal factors is just a baseline model. Variables may interact with each other to produce synergistic effects, for instance, and that level of complexity is beyond the scope of the current overview of factors drawn from respective levels of analysis and their putative connection to the outbreak of war. An example of a research enterprise (James 2002) that includes synergistic effects is neo-Kantianism, which takes the factors identified by the great philosopher Immanuel Kant and combines them into a large-scale data analysis. As described by Kant, democracy, economic interdependence, and membership in international organizations will have synergy, and states with these characteristics will be much less war prone than otherwise (see the online appendix for a relevant IR textbook discussion).

The section that follows applies levels of analysis to organize explanatory factors for the causes and characteristics of the War of the Ring. After that, the same task is carried out in subsequent sections for treatments of World War I and the War in Iraq. All three wars then are compared to each other, with levels of analysis once again organizing the presentation. The final section of the chapter sums up its contribution to the study of international conflict as informed by levels of analysis.

LEVELS OF ANALYSIS AND THE CAUSES OF WAR

System Level

We start analysis at the system level and move upward from there (see fig. 4). The international system is the broadest context for action; its explanations apply on a cross-national basis, so it makes sense to begin with that level. Among international (or global) factors, anarchy is the starting point. Anarchy is the absence of an overarching governing structure—for example, world government. It is regarded as an enabling cause of war because lack of an ultimate arbiter in the system encourages use of force as the final determinant of disputes. This is the standard way of thinking for all variants of realism. The resulting "security dilemma" is a long-standing concept in IR. It refers to the "difficult choice faced by states in anarchy between arming, which risks provoking a response from others, and not arming, which risks remaining vulnerable" (D'Anieri 2010: 64; see also Baylis, Smith, and Owens 2008: 102; and Russett, Starr, and Kinsella 2010: 240–41). In a world of anarchy the security dilemma represents the norm among states, and hence the basic conditions for war always are in place.

Given the constant possibility of war under conditions of anarchy, how power is distributed among states becomes important. Although it is possible to assess the distribution of capabilities in any number of ways, war-related theorizing tends to focus on the number of great powers and concentration of power in the international system. Unipolarity, a condition with just one great power, is regarded as unnatural and likely to be ephemeral. It results from either a lack of willingness or presumably temporary inability to engage in balancing. The act of balancing refers to efforts to deter aggression by joining in with the weaker side in a dispute. A great power with no rivals can be expected to engage in warfare at will, so the system is likely to experience predatory attacks from its unchecked leader.

More controversy exists over whether a system with two (bipolar) or a higher number of great powers (multipolar) will be less warlike. Arguments favoring bipolarity emphasize the simplicity of a system with just two great powers; it should be easier to manage and more stable as a result. Advocates of multipolarity stress the confrontation inherent in a system with two great powers; shifting coalitions, feasible only with three or more such entities, are regarded as the best means of achieving stability. A related discussion concerns the concentration of capabilities in the system: high versus low in relation to likeliness to engage in war. Research on the subject, interestingly enough, supports neither contention. Instead, major *shifts* in capabilities are associated with war.

Power dynamics, as revealed regarding the effects linked to concentration, can be just as important as statics in accounting for war. Prominent in thinking here are theories of power cycles and transitions.

Power Cycle Theory focuses on how great powers go through upward and downward trends in standing among their peers. Movement along the cycle resembles a sine wave (i.e., a roller-coaster type of movement) over the course of multiple decades. When the trend changes, as with reaching a high or low point in the cycle, leaders may be unprepared for what seems like a sudden change in their state's foreign policy role. Qualitative change in relative power—a shift in kind rather than mere degree—makes conflict management more challenging. Involvement in war therefore becomes more likely.

Power Transition Theory focuses on the distribution of power between the first- and second-place states in terms of national power, known, respectively, as leader and challenger. War becomes more likely when there is a power transition, that is, when the challenger is overtaking the leader. This development creates maximum tension because it represents a "changing of the guard" vis-à-vis management of the international system.

Degree of satisfaction with the existing Order is the other key element of power transition theory. War becomes more likely, all other things being equal, when the rising power is dissatisfied. A classic case of war not happening, in spite of a transition, is movement of the United States past the United Kingdom around the end of the nineteenth century vis-à-vis the standard metrics regarding national capabilities. While some tensions did arise, these states did not fight a war with each other. The United States, with minor exceptions, found that the UK-led international system worked in its interests. These leading capitalist, democratic great powers had much more in common relative to their occasional disagreements and cooperated to manage the world to their mutual advantage.

Research on alliances reveals some interesting patterns about the clustering of states in the system and how that relates to the outbreak of war. Creation of alliances, a standard practice in power politics, may be a signal that war is coming. An alternative point of view is that the effects of alliance formation can vary. Thus it becomes possible to discourage war by *balancing* power. One or more potential aggressors may be deterred by a sufficiently capable alliance of status-quo-oriented states (i.e., those generally content with the existing Order). By contrast, *bandwagoning* refers to joining an already superior coalition, with the obvious desire to share in the spoils from an even more likely victory. This type of alliance formation clearly is associated with a greater likelihood of war.

Another capability-related factor is the balance in technology between offense and defense. An advantage to the offense over the defense—even a false belief in it—should encourage invasion and conquest. The invention of artillery, for example, is linked to warfare in late medieval Europe that resulted in gradual consolidation of diverse entities into larger political units. Modern states such as France came about through such processes. By contrast, an advantage to the defense is expected to discourage war because casualties will be much greater for the invading force. Improvement in fortifications and defensive weaponry also can have the effect of lengthening a conflict, as with the American Civil War and World War I.

Factors identified so far reflect statecentrism and power-oriented, realist thinking because the realist tradition focuses on international conflict and war. However, the liberal tradition, which focuses more on international cooperation, is also relevant. From a classical liberal or neoliberal standpoint, international norms and law can play a role at the system level in identifying alternatives to the use of force. International organizations, along with transnational networks, can serve to inhibit war. Through such entities, cooperation may be promoted over confrontation in meeting global challenges. These factors can be summed up under the concept of interdependence, economic or otherwise. Thus the relative *absence* of institutional networks is regarded as a potential cause of war.

In addition to the realist and liberal traditions, critical scholarship also addresses war. As one example, scholarship in the Marxist tradition suggests that, within the context of class conflict, capitalism can produce imperialist war as a result of intensifying competition. As another example, feminist scholarship suggests that militarized masculinity leads to war, as well as other forms of violence. However, as Nau (2009) notes, overall, critical scholars tend to object to the idea of levels of analysis; instead, they see factors "interrelated as an inseparable whole" (133). In other words, the focus of critical approaches on emancipation frequently puts them at odds with conventional ways of describing the world, which are seen to reinforce the existing Order. Because of this, discussions of "class" and "gender" or other social institutions do not fit cleanly into the analytical framework of "levels of analysis."

State Level

Analysis at the level of the state focuses on government and society. The state appears one level up from the system in figure 3 because it is a closer proximate cause of action that includes war, that is, the state is a level less foundational than the system. Research on the causes of war over the last few decades has produced many connections with the type of political system of a state. The most robust finding is that democracies are very unlikely to fight each other. In fact, research on interstate "matchups" reveals that democratic states eschew full-scale war with each other altogether.

Diversionary thinking may encourage war. Extensive research confirms the idea that a national leader in trouble may consider an external conflict to divert the public's attention away from problems at home. Thus a state with internal economic problems or other forms of instability may find its leadership attempting to use a foreign conflict to achieve a "rally 'round the flag effect." Evidence suggests that the effects of such tactics on public support are mild and ephemeral. However, many leaders still *believe* that it can work. Attempted diversion, therefore, can be a cause of war because of leaders who escalate low-level conflict into an unwanted major war.

Another important aspect of government is the policy-making process. Are political and bureaucratic structures in place to provide leaders with access to expertise in an effective way? Given the range of issues impacting foreign policy, a "Lone Ranger" approach to decision making can invite error, misunderstanding, and warfare. At the other end of the continuum, bureaucracies that are vast and powerful can exercise influence independent of the top leadership, possibly even in favor of war (consider, e.g., Dwight Eisenhower's famous warning to beware of the "military-industrial complex").

With regard to society, public opinion and the nature of the economic system stand out as important. As a background condition, does the economic system tend to encourage expansionism, imperialism, or colonialism or are its features more benign? The need for raw materials, for instance, can drive efforts to take over territory by force. More directly, at the stage of confrontation itself, key questions are these: Does the person in the street want war or peace and how much are people willing to suffer? An unpopular government may be tempted to choose war over other options in the hope that victory will restore its position with the public.

Individual Level

Most intricate and immediate as a cause of action is the individual level of analysis. It appears at the top of the pyramid in figure 3—most proximate but least foundational among the three levels. High complexity at this level is not surprising, perhaps, in that the focus here is on the range of individual traits and social effects that can influence decision making. Both individuals and groups are of interest in deciphering decisions about war.

Human nature is deemed crucial by classical realism in explaining the recurrence of warfare; it assumed that people are naturally prone to conflict and states can therefore be expected to clash on the field of battle. Biologically oriented theorizing refers not to human nature but instead to a drive to control territory—and ends up with the same conclusion as realism, namely, that war will recur.

Belief systems, personalities, and perceptions of leaders can matter as well. These factors should influence war in more complicated ways than simply saying to expect more of it because of human nature. Competence and a belief that some viable alternative to war exists may be key considerations in determining outcomes in a crisis setting. Among the problems decision makers may face, exacerbated by a situation of crisis, are wishful thinking, stereotyping, enemy images, and inappropriate use of analogies. In addition, the physical and mental health of leaders can play a role. Leaders suffering from these kinds of problems become less likely to perform well under the extraordinary pressure that arises at the brink of war. Escalation thus becomes more probable.

Group factors also can make a difference. Government bureaucracies can help or hinder efforts to stave off war, as alluded to earlier. For example, groupthink, or the tendency toward premature consensus in a decision-making entity, can increase the likelihood of war. This decision-making malady is caused primarily by closing off the group to evidence contradicting its consensus position. Highly homogeneous groups—or groups made up of people who are very similar—can be particularly vulnerable to that syndrome. Increasing the diversity of groups and ensuring that someone takes on the role of "devil's advocate" can help. For example, increasing numbers of women in leadership above marginal levels (e.g., greater than 30 percent) can change the dynamics of decision-making processes. Another consideration is foreign policy role-playing. Those who occupy specific positions are likely to be influenced by more parochial concerns—this is a standard application of Miles' Law (Miles 1978) regarding point of view (see fig. 2 in chapter 2). A classic and ongoing example of this problem is conflict between the State and Defense Departments in the United States, which respectively tend to favor diplomatic versus military options, all other things being equal, as a by-product of bureaucratic rivalry.

LEVELS OF ANALYSIS AND THE WAR OF THE RING

The politics of Middle-earth can illustrate the previous discussion in a number of ways. However, as previously discussed, political life and political theory rarely map perfectly onto each other. For one thing, there can be some ambiguity among texts regarding where a particular causal variable might appear. The proper place for a factor can change because of the way in which it is articulated. For example, weak leaders such as Denethor and others in *LOTR* might be enumerated as either individual- or state-level factors because they exist as individuals but also are produced by a particular kind of political system that eschews meritocracy. Similar ambiguities arise when abstract concepts overlap—whether the impact of imperialism (system level) and economic system (state level) on war or whether group-related effects such as bureaucratic rivalry belong at the individual or state level. Applying these concepts to Middle-earth can both clarify theoretical understandings and highlight the limitations they involve.

System Level

In Middle-earth, anarchy is the norm among political entities. The security dilemma is both discussed and manifested in a variety of ways. When the members of the Fellowship arrive in Lothlórien and must walk blindfolded as a result of having a Dwarf among them, Haldir the Elf explains, "Indeed in nothing is the power of the Dark Lord more clearly shown than in the estrangement that divides all who still oppose him. Yet so little faith and trust to do we find . . . that we dare not by our own trust endanger our land" (I: 339). Previous warfare between the Elves and Dwarves explains that specific instance of mistrust, but the security dilemma is also often implicit in the international relations of Middle-earth.

One literary observer addresses the effects of anarchy and operation of the security dilemma in Middle-earth in language paralleling that of IR: "The question Tolkien addresses is this: how can individuals and nations so different from another coexist in harmony?" (Chance 1992: 119). Suspicion among the polities of Middle-earth is the norm because of a lack of positive integration; one commentator observes, insightfully, that the inhabitants of Middle-earth "frequently lose contact with each other" (Gray 1980: 3). This is a natural breeding ground for the security dilemma and helps to explain one of the main challenges faced by the Free Peoples in opposition to Sauron. Can they put aside their suspicions and rivalries long enough to stand effectively against him?

Lack of contact and fear of others, consistent with the security dilemma in operation, are pervasive themes in the trilogy (I: 7). Given its otherwise friendly character, instances of this type of thinking in the Shire especially are revealing. To Hobbits in general, Gandalf and Dwarves are regarded as outsiders, against whom one might have to be ready for just about anything (I: 10). Even Sam Gamgee, a character as purely good as virtually any encountered in the world of fiction, is suspicious of outsiders (I: 91).

While hardly militarized compared to other places in Middle-earth, the otherwise idyllic Shire is not without some capacity to defend itself. Known as the "Hobbitry-in-Arms," the Shire militia is led by the Thain, an otherwise vestigial officeholder, as needed. The "bounders" stand ready at the outskirts of the Shire to eject those deemed undesirable (Tyler 1976: 69, 227). While limited in comparison to standing armies and security forces elsewhere, these Hobbit-oriented examples are especially compelling because this is the race within Middle-earth that intuition would suggest is *least* likely to exhibit traits associated with the security dilemma.

Examples of the security dilemma abound in the pages of *LOTR*. Its impact is to create distrust and conflict far beyond levels noted for the Shire. Saruman's fear that King Théoden will find and use the Ring is the reason why he assaults Rohan (fear leading to conflict) (II: 487). When betrayed by Saruman and imprisoned in Orthanc, Gandalf questions Rohan's allegiance before ultimately deciding to fly there with Gwaihir the eagle (I: 255). As it turns out, sometimes suspicion is called for, as with the treachery of Saruman, and sometimes it is not, as with the true allegiance of Rohan. This rings true with the complexity of alliance politics in a world where the practice of IR is always conducted against the backdrop of the security dilemma.

Multiple security dilemmas are manifested in Middle-earth. Most obvious is the rivalry and suspicion between Mordor and Gondor, which among the lands of Middle-earth are the most powerful. The war potential of this pairing is increased precisely because of other security dilemmas that operate between and among the Free Peoples. Their inability to overcome rivalries weakens the overall effort to balance the power of Sauron. For example, suspicion exists between Gondor and Rohan, its principal ally among Men.

Consider also the distribution of capabilities as related to war. Middle-earth shows how capability distributions evolve and influence war's likelihood. At the time of Sauron's defeat and loss of the Ring, which marked the end of the Second Age, Middle-earth had been multipolar. Men and Elves had aligned against Sauron. Gondor at the height of its power could count on substantial support from the Elves, who collectively represented a second great power with multiple bases that included Rivendell and Lothlórien. So three great powers existed. With the passing of time in the Third Age, however, most Elves left Middle-earth, with the relatively few who remained preferring isolation. A unipolar world led by Gondor gradually saw the rise of new powers: a restored Mordor, with Sauron gaining strength more rapidly with time; the Kingdom of Rohan, led by its horsemen; and Isengard, with the treacherous Saruman at the helm. This is the profile of power during the decades leading up to the War of the Ring: a multipolar world.

With regard to the dynamics of power, Mordor is on top and still rising as the War of the Ring draws closer: "Gandalf and Aragorn have long been concerned with the growing presence of Sauron, even before the One Ring of Power is discovered" (Hall 2006: 185). *The Lord of the Rings* is full of references from various characters to the overwhelming military might concentrating in the hands of Mordor. Boromir, for example, articulates on numerous occasions the difficult situation of Gondor, which has responsibility for standing between Sauron and the Free Peoples. In the movie version of *The Fellowship of the Ring*, Boromir tells Aragorn, "My father is a good man, but his rule is failing." This perception of weakness relative to Mordor is reinforced as Gondor becomes more familiar throughout the story.

Located at a strategic position and once the jewel of Gondor, the city of Osgiliath changes hands between the two great powers in a flashback scene from the movie version of *The Return of the King* about the period immediately preceding *LOTR*. Forces led by Boromir are able to take back the city from an occupying force of Orcs but at great cost and with a sense that time is running out for a Gondor permanently on the defensive. Without a major reversal in the ongoing shift of capabilities toward Mordor, Gondor soon will have no hope against Sauron. The resulting sense of desperation is what drives Boromir to argue so vehemently at the Council of Elrond in favor of using the Ring. Later he even attempts to seize it from Frodo.

Quite memorable are the reflections of Frodo, gifted with enhanced vision when he puts on the Ring to escape the madness of Boromir toward the end of *The Fellowship of the Ring*. Consider the perspective gained by Frodo from a high elevation at Amon Hen. He sees the range of capabilities deployed by Sauron, and pauses to become impressed with Minas Tirith, but ultimately feels hopeless when his view shifts back to the overwhelming military might of Mordor (I: 391–92). This impression, along with the sense of urgency felt by Boromir after long experience in holding off the forces of Mordor, is consistent with a noteworthy shift of capabilities in favor of the Dark Lord.

Power Cycle Theory would explain the War of the Ring in terms of its proximity to critical points for the leading powers of Gondor and Mordor: it argues that war becomes more likely in proximity to critical points of changing relative capabilities for great powers. This would highlight the importance of Sauron's strike at Gondor after a long period of decline for his rival. Arguably, Gondor had reached its approximate nadir in terms of capabilities relative to Mordor. Perhaps this weighed on Sauron's mind and can help to explain the timing of initiation for the War of the Ring. Consider Aragorn's observation about Sauron: "He is not so mighty yet that he is above fear; nay, doubt ever gnaws him" (III: 763). Could this be an allusion to Sauron's perception of a critical point in power? Could he have feared that waiting would equal waning with respect to relative capability? This would be a reasonable belief, with the Ring unaccounted for and the potential for a return of the king to the throne of Gondor. While we cannot test this assertion, the timing of Sauron's attack is interesting to contemplate from the point of view offered by Power Cycle Theory.

Power Transition Theory would explain the timing of the War of the Ring as a product of long-term trends in relative capabilities for the leader and challenger in the system: this approach accounts for war when the second-most-powerful great power is moving past the most powerful. After his defeat at the end of the Second Age, Sauron existed in a weakened state and moved into the smaller, less conspicuous fortress of Dol Guldur. He worked slowly, through third parties, to weaken the northern Free Peoples. This allowed him eventually to move back into Mordor and focus on making gains at the expense of a gradually more isolated Gondor. Meanwhile, Gondor, once in a unipolar position, saw its power wane throughout the Third Age. Discovery of the Ring sets in motion the final set of events leading up to the great war that is the subject of *LOTR*. Mordor surpasses Gondor in power and strikes hard under what appear to be optimal conditions. Note that, as per Power Transition Theory's expectations, Mordor fits the description of a *dis*satisfied power that chooses war as its option for fundamentally changing the existing Order.

With regard to alliances, both balancing and bandwagoning occur in Middle-earth. Balancing of power in *LOTR* is most evident by the Free Peoples represented by the Fellowship against the rising threat of Sauron. At his Council, Elrond tells those attending, "[Y]our trouble is but part of the trouble of all the western world" (I: 236). This shared threat is what glues different groups of people together (see also Drury 1980), even though they do not always trust each other. For example, in the movie version of *The Fellowship of the Ring*, debate at the Council of Elrond over who should be the Ring Bearer focuses on mistrust between and among races of Free People. References to antagonism between races are legion in the trilogy. (See, e.g., I: 7, 10, 222, 288, 249, 295, 346; and II: 422, 664. See also Chance 2001: 48; and Scull 1992: 151).

From this perspective, it is interesting to consider the choice of Frodo to carry the Ring. In the movie version of *The Fellowship of the Rings*, it becomes obvious from the Council that none of the significant players would have trusted one of the others to serve as Ring Bearer. Thus a Hobbit ends up in that role because of the uniquely nonthreatening nature of this race among the Free Peoples. Security dilemmas plague all other combinations of Free Peoples as they attempt to collaborate with each other in even a minimal way against the life-threatening power of Mordor.

Gandalf repeatedly notes the importance of joining together in an alliance against Mordor (e.g., II: 500, 501) and tries to keep Sauron "off balance" (Lense 1976: 6). In this effort at balancing, Gandalf asks a fellow Wizard, Radagast the Brown, to use his special gift of interspecies communication to ask the beasts and birds that are his friends to ally against Sauron (I: 251). In addition, Denethor, Steward of Gondor, asks Théoden, King of Rohan, to remember their alliance in the face of the rising Shadow (III: 782), and the Wild Men of the Woods offer to ally with Théoden (III: 813). In each instance, the security dilemma is in play: can these actors follow their real interests or will mutual mistrust prevent them from allying against their most dangerous enemy?

Finally, the classic balancing formula of "my enemy's enemy is my friend" is demonstrated by Treebeard the Ent. Although Treebeard claims he is not on any particular "side" (II: 461), his Huorn companions help to finish off the Uruk-hai after the Battle of Helm's Deep (II: 556) because they so hate the Orcs, who also happen to be attacking Rohan. Overall, balancing by the heroes against the villains is a recurrent theme in *LOTR*, albeit insufficient to head off war.

Bandwagoning is also evident and is portrayed in a negative way in each instance. It is exemplified by Saruman's side switching (II: 427) and his exhortation to Gandalf to follow suit and ally with Sauron. Another example is the alliance of the Southrons (II: 625), along with other lesser powers bent on making gains at the expense of the Free Peoples, with the Dark Lord. In the movie version of *The Two Towers*, one character, Gollum—hardly a paragon of virtue himself—describes the Southrons as "wicked." Along with the Southrons, Sauron is supported by armies of Easterlings and the seafaring Corsairs of Umbar. In an overall sense, bandwagoning effects, along with the military power of Mordor itself, overwhelm efforts at balancing, with the exception of Aragorn's enlistment of the Army of the Dead. The war that ensues is consistent with theoretical analysis that warns against the inducement of war via bandwagoning.

The offense/defense balance in Middle-earth raises some questions about IR theory. On average Middle-earth institutions tend to favor defense. Minas Tirith and Helm's Deep, for instance, are very well fortified and extremely difficult for an army to attack without suffering massive casualties. One way of explaining the wars of conquest launched by Sauron and Saruman is to look at the interaction between military technology and a national-level characteristic, namely, the willingness to suffer. The Dark Lord is bent on dominion over Middle-earth and places no value on the lives of his minions. Thus many thousands of Orcs perish throughout *LOTR* with no effort to limit losses. While Sauron seeks to win the battles he fights, casualties are absorbed without comment (e.g., III: 809–10). One of Sauron's greatest advantages is that he is willing to sacrifice entire armies, which he can replace with relative ease, in order to come out on top. Saruman behaves in the same way until that capability is destroyed by the Ents. The Free Peoples, by contrast, place a much greater value on life and are less numerous in the first place. Thus the very high willingness to absorb casualties can explain why wars of conquest could be launched even in a world approximating defensive dominance.

With regard to international organizations, Middle-earth appears to contain just one: the White Council. This Council of the Wise met on an *ad hoc* basis and featured elite membership consisting of Wizards and the highest of the Elves. It existed to manage the response to Evil in Middle-earth, most notably as manifested by Sauron. The Council's story is unfortunate because of a traitor in its midst: Saruman, who served as its first chief. The Council had the right idea about Sauron, but Saruman blocked an attack on the Dark Lord at a time when the Free Peoples still had much greater power and could have preempted his later actions. Suspicion built that Dol Guldur had become the place where Sauron attempted to rebuild his power after losing the Ring. By the time Saruman later agreed to an attack by the Wise on Dol Guldur, Sauron, who had been there all along, "withdrew to Mirkwood and re-entered Mordor long prepared for him." By the time of the War of the Ring, members of the White Council itself had become quite suspicious of Saruman, who, as it turned out, had undermined their efforts to protect Middle-earth against Sauron (Tyler 1976: 517–18).

Interdependence is at a very low level in Middle-earth. Its inhabitants, as the discussion of the security dilemma brings out, harbor suspicions about each other. The Common Speech permits communication among virtually everyone, but that does not translate into sustained and significant interactions. While trade exists, autarky (i.e., a self-contained economy) seems closer to the norm, economically speaking. This is connected to technology, since travel is time consuming and can even be dangerous, especially if the destination is distant from home.

State Level

Middle-earth is populated overwhelmingly by autocracies. The most extreme example is Mordor, which is under the total domination of Sauron. Political entities allied with Mordor are under dictatorship by puppet regimes. Gondor and Rohan are monarchies. The Order among the Elves contains elements of hereditary aristocracy (Elrond and Galadriel are preeminent in Rivendell and Lothlórien, respectively), although the little information that is available about how power is institutionalized makes categorizing them difficult. Two exceptions exist to the overall pattern of autocracy: Fangorn Forest and the Shire.

Within Fangorn Forest, the Ents live in a state of peaceful anarchy. Known as "Entmoots," their rare meetings are intended to produce consensual agreement. These gatherings occur only under pressing need for major decision making. In that sense, Fangorn Forest lacks a key property of a political system per se: regular interaction.

Among political entities in Middle-earth, only the Shire resembles a democracy in even a limited way (but see Barnett 1969). The Shire's most important official, the mayor of Michel Delving, is elected every seven years and plays a largely ceremonial role. The mayor's responsibilities included presiding at banquets and supervising the Shire's only services: messengers and a watch kept on the borders (the bounders, noted earlier). More important are the hereditary leadership roles of two families: the Tooks and Brandybucks (Tyler 1976: 286). In particular, the "thain" of the Tooks had authority to take over from the mayor under crisis conditions—a shift in decision-making power in response to security-related needs. In sum, only in a very minimal way does the Shire look like a democracy; it might be regarded as such strictly in comparison to the other Free Peoples. What the label of "Free Peoples" means in Middle-earth as opposed to our contemporary world remains an interesting question.

Given the political systems prevailing in Middle-earth, wars between and among them come as no surprise. The pacifying effects of the democratic peace do not apply in a world with only one quasi-democratic political system.

Policy making in Middle-earth reveals the dangers of unchecked personal power. Neither Rohan nor Gondor, the two powers principally resisting Mordor, possesses anything that resembles an advisory council. Instead, rulers are in a position to go their own way.

Take, for example, King Théoden's power to decide unilaterally the foreign policy of Rohan. The policy-making process there became hopelessly corrupted prior to the arrival of members of the Fellowship; the king consults only with a traitor, Wormtongue, who does all that he can to bring about isolationism and a lack of preparedness in Rohan. Wormtongue's agenda favors war—that is, a successful one for Isengard, not Rohan. Given that Saruman cast a spell on the king, causing him to accept Wormtongue's deceitful advice, it is not surprising that Rohan is in rapid decline.

Things are no better in Gondor, where the Steward, Denethor, holds sway. *The Return of the King* conveys an elderly, bitter man, broken by the loss of Boromir and increasingly out of touch with reality. Faramir, his surviving son, is blamed unfairly for Boromir's death, the loss of Osgiliath, and seemingly whatever else upsets Denethor at a given moment. This poor judgment comes out vividly in a movie scene in *The Return of the King*. Denethor rejects Faramir's good advice and instead insists on a suicidal attempt, led by his son, to retake Osgiliath. This is just one example of Denethor's incompetent leadership, which is coupled with an overall lack of preparedness and sporadic instances of aggression. All of this is a product of Denethor's use of one of the *palantíri*, the seeing stones, through which he comes under the powerful and destructive influence of Sauron, who also possesses one of these stones.

Even with more capable leadership, it would have been challenging to produce a minimally competent treatment of the issues and options for dealing with them under the conditions that existed for decision making in Rohan and Gondor. No structure for advising is available in either kingdom. The increasingly precarious position of the Free Peoples, in part, is a commentary on the inadequacies of monarchical systems. Gondor and Rohan, poorly led autocracies, pursued policies that have made them vulnerable to attack.

This point spills over into a consideration of public opinion, in which both Gondor and Rohan can be characterized as defeatist, in keeping with their leadership. In the movie version of *The Two Towers*, Gimli notes the demoralized appearance of the people looking on as he and the other members of the Fellowship enter Edoras and approach King Théoden's hall. Gandalf tells Pippin in *The Return of the King*, represented on screen in tones of exasperation, about the decrepit condition of Gondor, with a leader more focused on the past than the future. It almost goes without saying that such a mind-set reduced the level of preparedness for war attained by each Kingdom, even though the ill intentions of Sauron and Saruman had been obvious for some time.

Despite these limited institutional advising structures, it is interesting to note that both Gondor and Rohan do have a hierarchical "officer corps" in place, ready to act as needed. However, both kingdoms end up paralyzed because of (in)actions by those at the top. In the movie version of *The Return of the King*, Théoden banishes Éomer and his horsemen, while Denethor fails to set in motion defensive actions that military officers in Minas Tirith would have been ready to take. War becomes more likely under such conditions because neither Gondor nor Rohan balanced effectively against its adversaries.

Economic issues are relatively absent in *LOTR*. This is noted already vis-à-vis low levels of interdependence in the international system. Some information is available, however, about economic systems at a general level. Extremes in terms of economic organization come out when comparing Nurn and the Shire, both agrarian. Nurn is the name given to the greater part of Mordor, "filled with endless acres of regimented fields, which were worked by Sauron's slaves to feed his numerous armies" (Tyler 1976: 347). The Shire, by contrast, is made up of family farms. It engages in limited trade with the neighboring village of Bree and is remarkably self-contained otherwise. In accord with what scholars in the Marxist tradition would argue, Sauron's expansionist foreign policy dovetails with his exploitative economic system. After Sauron lays waste the natural resources in Mordor, he must extend his grasp into less exploited resources beyond its boundaries to sustain his power. This expansive and unsustainable approach comes first at the cost of the inhabitants of Mordor and then targets the Free Peoples beyond its borders. Observe, for example, that pipeweed from the Shire's Southfarthing made it all the way to Isengard, a puppet regime seemingly under the direction of Saruman but ultimately controlled by Sauron. This reveals the spread of Sauron's geographic reach as the time of war approaches. From the standpoint of the Dark Lord, expansion involves the need for more food, which in turn facilitates greater conquest. It is a classic vicious circle.

Except for Isengard, which Sauruman leads in alliance with Mordor, other entities in Middle-earth do not feature this imperative toward expansion. This returns to the neo-Marxist perspective, which would explain expansionism on the basis of the forces of imperialism. The economic superstructure of Mordor might cause it to initiate wars of conquest even if led by someone less evil than Sauron.

Individual Level

Classical realism finds its views about human nature lived out to the extreme in the actions of Sauron. The Dark Lord is bent on conquest and represents Evil with a capital *E*. More than anything else, the War of the Ring comes about because of Sauron's desire to dominate Middle-earth. His master creation, the Ring of Power, is able to tempt all who encounter it into evil as well. Sauron's disposition toward war is clear, yet he does not attack at all times. Although he is in error about the other side's ultimate strategic goal, Sauron tempers his desire for conquest with a remarkable ability to wait out events. He waits literally thousands of years to attack Gondor in full force, after long efforts to weaken it sufficiently. Perhaps it could be said that Sauron waits because he must; in spite of an urge toward conquest the Dark Lord is able to show great patience and strike when the real opportunity comes his way. Thus the timing of the War of the Ring may be more interesting to consider than the issue of whether or not it would occur.

The beliefs, personalities, and perceptions of Denethor and Théoden can help clarify the issue of timing. Each leader suffers from influences that induce fatalism, most notably, a belief in inevitable defeat. Théoden is subject to the spell of Saruman, conveyed through Wormtongue. He comes to believe, falsely, that friends are enemies and Saruman is an ally. Denethor's malady comes about through use of the *palantír*. He is overwhelmed by the will of Sauron and comes to believe that no hope exists for Gondor. Denethor becomes subject to a peculiar combination of defeatism and wishful thinking and does not prepare Gondor properly for the coming assault from Mordor. A memorable scene from the film version of *The Return of the King* reveals the shock experienced by Denethor when he sees the Dark Lord's enormous military forces forming a ring around Minas Tirith. Denethor panics, calls out for people to flee for their lives, and is knocked unconscious by Gandalf, who instead urges the forces of Gondor to stand and fight.

Effects from personality come out dramatically through Saruman's descent into evil. He once had been a great force for good—head of the White Council itself. Yet his ambition knew no bounds. He looked into the *palantír* and fell under the influence of Sauron. Saruman's bandwagoning significantly increases the strength of Mordor and helps to explain the timing of the war. Without the power built up in Isengard, Rohan would have been free to assist Gondor directly and not forced to fight a separate war beforehand against Saruman.

What about the role of women in decision making? Even Galadriel, the most powerful woman in *LOTR*, does not participate in the Council of Elrond. In Middle-earth, women appear to exert political influence only indirectly through marriage or other family connections. Their official role appears to be virtually nonexistent; a major exception is Galadriel who, for example, initiated the White Council. In most other instances, the amount of influence exerted, institutional or otherwise, is unknown.

Despite this, clues available in *LOTR* suggest that—as in our world—simply including a woman decision maker in decisions of war and peace would not reduce the likelihood of war in Middle-earth (Rourke and Boyer 2010: 60). First, while Galadriel is able to refuse the Ring, she does so knowing that she could not resist its evil influence if it came into her possession. This is a trait she shares only with Gandalf, Faramir, and presumably just a few others in Middle-earth. Second, the character of Éowyn, a member of high nobility in Rohan, contradicts notions that women are pacifist because of their biological characteristics. She wants, more than anything else, to participate in Rohan's martial culture rather than being left behind to take care of women and children while the men go off to fight.

Consider an exchange between Éowyn and Aragorn over this issue. Aragorn urges her to take satisfaction in the role of shepherding women and children through the battle to come rather than participating in it. Éowyn expresses no fear of pain or death but does say that she fears one thing: "'A cage,' she said. 'To stay behind bars, until use and old age accepts them, and all chance of doing great deeds is gone beyond recall or desire'" (III: 767). She even goes so far as to disguise herself as a man in order to participate in battle and plays a critical role in the defeat of Sauron's forces at the Fields of Pelennor. As such, the few women who are highlighted in Middle-earth support feminist IR arguments about our world that suggest that gendered "martial culture" (such as that participated in by Éowyn) and gendered institutions that support dominating relationships (such as Galadriel wielding the Ring) are more important in influencing opportunities for war and peace than decision makers' genetic makeup.

WORLD WAR I

The Great War

World War I, known as the Great War until it was renamed over two decades later, stands as one of the great tragedies in human history. It lasted from August 1914 to November 1918. The Great War involved all of the great powers of its time. While it started in a remarkably innocuous way, it mobilized more than seventy million military personnel, unfolded as a hellish war of attrition, and left over fifteen million people dead. The main European battlefronts in Europe, which featured trench warfare, produced utter devastation and changed the continent forever. World War I produced the Versailles Treaty, which enraged a defeated Germany and set the stage for efforts to even the score (and beyond) in World War II. The Great War's suffering and chaos extended to respective home fronts and produced, most notably, the Russian Revolution of October 1917—the birth of world communism—and brought to an end the Ottoman and Austro-Hungarian empires. (Nau 2009: 109; Rourke and Boyer 2010: 37).

Efforts to unravel the causes of the Great War continue to this day. "More has been written on the origins of World War I," observes D'Anieri (2010: 38), "than on those of any other war." Still, the causes of the Great War "remain in dispute" (Kegley and Blanton 2010: 92). No effort will be made here to offer a definitive treatment and thereby resolve points of disagreement that linger on about World War I. Instead, we seek to bring out its complexity using all levels of analysis and thereby to facilitate comparison of cause and effect with the War of the Ring and War in Iraq).[1]

---

1. For related textbook discussions, see Baylis, Smith, and Owens 2008: 56, 57; Bueno de Mesquita 2010: 413; D'Anieri 2010: 39, 40, 185; Goldstein and Pevehouse 2009: 26; Kegley and Blanton 2010: 91, 92; Mansbach and Rafferty 2008: 102, 103, 104–5, 106, 108, 115, 116; Mingst 2008: 209, 213; Nau 2009: 121, 128, 129, 132, 133; Ray and Kaarbo 2008: 188, 197, 201, 202, 203, 257, 293; and Steans, Pettiford, and Diez 2005: 81.

System Level

Ideas about the origins of the Great War emerge primarily from realist expositions. However, neoliberal and critical approaches provide explanations as well.

Anarchy stands as an enabling condition for war because of the lack of any overarching international authority. Security dilemmas abound in the world of early-twentieth-century Europe, home at the time to most of the great powers and therefore the central subsystem of world politics. At the top of the list is the enmity between France and Germany over the latter's victory in the Franco-Prussian War, which had included the transfer of Alsace-Lorraine. Loss of this territory by France stood as a national humiliation and ongoing grievance against Germany. Russia and Germany also eyed each other with suspicion. In the Balkans, rivalry played itself out between the Austro-Hungarian and Russian empires. Slavs chafed under Austro-Hungarian rule and inspired ethnically driven sympathy from Russia. Tension also built between Germany and the world's leading naval power, Great Britain. The British viewed the impressive navy built by the Germans with great concern because of the threat it could pose to their far-flung empire. Taken together, this series of conflicts, among others, caused many observers to refer to Europe at the time as a "powder keg"—ready to explode at a moment's notice.

World War I stands as the archetypal case for the bipolarity argument in the debate over stability and polarity. Europe plunged into war for reasons that follow from its multipolar nature. Consider all of the problematic pairs of states just discussed. Complex relations among the conflict-laden great powers produced uncertainty, fear, and an urge to act under time pressure. From the standpoint of bipolarity, complications in pre–World War I European diplomacy eventually added up to polarization into two hostile camps and escalation to war.

Rapid and qualitative change in the concentration of power drove European politics toward confrontation in the decades leading up to the Great War. Germany, in particular, was transformed from a collection of minor states to the greatest power on the continent in just three decades. It surpassed Great Britain as the leading industrial giant and had by far the most impressive land forces among the great powers. Not surprisingly, Germany's rapid rise created efforts to balance against it. Russia and France both felt threatened by Germany and signed a defense pact directed against this ascendant power.

At the other end of the scale from Germany, dramatic decline beset both the Austro-Hungarian and Ottoman empires. Conflict in the Balkans heated up in the early twentieth century and represented a response to the emerging power vacuum in that region as the old empires lost their grip. Russia, in particular, hoped to make gains at the expense of Austria-Hungary, in spite of its own primarily economic challenges.

Dynamics of power also point in the direction of war. Power Cycle theorists have charted critical points for the great powers and find several in proximity to the outbreak of World War I. In a relative sense, Great Britain had peaked and entered a phase of relative decline while Germany was approaching its apogee. This, perhaps, helps to explain why Great Britain went to war in 1914: it would be better to fight then than later. Also consistent with Power Cycle Theory, German leaders expressed anxiety about the rise of Russia. A similar logic then drove the German position: fight now rather than later when relative power is in decline. German power by most accounts peaked a few years prior to World War I. While Russia's collapse in the war reveals the projection regarding that empire to be off base, perceptions, not reality, are what matter under such conditions.

Power Transition theorists emphasize the passing of the torch from Great Britain to Germany as the leading power, shortly before World War I, as a dangerous development. The international system as managed by Great Britain had little appeal for Germany, to put it mildly, a late and somewhat disadvantaged entrant into colonial competition. Known as the Pax Brittanica, Order certainly existed, but it lacked Justice from a German point of view. Tensions between the leading state and the challenger built as the transition between them took place.

Alliances factor significantly into the story told here. Noted already is the defense pact signed by Russia and France. This agreement, however, represented just one of a dense network of alliances formed between and among European powers. The rate of formation of such agreements was much higher in Europe in the period after the unification of Germany than it had been in preceding decades. In addition to the sheer quantity of alliances—perhaps a signal of oncoming war in and of itself—the structure of these affiliations proves revealing. The alliance system of early-twentieth-century Europe may be summed up as highly polarized. Composed of Germany, Austria-Hungary, and Italy, the Triple Alliance faced off against the Triple Entente, which included France, Russia, and Great Britain. No agreement with any real "teeth" in it—

meaning a defense pact, which would obligate assisting the ally if attacked—overlapped between the two alliances. This is why the alliance system is described as polarized and regarded as an important contributing factor to the Great War.

What about the offense/defense balance? This is perhaps the cruelest part of the story, given how the war worked out in practice. All major powers believed in offensive dominance in 1914. This now is known as the "cult of the offensive." Railroads, automobiles, and airplanes made it possible to move much more quickly than in the past, so this revolutionary change in transportation led to the mistaken belief that striking first and quickly would lead to rapid victory. Unfortunately for all concerned, this made war more likely because it reduced the time for, and interest in, negotiation.

This fixation on striking quickly occurred despite the fact that, at a tactical level, the fighting in the Great War turned out to be dominated by defensive weaponry: huge armies faced off against each other in thousands of miles of trenches, separated by barbed wire, with artillery, poison gas, and machine guns inflicting devastating casualties. The trenches cut across Europe from the English Channel to the Swiss border. Tolkien himself experienced the Battle of the Somme, in which hundreds of thousands died because of senseless infantry charges into heavily defended positions. The conundrum of *why* states overestimate offensive dominance capabilities—both in World War I and otherwise—is not addressed in traditional accounts of the cult of the offensive but is addressed by feminist scholarship.

Liberal theorizing, not surprisingly, emphasizes the role of international institutions in explaining the Great War. Perhaps a better way of putting this is to say that a *lack* of institutional networks is the fundamental explanation for the war from a liberal point of view. While conferences did occur at the Hague in 1899 and 1907, the European powers lacked a regular forum for discussion. They had scheduled a further meeting—but not until 1915. War intervened in August 1914.

Critical perspectives on World War I in the Marxist tradition emphasize imperialism. This line of reasoning is associated most closely with the principal figure of the first Russian Revolution, Vladimir Lenin. This Marxist-Leninist perspective, articulated by Lenin in *Imperialism*, a book published in 1916—before the revolution of 1917—regards the capitalist economic system practiced by the great powers as the principal underlying reason for war in August 1914. Driven by the need for new markets and raw materials, great powers competed with each other at high levels of intensity around the globe. The friction created by this competition eventually could be expected to produce a general war. Thus Anglo-German naval rivalry, along with other pairings that led to war in 1914, could be subsumed under the larger heading of imperial rivalry. The fact that workers with rare exceptions fought under their respective flags for nationalist purposes rather than rising up against the exploitation of capitalism is a problem for traditional Marxist theory, which focused primarily on *material* economic inequalities. This kind of anomaly helped instigate reinterpretations of Marxist theory such as Gramscianism and Frankfurt School Critical Theory, which emphasize how dominating *beliefs* (e.g., nationalism) circumscribe efforts to combat exploitation.

State Level

Factors at the state level also influenced the start of World War I. Nationalism, as previously mentioned, and internal political developments and bureaucracies are the most commonly cited causal forces at this level.

Nationalism pervaded the thinking of elites and mass publics alike in the Europe of the early 1900s. A perversion of the theory of natural selection, known as "social Darwinism," had gained extensive popularity. This misapplication of Charles Darwin's scientific principles encouraged people to think of themselves as superior based on their nationality. (This corresponded to beliefs about the superiority of masculinity over femininity.) Such beliefs created the disposition toward conquest of those deemed inferior and thereby encouraged war. This reinforced rivalries based on power politics. It also encouraged the mistaken view, held across the board in both the capitals and streets of Europe, that war would be short, easy, and glorious. All believed that their favored version of a new Order could be imposed with ease.

What about regime type? No effects from collective democracy among states mitigated conflict here. Among the major participants at the outbreak of the war, only Great Britain and France qualified as democracies. The United States, also a democracy, joined the war later. At the outset, the two coalitions featured a mixture of regimes, so the democratic peace does not apply here as a condition inhibiting war.

Domestic disintegration of the Ottoman, Russian, and Austro-Hungarian empires opened the door to war. Internal problems reduced the capabilities of each of these polyglot entities significantly; in fact, the Ottoman Empire of this era became known as the "Sick Man of Europe." Declining ability to control their territory produced separatist movements in the Austro-Hungarian and Ottoman empires, which in turn exacerbated great power rivalries because other great powers tried to exploit the problems. Turmoil also may have encouraged leaders of these beleaguered states to look at war as a more attractive option. Victory might distract the public from ongoing problems and enable the leadership to regain control of a deteriorating situation.

Domestic problems can facilitate war for relatively strong, as well as weakening, states. The rising power on the continent, Germany, had some of the same motivations concerning war. Unlike the great powers just noted, Germany featured a very successful economy and had been gaining power and influence. However, it also faced internal tensions that could get out of control if left unchecked. Concerned for their positions of power, industrial and agricultural interests worried about efforts by the working class to obtain political influence. Thus war could serve multiple interests: A successful war could take attention away from class conflict, as well as make gains at the expense of other great powers. In addition, those in power at the time favored policies that tended to cause strife with other great powers anyway. The landed aristocracy wanted high tariffs to prop up grain prices, and industrialists benefited from the military buildup. Backed by the new navy, German colonial ambitions worsened relations with the British in particular.

Add it all together and the German domestic situation and associated policies had many ingredients that encouraged war. Germany did not go looking for war directly, but its characteristics made this state more likely to be opportunistic. Rather than being averse to conflict, Germany did not make much of its chances to slow or prevent escalation. Instead, the German leadership backed increasingly aggressive Austro-Hungarian behavior in the Balkans to the point of no return.

Bureaucracy—or perhaps lack of it—plays a significant role in the story of the war's outbreak. Most apparent is the fact that modern foreign policy administration did not exist at the time. A handful of overworked and ultimately exhausted leaders attempted to manage the mounting crisis that produced a general war. Neither expert opinion nor possibilities for delegation existed in the way they did later in history; for example, none of the adversaries could rely on anything like the Department of State in the United States today, where experts on a comprehensive range of regions and subjects stand ready to advise the president. Lack of infrastructure increased the likelihood of misperception and error and thereby enhanced the probability of war. Notable in particular is how rapidly the situation in the Balkans fell apart. An apparently minor incident in late June had escalated to all-out war by early August.

Individual Level

Explanations for World War I also are plentiful at the individual level. Among the standard factors noted are the assassination of the Austrian archduke in late June 1914, defects of the key decision makers, misperception, and the role played by bureaucracies.

Gavrilo Princip, a Serbian nationalist, assassinated Archduke Franz Ferdinand of Austria on 28 June 1914 in Sarajevo. The Balkans had been unstable for some time, and this event, regrettably, did not seem to represent anything out of the ordinary. However, the assassination is remembered as the proximate cause of the war because multiple great powers became involved and handled the ensuing crisis in a manner not conducive to its peaceful resolution. Austria-Hungary gave Serbia, a component of the empire associated with the assassination, an ultimatum. The Serbs complied with most of the empire's demands but suffered invasion anyway because Austria-Hungary had no intention of backing away from war. The ultimatum had been written, in fact, to be rejected. The ultimatum and its partial rejection constituted the spark that ignited a general war.

Leadership at the time of the July Crisis, as it became known, seems quite unimpressive and constituted a significant cause of war. Emperor Franz Joseph of Austria-Hungary emerges from the pages of history books as a tired old man. Isolated and highly autocratic in his ways, Czar Nicholas II of Russia fared poorly in crisis management. Perhaps the worst of all throughout accounts of the decades leading up to the Great War is Kaiser Wilhelm II of Germany. His bombastic style of diplomacy exacerbated tensions and inspired dislike for Germany. Some critics even have characterized Wilhelm and Theobald von Bethmann-Hollweg, his principal adviser (with the use of gendered "enemy images"), as emotionally unstable or evil. They certainly appeared to be out of touch with reality in continuing to believe that Great Britain, and perhaps even Russia and France, could be kept out of the war as the July Crisis wore on. At a deeper level, of course, the weak leadership in these autocracies can be linked to the dynastic systems that produced them. Without meritocracy, it is not surprising that mediocre leaders might end up as the rule rather than the exception, with harmful consequences at times that called for adroit diplomacy to avert war.

Finally, misperception also contributed to war in other ways. Italy had a nonaggression pact with France and, when war came, stayed out of the fighting until 1915, finally siding with the Triple Entente. (The Ottoman Empire ended up fighting on the side of the Triple Alliance.) As this illustrates, not all states met their commitments. The Germans reasonably could have concluded (and did) that Great Britain would stay out of the fighting, but that inference turned out to be incorrect (Bueno de Mesquita 2010: 120).

WAR IN IRAQ

War and Occupation

Led by the United States and United Kingdom, a temporary alliance of states referred to as the "Coalition of the Willing" invaded Iraq on 20 March 2003. The war became known under several labels, which correspond to how one might see its context: the War in Iraq (put most simply), Operation Iraqi Freedom (obviously a label favored by those who supported the military effort to overthrow Saddam Hussein's dictatorship), and the Second Gulf War (which connects the events of 2003 with George H. W. Bush's military-backed eviction of Saddam Hussein from Kuwait, i.e., the First Gulf War). Perhaps a proliferation of names is fitting for a conflict that continues to be so controversial. The Coalition of the Willing—from a military standpoint, overwhelmingly made up of forces from the United States and United Kingdom—defeated Saddam's forces on the battlefield in short order. While initially well supported by the public in most of the states in the coalition, failure to discover weapons of mass destruction—a key reason provided for the need to remove Saddam Hussein from power—caused great concern and eroded poll numbers. Sectarian violence ensued, with many civilian casualties and a growing sense that the United States and its allies had not planned properly for what would ensue after the overthrow of Saddam. The new Iraqi government—nominally democratic but very troubled—put Saddam on trial and executed him. Coalition forces no longer play a combat role in Iraq, with the United Kingdom and United States having ceased such operations in 2010 and 2011, respectively.

The War in Iraq continues at this time of writing as low-level civil strife.[2] The United States continues to occupy the country. While it won an easy victory over Saddam Hussein's forces in the conventional stage of interstate war, the same cannot be said for the struggle to create a stable democracy in what had been an odious dictatorship. Thus the War in Iraq is an especially interesting contemporary case to study because it involves the system-leading United States in a complex conflict.

System Level

System-level factors linked to the War in Iraq include anarchy and the security dilemma, the unusual distribution of power in the post–Cold War era, bandwagoning, limitations on international institutions, and emerging global norms regarding intervention.

Anarchy and the security dilemma are at work in this case. Iraq and the United States worried about each other's capabilities and acted accordingly. While this might seem odd, given the much greater power of the United States, the possibility of being struck with WMDs weighed heavily on leaders in Washington.

Unipolarity is prominent in virtually all accounts of this war. The unusual configuration of power that followed the collapse of the Soviet Union left the United States by far the preeminent state in the international system. This permitted it full discretion in intervening around the globe and served as an enabling condition for war. The explanation is consistent with realist principles; with no power to balance the United States, it could be expected to do as it pleased.

Bandwagoning strongly outweighed balancing in this case. Without United Nations (UN) approval, the United States invaded Iraq with assistance from the many states that collectively made up the Coalition of the Willing. Among those involved, only Great Britain would qualify as a great power. With the enormous power of the United States, however,

---

2. These textbooks provide the basis for the discussion that follows: Baylis, Smith, and Owens (2008: 84), Bueno de Mesquita (2010: 161, 169, 235), D'Anieri (2010: 185, 186), Goldstein and Pevehouse (2008: 18), Mingst (2008: 59), Rourke and Boyer (2010: 19, 220), Steans, Pettiford with Diez (2005: 33, 98) and Viotti and Kauppi (2009: 83, 84).

participation by others had a largely symbolic value. France, Russia, and China opposed the US action at the UN but went no further in attempting to assist Iraq. Saddam Hussein stood alone against the United States and then an even larger bandwagon of states.

With regard to international institutions, the UN plays a central role in this story. Various UN resolutions condemned Iraq and called for its strict supervision. These resolutions, however, became subject to controversy when the United States and Great Britain claimed that enough authority already existed for an invasion to get under way. When the US-led assault on Iraq took place, it occurred without UN support—instead, with the ad hoc Coalition of the Willing. As in so many other cases, the UN could not act on Iraq because any policy it voted on would be assured of a veto by one of the five members of the Security Council with such power. The United States and Great Britain, its principal ally, wanted an invasion, while France, Russia, and China, the other permanent members of the Security Council, did not.

State Level

State-level factors pertain to both government and society. Among those cited most frequently are the perceived WMD threat, the legacy of 9/11, economic concerns, and interest in nation building. Under conditions of unipolarity it is not surprising that the United States is the focal point of this part of the analysis.

First and foremost is the perceived threat of WMDs in the possession of Saddam Hussein. The Iraqi dictator had been under UN sanctions, which included some degree of aerial harassment from the United States and Great Britain, since his defeat in the First Gulf War in 1991. All parties had expressed concerns about renewed aggression from Saddam and thus the need for vigilance. Statements by the George W. Bush administration leading up to the war reinforced public concerns that WMDs might be used by Saddam directly or passed on to terrorists. Secretary of State Colin Powell claimed, at a crucial speech given to the UN Security Council, that the United States had strong evidence of Saddam's efforts regarding chemical and biological weapons. The Iraqi dictator seemed to be pursuing a nuclear program as well, given intelligence reports about his efforts to obtain fissionable materials.

American society after 9/11 lived through an era of hypervigilance regarding potential large-scale attacks. This (militarized, masculinized) discourse created in both elites and the mass public a tendency to accept evidence of the hostile possession of WMDs at face value rather than challenging it. The discourse of the War on Terror encouraged this mind-set because the United States did face a real and ongoing threat from al-Qaeda, the perpetrator of 9/11. Thus President Bush and others found the public relatively willing to go to war, that is, "Let's not take any chances with Saddam Hussein" stood as the prevailing mind-set when it came to WMDs.

Consistent with arguments in the Marxist tradition about wars of imperialism, potential economic gain for the United States is cited as another explanation for the war. Iraq in 2003 ranked among the world's top oil producers. Some have argued that the United States went to war at least in part to improve its situation as a principal importer of energy. Saddam previously had invaded Kuwait, another key oil exporter, and had expressed ill intentions toward Saudi Arabia, the world's leading producer of oil, as well. For such reasons the United States might have regarded a war against Saddam as both a necessity and an opportunity from the standpoint of energy security.

Democratic peace is also consistent with the occurrence of the War in Iraq. Saddam ran a brutal dictatorship and had no allies. Thus the mitigating effects of joint democracy did not operate in a case in which a coalition with many different governments confronted a single autocracy.

Individual Level

Individual factors contributed significantly to the outbreak of the war as well. Among those highlighted are the tactics pursued by Saddam Hussein, misperceptions and misinformation about threat on the part of President Bush, the role played by advisers left over from the administration of George H. W. Bush, beliefs by US leaders about the ease of victory, and interest in the promotion of democracy abroad.

Saddam took a calculated risk in misleading the world about his possession of WMDs. It proved very difficult to discern at the time that he did not have such weapons precisely because of his behavior. He obstructed UN inspectors and gave every indication of possessing WMDs in the hope that doing so would deter invasion by the United States. (It also is likely that the claim played a role in Saddam's ongoing efforts to intimidate potential internal challenges to his power.) Ironically, the dictator's ploy had exactly the opposite effect. The tactics pursued by Saddam revealed a poor understanding of his adversary and led to the outcome he wanted least of all: defeat in war and his death at the hands of a new US-imposed regime.

President Bush found Saddam threatening and came to believe that war provided the only answer to problems created by the dictator. Flawed intelligence tells a great part of the story here. First, Saddam had no demonstrated connection to either al-Qaeda in general or the 9/11 attacks in particular. Second, his behavior suggested culpability regarding the possession, or at least attempted acquisition, of WMDs. Add in a belief in the (gendered) enemy image of Saddam as having an inherently evil and irrational nature and a vision of imminent danger easily arose for President Bush in the period leading up to the war. With such beliefs held by US leaders, preemption became the logical response.

Characteristics of the president interacted with those of his advisers to influence decision making. George W. Bush came to office with limited foreign policy experience. Lack of previous work in this area may have predisposed him to listen more uncritically to his advisers than some others who have sat in the Oval Office. Vice President Dick Cheney, along with Paul Wolfowitz as Deputy Secretary of Defense and Secretary of Defense Donald Rumsfeld, had held high-level positions in the George H. W. Bush administration and commanded great respect from the new president. These advisers strongly favored a military solution to the problems represented by Saddam Hussein. This disposition may have affected their reading of intelligence and, in turn, heavily influenced the president's ultimate decision in favor of preemptive war.

Another point in favor of war concerned its likely outcome. Saddam could expect no help from elsewhere, and thus the United States anticipated a quick and easy military victory. Experience in the First Gulf War of 1991 and the (gendered) framing of a dominant "us" over a subordinate "other" strongly supported the idea that the United States would win fast and with light casualties.

After 9/11, the Bush administration shifted toward beliefs in democracy promotion and nation building. This came after reflection on the root causes of Islamist extremism that had produced the tragic events of that day. As a result, a war against Saddam Hussein's dictatorship could be seen as an opportunity to implement and nurture a democratic regime—the first of its kind in the Arab world in particular. Add to this a sense that UN resolutions should be upheld (even if that took ignoring UN deliberative processes) and these beliefs all pointed toward war.

IMAGINARY, HISTORICAL, AND CONTEMPORARY
WAR IN COMPARATIVE PERSPECTIVE

Figure 4 permits visual comparison of the three wars. Note that four factors are common to all of the conflicts: anarchy coupled with the security dilemma, deficiency in international institutions, a lack of mitigating effects from joint democracy, and questionable leadership. Perhaps fittingly, the two system-level factors come from the realist and liberal traditions, respectively. Given its extremely high profile over the last twenty-five years in the academic study of war, it is interesting to see that regime type seems to matter even in the fantasy world of Middle-earth. At the individual level, the cast of characters in official leadership roles in both the real and imaginary worlds are grim to consider. (Gandalf and Aragorn are superb leaders but lack official status; as such, mainstream IR scholarship is set to interpret their contributions as secondary, à la "track two diplomacy," although feminist scholarship is set to recognize their greater impact.) Among the personality traits that combine to create the verdict of undesirable leadership across the board are evil, defeatism, incompetence, excessive ambition, age and fatigue, isolation, dictatorial tendencies, bellicosity, instability, and inexperience. Some of these unfortunate traits are found in more than one leader.

Now consider the traits common to two of three wars. The War of the Ring and World War I share seven traits: multipolarity; significant change in concentration of power; critical points in power cycles; power transition from leader to challenger; the presence of an expansionist economy and imperialism; lack of bureaucratic infrastructure and inadequate advising; and a monarchical, nonmerit political system. Note that these huge wars share many traits with each other; by comparison, the other two subsets are much smaller. The War of the Ring and War in Iraq have two common traits: bandwagoning and biased advising. Finally, World War I and Iraq—ironically, the two cases drawn from the real world—have just one other common trait: expectation of easy victory.

Unique features exist for each war. World War I is distinguished in seven ways: a high quantity of alliances, alliance polarization, the cult of the offensive, hypernationalism (i.e., social Darwinism), disintegrating empires, diversionary motives for war, and an assassination as the triggering event. Five unique traits appear for the War of the Ring: secondary-level security dilemmas that inhibit balancing against the main adversary, low interdependence, unlimited willingness to suffer, defeatist

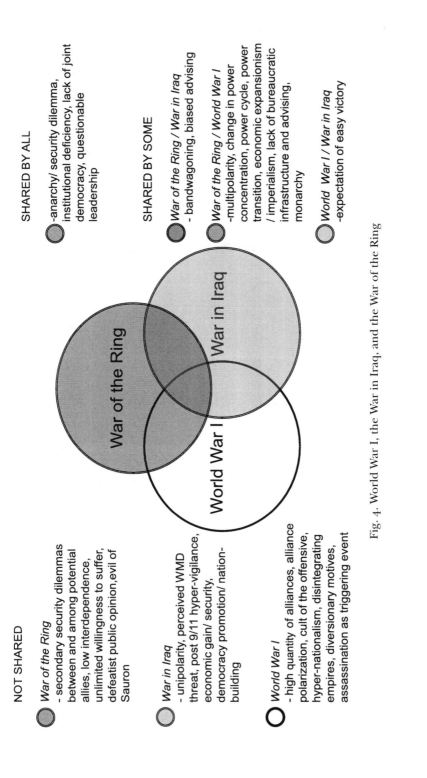

SHARED BY ALL

-anarchy/ security dilemma, institutional deficiency, lack of joint democracy, questionable leadership

SHARED BY SOME

War of the Ring / War in Iraq - bandwagoning, biased advising

War of the Ring / World War I -multipolarity, change in power concentration, power cycle, power transition, economic expansionism / imperialism, lack of bureaucratic infrastructure and advising, monarchy

World War I / War in Iraq -expectation of easy victory

War of the Ring

War in Iraq

World War I

NOT SHARED

War of the Ring - secondary security dilemmas between and among potential allies, low interdependence, unlimited willingness to suffer, defeatist public opinion, evil of Sauron

War in Iraq - unipolarity, perceived WMD threat, post 9/11 hyper-vigilance, economic gain/ security, democracy promotion/ nation-building

World War I - high quantity of alliances, alliance polarization, cult of the offensive, hyper-nationalism, disintegrating empires, diversionary motives, assassination as triggering event

Fig. 4. World War I, the War in Iraq, and the War of the Ring

public opinion, and the ultimate evil of Sauron. Finally, the War in Iraq also features five unique traits: unipolarity, a perceived WMD threat, post-9/11 hypervigilance, economic gain/security, and democracy promotion/nation building.

Consider the sheer number of causes associated with each war: eighteen for the War of the Ring, nineteen for World War I, and twelve for the War in Iraq. While too much should not be made of these numbers, it makes sense that the two wars of great scope would have more intricate causes. Even the lesser, regional War in Iraq is explained with a dozen factors, of course, and this serves as a lesson that applies across the board in studying war: beware of simplistic explanations. Such accounts probably are politicized, while more accurate and comprehensive causal analysis is complex and multilevel—even more so for the most destructive wars.

SOLVING THE PROBLEM OF WAR

Comparing real wars to each other and the War of the Ring highlights the need to respect the intricate nature of such events. Although certain strands of problem-solving approaches within IR emphasize the utility of "parsimonious" (elegant or simple) explanations, this analysis supports alternative calls for recognizing complexity within international politics: here, the message is to avoid oversimplification. The temptation is to jump to a conclusion such as "World War I happened because of the archduke's assassination." Examples of overemphasis on the proximate causes of war, such as this one, are legion.

Rather than giving into such temptations, this analysis supports criticism of mainstream approaches to IR theory, especially of realism, which rejects excessive emphasis on parsimony. Instead, this highlights the importance of making tradeoffs between and among description, explanation, and prediction on one hand and complexity of theorizing on the other (James 2002). As such, it recognizes how—even within the problem-solving tradition—drawing insight from different kinds of lenses or perspectives is important for stronger understanding. Consider, for example, the case of neorealism. Critics have pointed out that its parsimony is carried to an extreme; neorealism would be well-advised to permit elaboration in order to explain more than a minimal number of things. While neorealism can account for power balancing and recurrent warfare, it lacks propositions about foreign policy. Thus saying more about the possible reactions of states to system structure, with a higher degree of specificity than seen so far, becomes a priority for neorealist theorizing (James 2002).

This is a good point at which to revisit figure 2, which conveyed how one might think about IR. Multiple paradigms and levels of analysis turn out to be the rule rather than the exception in explaining war. It also is easy to see a place for multiple methods in the long-standing research program on war. Liberals and constructivists might focus on how institutions and institutionalized belief systems lead to or limit war, while strategic interaction becomes the domain of realists. Critical scholars might in turn emphasize a perceived lack of underlying Justice in whatever Order is observed, within which forces might arise to overturn the system. Efforts of all kinds can be expected to enhance further the understanding and explanation of war. Notable also is the range of evidence, historical and contemporary, available for study. This chapter's unique contribution is to introduce the War of the Ring in Middle-earth to complement what can be learned from our world about the causes of war. Comparative analysis confirms the existence of common causes for wars from the real and mythical worlds while also identifying unique reasons for these horrific events.

This chapter and the two preceding it have used *LOTR* to illuminate mainstream IR paradigms and the problem-solving analytical framework of levels of analysis. The next chapter uses *LOTR* to illuminate feminist IR scholarship as one example of a critical approach to IR.

CHAPTER 5

Middle-earth and Feminist Theory

And in the end, of course, a true war story is never about war.
—*Tim O'Brien*, The Things They Carried

PROBLEMS OF "WAR"

In *The Things They Carried* (1990), Tim O'Brien draws on his experience as a veteran in the American war in Vietnam to tell what people often interpret as "war stories." But he argues that they are *not* war stories and suggests that people who interpret them that way simply are not "listening" (85). Instead, he describes what a "true" war story is about for him.

> It's about sunlight. It's about the special way that dawn spreads out on a river when you know you must cross the river and march into the mountains and do things you are afraid to do. It's about love and memory. It's about sorrow. It's about sisters who never write back and people who never listen. (85)

As O'Brien suggests, thinking about war from the perspective of war stories often misses the point. It misses myriad other stories that make war possible and influence and interact with war's buildup, conduct, and aftereffects. And its abstraction misses the emotional impact that "makes the stomach believe" (78).

Feminist IR scholarship addressing war and other issues on the problem-solving IR agenda similarly suggests that traditional IR analyses tell only part of the story. Like O'Brien's quote suggests, such feminists argue that war stories are just the view of one narrow lens on a much more colorful world and a narrow account of what needs to be addressed for "accurate, rigorous, and ethical scholarship" that provides a full and reliable account of both war and other issues of international relations (Sjoberg 2009: 186; see also Agathangelou and Ling 2009; Enloe 2000b: 213; Enloe 2004: 23–24; Pettman 1996; Zalewski 2010: 36, 349; and Zalewski 2000). Rather than using "levels of analysis" to structure analysis of the causes and effects of discrete wars, IR feminists use "gender-sensitive lenses"[1] to organize understanding about both the foundation for and the causes and effects of a *spectrum* of violence—ranging from "peacetime" through the lead-up, duration, and aftereffects of "war" (see, e.g., Sjoberg 2009). In doing so, they participate in feminist IR research more generally, which argues that "the worldwide institutionalization of gender differences is a major underpinning of structural inequalities of significance to world politics" (Peterson and Runyan 1999: 7).

These scholars also suggest that traditional IR accounts are limited significantly both because such perspectives oversimplify and reduce the richness of our understanding of the political system and because they consequently are unable to make accurate predictions, especially about political change (see Enloe 2004: 23–24). With many critical theorists, IR feminists tend to be open about having a strong "emancipatory knowledge interest" (Tickner 1997; Alker 2005)—a commitment to social justice (see also Baylis, Smith, and Owens 2008: 264). As such, they suggest that focusing on the perspectives and knowledge of people at the margins rather than the mainstream (e.g., those oppressed by hierarchical structures such as gender, ethnicity, class, postcolonial status, religion, or disability) is both intrinsically and instrumentally valuable.

In this chapter, we provide a brief overview of what it means to use gender-sensitive lenses to organize our understanding of global politics before reviewing current feminist IR scholarship within the context of the "waves" of the feminist political movement. This provides the background for the next chapter, where we apply a gender-sensitive lens to *LOTR* and compare this to feminist analyses of World War I, the US War

---

1. See, for example, Zalewski 2010: 29–30; Hunt 2010: 117; Tickner 2008: 266; and Steans, Pettiford, and Diez 2005: 256. See also Edkins and Zehfuss 2009: 76–77; Mansbach and Rafferty 2008: 37–38; and Weber 2005: 89–90.

in Iraq, and the War of the Ring. In that way we go beyond the problem-solving approach taken in the preceding chapter toward these events and apply one kind of critical approach. We conclude by reviewing how feminist analyses that bring to bear a gender-sensitive lens on politics create a stronger, more inclusive basis for understanding and explaining Order and Justice from the personal to the international.

GENDER-SENSITIVE LENSES

Many feminists point out that different theoretical perspectives involve different "lenses," which find different aspects of reality problematic, and use different explanations to address these problems; consequently, they "act to foreground some things, while backgrounding others" (Peterson and Runyan 1999: 21). For example, realist lenses emphasize interstate conflict, liberal lenses emphasize interstate cooperation, and neo-Marxist lenses emphasize class inequalities—while each approach at the same time at least implicitly deemphasizes other frameworks and issues (21). In other words, each approach tells a different kind of story, through different colored glasses, while all ostensibly address global or international "politics."

Feminist analysis, on the other hand, puts together its ideas about the world—including but not limited to war—by organizing analysis using a gender-sensitive lens. To do this means "to focus on gender as a particular kind of power relation, or to trace out the ways in which gender is central to understanding international processes" (Steans 1998: 5; see also Peterson and Runyan 1999: 1). Within this framework, it is important to recognize that "gender" is not the same as "sex." Particularly, *sex* can be understood as "the biological distinction between males and females" (Peterson and Runyan 1999: 5). However, *gender* can be understood as a system of symbolic meaning that creates social hierarchies based on perceived associations with masculine and feminine characteristics (Sjoberg 2009: 187). While gender most plainly institutionalizes inequalities between (dominant) men and (subordinate) women, it also supports inequalities between other groups (e.g., through the feminization of race, class, sexuality, and postcolonial position).

Using a gender-sensitive lens can start with asking a simple question such as "Where are the women?" This is an important place to start, as women's experiences and stories are regularly devalued and deprioritized. For example, in May 2011, a Hasidic newspaper in Brooklyn, New

York, actually *erased* the images of US Secretary of State Hillary Clinton and Director for Counterterrorism Audrey Tomason from an iconic photograph of the situation room during the 2011 US Special Forces raid that killed al-Qaeda leader Osama bin Laden. According to the newspaper, erasing the women's images was done to foster sexual restraint and was an act that should be supported as part of multicultural freedom (Michaeli 2011).

Although this instance could be discounted as bizarrely exceptional, it is consistent with the marginalization of women's stories and experience more broadly. For example, of forty-five Oscar winners for Best Film between 1965 and 2010, only five "tell a story through the life of someone who is female": *Chicago, Out of Africa, Terms of Endearment, The Sound of Music,* and *Million Dollar Baby*—with *Crash* (because of its complex story line) being a possible sixth (Johnson 2005: 11).[2] As such, the seemingly innocuous question "Where are the women?" frequently raises other issues, which highlight the work that masculinity and femininity are doing, such as "Why?," "Who put them there?," "Who benefits from them being there and not someplace else?," or "What do they think about being there and what do they do with those thoughts?" (Enloe 2004: 4–6; Zalewski 2010).

These kinds of questions highlight how international processes are influenced and defined in "gendered" ways—or how characteristics defined as "masculine" are defined as different from and superior to characteristics defined as "feminine." Characteristics perceived as masculine have included power, autonomy, rationality, and public, while characteristics perceived as feminine have included weakness, dependence/connection, emotionality, and private. However, the specific characteristics associated with masculinity and femininity change over time (Tickner 2008: 265).

Feminist analysis argues that gendered institutions support a variety of relations of domination in world politics. A key example is through processes of "masculinization." A group is masculinized to the extent that (1) group composition is predominantly (but not exclusively) made up of men, (2) group leadership is predominantly (but not exclusively) composed of men, (3) strategies and goals are adopted that are associ-

---

2. Johnson's analysis examines Best Picture winners from 1965 to 2003; our own examination expands it into the 2004–10 time period.

ated with stereotypical traits of manliness, and (4) relationships among members are rooted in ideas about shared manhood (Enloe 2010: 115).

In our world today, gendered institutions make women particularly vulnerable. Despite recent improvements in literacy and voting rights, an absolute *decline* in the quality of life has occurred over the past decade for many women worldwide (Seager 2003: 7). Many factors contribute to this kind of discomforting trend: "flexible" global markets of underpaid, often female, workers; an increased gap between the rich and the poor, with women remaining the poorest of the poor; increased social demands for picking up the slack when governments slash social programs (e.g., as part of "structural adjustment" programs or transitions from socialist to "free-market" societies); mass rape, erosion of rights, and increasing burdens to sustain households during wartime; increasing violence, sexual exploitation, and unemployment with decreased political representation in the transition from socialist to free-market societies; resurgent fundamentalism; and enslavement, including sex-trafficking (7). While these vulnerabilities are particularly apparent in the developing world, women in industrialized countries also are vulnerable: battery and sexual assault, wage gaps, glass ceilings in public and political participation, limits to health care, and restrictive gender stereotypes in the media all contribute (Ruane 2010: 136–37). As a whole, feminist scholarship suggests that these vulnerabilities are part and parcel of gendered systems of domination that support unequal gendered relationships worldwide.

While the impact of gendered institutions on women is particularly evident, gendered relations of domination are apparent everywhere from individuals (e.g., particular women and men), to groups (e.g., based on ethnicity, class, religion, sexuality, or disability) to states (e.g., "first world," "third world," or "postcolonial"). For example, feminized images of "Oriental" countries have frequently supported Western efforts to protect or dominate them. Here unequal relationships that are assumed to be natural among men and women are projected onto states, and, like with men and women, assumptions that masculine actors will "protect" feminine ones become especially problematic when "protectors" paternalistically take away their ability to make their own decisions or become the source of violence for those in their care (Hunt 1987). These problems are obscured by positions of privilege—location within a "structure of unearned assets" that is taken for granted (Edkins and Zehfuss 2009: 80). Privilege can exist in multiple dimensions, for example, due to race, class, or country of origin's level of development, as well as gender. It is insidious because, from a position of privilege, access to those unearned assets is assumed to be normal; however, for others, this is anything but the case.

As this discussion suggests, looking at the world through gender-sensitive lenses allows feminists to listen to a variety of marginalized voices in their work across a number of areas, including but not limited to the problem of war. In doing so, applying a gender-sensitive lens encourages a feminist curiosity that avoids intellectual laziness and aims to illuminate privilege that is otherwise invisible because of assumptions that it is normal and/or unimportant (Enloe 2004: 4–6; Peterson and Runyan 1999).

Feminist IR in Context

Feminist IR asks both how to theorize the state and IR and how to theorize gender (Hansen 2010: 18; see also Agathangelou and Ling 2009; Pettman 1996; and Zalewski 2000). However, the political movement out of which feminist IR grew was dedicated to achieving equality for women in all aspects of life and focused on explaining and ending women's political, social, and economic subordination throughout the world (Tickner 2008: 264). As such, in this section, we first review the "waves" of the broader feminist movement that current feminist IR approaches build on. Next we outline their related current feminist IR approaches. Finally, we use *LOTR* characters to illustrate feminist political movement approaches and the current IR feminist scholarship that draws on them.

Feminist IR scholarship today builds on the broader feminist political movement, which itself includes a variety of different perspectives. Feminists "disagree on why women are subordinate" and therefore have different recommendations for improving the status and well-being of women (Tickner 2008: 264). As noted in chapter 2, different approaches can be thought of as what the great social theorist from a century ago, Max Weber, described as "ideal types"—simplified, abstract versions of phenomena that highlight their characteristic features, even while the particular phenomena involved always are manifested in more historically varying ways. Our discussion here focuses on these abstract ideal types in order to highlight major differences across historical time periods. However, this simplifies discourse and by no means exhausts all those from within either the waves of the feminist political movement or current IR feminist scholarship.[3]

Background Political Movements

Within this context, the broader feminist movement has frequently been characterized as including three historical waves, which overlap and interact but also involve their own distinctions (e.g., Krolokke and Sorensen 2005; other viewpoints include Zalewski 2000; and Hewitt 2010). In the first wave, feminist mythology defines the dominant discourse, especially from the 1860s through the 1930s, as focusing on officially mandated inequalities by what are now called "liberal feminists" but then were called "women's liberation" activists. This wave frequently drew on women's experiences in resisting slavery (especially in the 1770–1870 era of slave emancipation), resisting oppressive marriage laws (especially eighteenth- and nineteenth-century prohibitions on married women being able to divorce or own property), and resisting colonialism (ushering in the decolonization of the 1950s and 1960s) as their motivation for demanding the vote (Whittick 1979; Jayawardena 1986; Rupp 1997; Sklar, Stewart, and Lehrman 2007). Frequently cited exemplars include Mary Wollstonecraft's (1792) *A Vindication of the Rights of Women* in Britain, Olympe de Gouges's (1791) *Declaration of the Rights of Woman and the Female Citizen* in France, and Elisabeth Cady Stanton's (1848) *Declaration of Sentiments* in Seneca Falls, New York.

In the second wave, the story goes that the dominant discourse focused on unofficial inequalities, especially from the 1960s through the 1980s. As part of this second wave, radical and socialist feminisms critiqued structural patriarchy, including the gendered division of "productive" and "reproductive" labor. Feminist thought during this time underlined cultural contradictions within societies. In the United States, Betty Friedan's best-selling (1963) *The Feminine Mystique* brought attention to the widespread unhappiness of American housewives despite the cultural myth that women should be wholly fulfilled in their role. In the Arab world, books such as Fatema Mernissi's (1975) *Beyond the Veil* and Nawal El-Saadawi's (1977) *The Hidden Face of Eve* highlighted how cultural practices in Islam—rather than original premises—limit equal rights for women.

---

3. For the development of historical discussions, see Tong 1998; Peterson and Runyan 1999; Tickner 2001; Sylvester 1994b, 2002a; and Dietz 2003.

Finally, in the third wave, the myth is that the dominant discourse focused on the multiple and varying forms of gendered oppression, especially from the 1980s onward. This wave frequently drew on the experiences of women of color and women outside the Western world to reassess gender problems without assuming that all experience was the same as that of upper-class, white, Western women. For one example, Chandra Mohanty's (1988) essay "Under Western Eyes" critiqued Western feminist depictions of the "Third World Woman" as excessively simplified and ignoring how oppressions are diversely manifested. For another example, Judith Butler's (1990) *Gender Trouble* argued that we are all basically in "drag"—sex and gender are performed, not innate—and consequently, feminist activists should trouble gendered categories with subversive performance rather than focusing on particular kinds of "women's interests."

As a whole, recent feminist conversations highlight how the traditional "wave" analogy is a simplified way of understanding a more complicated history. As such, a more accurate understanding of this evolution would recognize how feminist discourse overlapped and interacted in varying historical contexts—perhaps more along the lines of radio waves or hip-hop—as influenced by diverse voices from different races, classes, and sexualities (Hewitt 2010).

Feminist IR Theory

Current feminist IR analysis draws on different approaches within these waves to investigate how gendered relationships of power structure politics from the personal to the international (Sylvester 1994b: 30; Agathangelou and Ling 2009; Hewitt 2010; Pettman 1996; Zalewski 2000). Different approaches involve different assumptions about what exists (ontology), what we can know and how we can know things (epistemology), and the concrete steps that should be taken to achieve knowledge (methodology) (Hansen 2010: 25; Harding 1986; Sylvester 1994b: chapter 1).[4] The following overview integrates and adapts the reviews by Hansen (2010) and Sylvester (1994b).[5]

---

4. Mainstream IR theory involves related discussions about method and epistemology, especially in its second and third "Great Debates." The focus of IR's Third Debate on epistemology is particularly relevant. It highlights what has been called the "fact-value distinction," or the question of whether arguments can be understood as based on pure facts or reason or whether they are to some extent based in normative or prescriptive value judgments (Mansbach and Rafferty 2008: 18–35).

5. Hansen focuses on poststructuralist IR feminism while Sylvester focuses on postmodern feminism and feminist postmodernism. Here we focus on postmodern feminism to parallel our discussion of postmodern IR more generally.

First, rationalist IR feminism can be understood as applying liberal concerns for equality as identical treatment to global politics. It does so by engaging in "positivist" research such as quantitative statistics or comparative case studies. This aims at establishing causal connections between gender and state action (Hansen 2010: 25; Sylvester 1994b: 31–42). For example, rationalist IR feminist scholarship may investigate whether levels of gender equality are correlated with the likelihood of going to war or whether democracy and human rights ensure women's human security (Hansen 2010: 20–21).

Second, standpoint IR feminism can be understood as building on radical-cultural, socialist, and postcolonial insights that value the experience of people marginalized by different "axes of oppression" (such as gender, ethnicity, class, postcolonial status, religion, or disability) as a basis for understanding global politics. It does so by engaging in standpoint or constructivist research. This includes fieldwork, hermeneutic or narrative analysis, interviews, and quantitative documentation and aims at starting research from women's lives in order to create less biased and distorted knowledge (see Hansen 2010: 25; and Sylvester 1994b: 43–52). For example, standpoint IR feminist scholarship may analyze how approaches to global ethics drawing on male experience (such as utilitarianism) support kinds of discussion and action that differ from those drawing on female experience (such as feminist care ethics).

Finally, postmodern IR feminism can be understood as building on socialist, postcolonial, and postmodern insights that highlight the differences among women. It engages in discourse and text analysis, fieldwork, and interviews in order to question dominant stories that reflect the perspective of dominant groups (Hansen 2010: 25; Sylvester 1994b: 52–67).[6] For example, postmodern feminist scholarship may analyze how narratives about (male) Just Warriors and (female) Beautiful Souls support traditional war stories, which support unequal and undemocratic relationships, and suggest how questioning, destabilizing, and rearranging such stories can cultivate new and hybrid identifications with rearranged relationships of power (Zalewski 2010: 126; Sylvester 1994b:

6. For related introductory text discussions, see Tickner 2008; D'Anieri 2010: 102–9; Wibben 2009; Goldstein and Pevehouse 2009: 105–18; Kegley and Blanton 2010: 46–47; Mansbach and Rafferty 2008: 37–38; Mingst 2008: 318–20; Nau 2009: 55–56; Rourke and Boyer 2010: 24–25; Ray and Kaarbo 2008: 18–21; Russett, Starr, and Kinsella 2010: 150–53; Shepherd 2010a; Steans 2003; Steans, Pettiford, and Diez 2005, chapter 6; Viotti and Kauppi 2009: 97–98; and Weber 2005: chapter 5.

55–63). (For a comparison of ontological, epistemological, and methodological perspectives, see tables 3 and 4.)

Despite these divergences, current feminist IR scholarship often draws on insights from multiple traditions and supports a multilayered approach to both understanding and taking action on issues of gender and global politics (Sylvester 1994b: 31; Cockburn 2010). Just as each political feminist wave built on the work of the previous one, so, too, feminist IR scholarship often recognizes the complexity of global politics today and integrates a broad range of insights to deal with this complexity. For

TABLE 3. Feminist IR and Assumptions about What Exists (Ontology)

Feminist Approach	Understanding of "Gender"	View of People	View of Politics: The Example of "Civilian Immunity"
Rationalist feminism	Gender is essentially linked to biology (essentialist).	All women are feminine and all men are masculine.	Translating "civilian immunity" in war as immunity for women and children is *politically appropriate;* e.g., it indicates that the "civilians" in need of immunity are almost exclusively women and children.
Standpoint feminism	Gender is mediated through social constructions of masculinity and femininity (constructivist).	Women tend to be defined in feminine terms and men in masculine ones. (Biology and language are intertwined.)	Translating "civilian immunity" in war as immunity for women and children is *politically meaningful;* e.g., it indicates that men will fight to protect "vulnerable" women during wartime.
Postmodern feminism	Gender is defined through language (discursive).	Women and men are not born (resulting from biology) but made (resulting from language).	Translating "civilian immunity" in war as immunity for women and children is *politically constraining;* e.g., it indicates that protector/ victim dichotomies involved in "civilian immunity" discourse empower (masculinized) soldiers, marginalize (feminized) civilians, and contribute to defining the politics of war.

Source: Hansen 2010: 25; Sjoberg and Peet 2011; Tickner 2011.

example, this could include support for developing and drawing on (rationalist-style) statistics about inequalities based in gender, ethnicity, class, postcolonial status, religion, or disability. However, this scholarship would supplement such information with (standpoint- and/or poststructuralist-style) fieldwork, interviews, or narrative analysis to highlight the experience of marginalized people or the way language is used to construct gendered worldviews (Shepherd 2010a). As such, this would incorporate the insight that men and women are treated differently (e.g., à la the essentialist ontology of rationalist IR feminism) but would develop this much further with the insight that masculin*ized* and femin*ized* actors are unequally constrained (e.g., à la the constructivist and discursive ontology of standpoint and poststructuralist IR feminism).

Because much feminist IR scholarship today draws on a variety of traditions and insights in analyzing global politics and critiquing traditional IR theory, we focus here first on illustrating different approaches in the waves of the feminist political movement using *LOTR* characters. We then discuss the wave myth and its implications for current feminist IR scholarship that draws on these "waves." This enables us to, first, highlight different points of emphasis across historical time periods. Second, it helps us recognize how the myth may imply that certain perspectives are more relevant than others and mask important conversation and debate among varying viewpoints.

TABLE 4. Feminist IR and Assumptions about What We Know and How We Should Learn (Epistemology and Methodology)

Feminist Approach	Basis for Useful Knowledge (epistemology)	Illustration (methodology)
Rationalist feminism	More accurate and less gender-biased scientific knowledge ("positivist" or "empiricist")	Using sex-disaggregated statistical methodologies to document those killed and wounded in war
Standpoint feminism	The experience of marginalized people ("standpoint")	Using interviews with civilians in conflict in order to highlight alternative forms of experience and create a stronger basis for "objectivity"
Postmodern feminism	Discourse evidencing meaningful gender norms in language ("discursive" or "postmodern")	Using interviews with civilians in conflict in order to suggest alternative kinds of "war stories" and highlight how existing forms of domination are enabled by and influence traditional stories

Source: Hansen 2010, 25; Sjoberg and Peet 2011; Tickner 2011.

Table 5 uses female characters from different races in *LOTR* to illustrate different feminist approaches. As noted previously, using female characters to illustrate these traditions does not mean their insights are restricted to women; however, it does suggest how such insights are more grounded in women's lives. "Starting thought from women's lives," rather than men's lives, as has typically been the case in IR, can provide a stronger basis for understanding our world (Harding 1990).

Within table 5, the waves of feminist approaches are broadly chronological: Early on, feminist political approaches were predominated by liberal discussion, while postmodern feminism has gained strength more recently. So, too, postmodern feminist IR scholarship has developed in response to earlier standpoint and liberal feminist IR scholarship. Despite this general trend, however, it is important to recognize that discussions have been diverse and eclectic both within waves (where alternate approaches exist, even if they do not predominate) and between waves (where discussion frequently integrates insights across time rather being limited to single, relatively narrow viewpoints). This eclecticism is evident in a small way in the table, which highlights how socialist feminism informs both standpoint and postmodern feminist IR scholarship. Understanding the historical context of each wave can clarify how each was shaped by the problems and priorities of its time.

TABLE 5. Waves of Feminist Approaches and Illustrative Characters

IR Feminist Approach	Feminist Political Approach	Ontology	Epistemology	Race	Female Character
Rationalist IR feminism	Liberal feminism	Rationalist/ essentialist	Positivist/ empiricist	Men	Éowyn
	Radical (cultural) feminism	Constructivist	Standpoint	Ent	Wandlimb
Standpoint IR feminism	Postcolonial feminism	Constructivist	Standpoint	Dwarf	Dís
	Socialist feminism	Constructivist	Standpoint	Hobbit	Lobelia Sackville-Baggins
Postmodern IR feminism	Postmodern feminism	Postmodern/ poststructuralist	Discursive	Elf	Galadriel

FIRST WAVE: HUMANS

The dominant first-wave ideal type approach was *liberal feminism*. According to the myth, this prioritizes the advancement of women through legal and social changes enabling them to compete with men on an equal (identical) basis rather than—as later approaches would do—reformulating biased social standards themselves. For one example, such activism paved the way for many countries to finally grant women the right to vote after World War I—a right not granted to all women citizens by *any* self-governing nation before New Zealand's extension of women's suffrage in 1893. For another, such activism also integrated "the woman question" into the agenda of the League of Nations instead as its "social questions" (Jang 2009); this broadened area of focus is still evident today in UN bodies committed to economic and social issues.

Liberal feminism and the rationalist IR feminism that builds on this tradition focus on gender roles as being equivalent to biological sex rather than being based in socialization or narrations of masculinity and femininity (an essentialist ontology). It also holds that we can learn more (e.g., overcoming women's oppression or understanding and explaining IR) by drawing on more accurate and less biased scientific forms of knowledge. Examples of such research would include obtaining information about sex distributions in different forms of paid work (a positivist or empiricist epistemology) (Hansen 2010: 25).

Liberal feminism as an ideal type is best illustrated by Éowyn, a Human of noble birth from Rohan. Éowyn experiences the formal constraints rejected by liberal feminists, as she is restricted from riding to battle with her brother and is treated as a piece of chattel rather than a person by Saruman, who promises her as a reward to Wormtongue (his henchman and spy within Rohan) for the latter's allegiance (II: 509, 513). However, she does not question masculine norms as superior but instead seeks equality with men: Éowyn is "strong" and "stern as steel" (II: 504) and rejects Aragorn's implicit argument that "you are a woman and your part is in the house" (III: 767). Éowyn does so by dressing as a man and riding in disguise into battle, despite admonitions from the men in her life (e.g., Théoden [in the movie version] and Aragorn) that she should stay behind.

Although she pursues her goals despite legal and social constraints, Éowyn's story illustrates how the wave myth defines liberal feminism as limited to negative-sum (i.e., losing out regardless of the option selected) problems of either choosing to be "equal" with men or renouncing that opportunity: Pursuing equality requires overcoming many obstacles and is constrained to masculine models. However, giving up equality requires accepting a less powerful, feminized position. This perspective cautions rationalist feminist efforts to engage "equally" (identically) with traditional IR scholarship—which values social scientific, falsifiable research—because it is limited to engaging in scholarship that may be equally valued but is based primarily in elite male experience (e.g., in assuming autonomous and masculine entities); the alternative to this is engaging in scholarship that is *dev*alued by the "mainstream" but draws more broadly on a variety of (often subordinated) kinds of experience as a stronger basis for "objectivity" (e.g., assuming relational and interdependent entities) (Keohane 1988, 1998; Tickner 1997, 1998, 2005). In Éowyn's case, she initially pursues equality with men but eventually sacrifices at least one form of equality by becoming a healer—perhaps as a result of her continuing admiration for Aragorn, who had that facility himself—and renouncing her shieldmaiden desires.[7]

This said, Éowyn's slaying of the Witch King Black Rider in battle also highlights a number of problems with the wave myth. First, it illustrates how attacking the clearest monsters is one important step in overturning oppression, even if it does not solve all of the problems. So, too, the "women's liberation" activism of liberal feminism took an important first step against women's broader oppression when it channeled anger against oppressive institutions regarding marriage, slavery, and colonial rule toward support for women's suffrage. Second, Éowyn's story illustrates the importance of recognizing everyone's role in challenging oppression: although Éowyn tends to get credit for slaying the Witch King, she cannot do so until Merry stabs him first, and it is only through their coordinated efforts that the Nazgûl is destroyed. So, too, the wave myth's focus on Western feminists obscures how many in the women's liberation movement were located around the world—including Egypt, Ceylon (now Sri Lanka), Vietnam, the Philippines, Mexico, Brazil, China, South Africa, Turkey, India, and elsewhere—and actively shaped the global

---

7. Key aspects of the story of Éowyn include her manifesto as a shieldmaiden (III: 766–67), her slaying of the Wraith King (III: 821–24), and her acceptance of Faramir's (brother of Boromir's) proposal of marriage, which brings together the kingdoms of Gondor and Rohan (III: 937–44).

feminist agenda (Badran 2001; Jaywaradena 1986). Overall, the wave myth obscures how liberal and rationalist IR feminisms still contribute significantly to understanding and struggling against gendered politics by addressing one part of a broader puzzle.

SECOND WAVE: HOBBITS AND ENTS

According to the myth, second-wave ideal type approaches such as *socialist feminism* and *radical feminism* develop the insight that "the personal is political" and focus on how social institutions create inequalities. As will become apparent, standpoint feminism, which emphasizes the impact of personal perspective, is related to Miles' Law but is situated within a normative context.

On one hand, socialist feminism and radical feminism, as well as standpoint IR feminism, which draws on them, holds "reality" to be something that is not "objective" but instead is something people create by attaching meaning to "facts" that are "out there" (a constructivist ontology): this means that hierarchical gender relations are created (i.e., not natural) through social constructions of masculinity and femininity. This also means that it is possible to learn more about international relations and overcoming women's oppression by drawing on the experience of people on the bottom rungs of society (including but not limited to women) in order to demonstrate how women's experience is different from but also valuable relative to men's experience (a standpoint epistemology) (Hansen 2010: 25).

On the other hand, postmodern IR feminism, which also relates to socialist feminism, does not share these ontological and epistemological assumptions. Instead, it supports socialist feminist insights in suggesting that because socialization (which results, e.g., in a "double burden" of reproductive and productive labor for women) is the source of women's oppression, changes to that socialization (e.g., through conversations in "women's groups") may also be the key to pursuing more flexible and less limiting understandings of ourselves and others.

Socialist feminism as an ideal type focuses on how productive labor relies on reproductive labor and argues that power should be redistributed globally to recognize more adequately women's nonmarket contributions. As such, this perspective highlights the standpoint of women whose unpaid or underpaid and unrecognized or underrecognized labor in the "reproductive economy" supports and gives a "free ride" (or a heavily subsidized one) to formal actors in the traditionally recognized "productive economy" (Peterson 2003; Waring 1988).

Tolkien pays relatively little attention to economics in *LOTR*, either of the productive or reproductive kind, which makes elaboration of material concerns difficult. However, socialist feminism can be illustrated by the Hobbit Lobelia Sackville-Baggins. Lobelia's concerns over economic security—most notably, ownership of the residence of Bag End after Bilbo's disappearance—illustrate socialist feminism's argument that sexism is inextricably linked to problems of class. As such, one of the last things Frodo does before departing on his quest is to leave the "washing up" for hundred-year-old Lobelia, who is about to move into Bag End.

This may represent broader trends, where Hobbit prosperity depends not only on formal work (farming and hunting or other endeavors) by Hobbit men but also informal work done, with little acknowledgment, by Hobbit women. Similarly, the Hobbits Rosie Cotton and Mrs. Maggot both manage households and engage in local community politics, yet these are not apparently valued as important contributions to either the economic or political stability of their communities. As drawing on experience from these seemingly minor characters illustrates, "public" work (whether performed for daily living or the quest for the Ring) relies on and is interconnected with devalued "private" work. Despite this marginalization, Lobelia demonstrates that she can stand up for herself when she takes on the ruffians who terrorize Hobbiton during the great war over the Ring that is the climax of the story. Lobelia resists a leader of the ruffians—lunging at this much larger adversary after he tells her to get out of the way—and is dragged off to jail as a result (III: 990). As such, she is active in defining her own life options, in spite of her constraints.

Although Lobelia's standpoint is influenced by the devaluing of her reproductive and informal work, it is also influenced by her other experiences; for example, her family is from a different part of the country than the heroes of *LOTR* (Hardbottle in the Northfarthing, not the Shire, like Bilbo and Frodo), and both her husband (Otho) and then son (Lotho) die during the period of Frodo's quest. Consequently, she shares certain concerns with other women in *LOTR* over some things (e.g., issues over who was responsible for doing Frodo's dishes and who had the time and ability to engage in "political" rather than "personal" activities); however, she also probably differs with other women on other things because of her other experiences (e.g., over relative valuing of inheritance rights—due to her being less well off than Bilbo and Frodo, at least in the beginning).

Lobelia's experience highlights how the wave myth defines early standpoint approaches, including forms of socialist feminism, as limited by focusing on just one kind of (e.g., Western rather than developing country) woman as representing the only "women's perspective." Although current standpoint approaches have moved beyond this kind of focus and now often highlight different intersecting bases of perspective (e.g., race, class, and nationality, as well as gender), Lobelia's story suggests that work that focuses on economic or other "women's concerns" is problematically oversimplified because it assumes an undifferentiated group without considering other important features of experience (e.g., historical time period, class, ethnicity, or geographical location) (Mohanty 1988). In Lobelia's case, her domestic work certainly contributes to limiting her opportunities to pursue her own adventures. However, it is her interpretation of her experience within the *context* of where her extended family lives and the death of her husband and son that shapes Lobelia's decision to return to Northfarthing at the end of the quest.

This said, the way Lobelia takes on the ruffians in Hobbiton at the end of the story also highlights how nontraditional heroes can take important actions. Her only weapon, as the story goes, is an umbrella! As such, the wave myth obscures how socialist feminism and standpoint feminist IR make important contributions. This is particularly the case regarding their recognition that drawing on women's experience enriches our understanding of gendered politics, even if "women's" experience is not all exactly the same.

Radical feminism includes a range of differing perspectives that focus on how culture and sexuality restrict women. Within this approach, cultural feminism as an ideal type rejects liberal assumptions that women and men are identical. It instead focuses on differences between—and the superiority of—femininity over masculinity as the basis for women's advancement. Even more explicitly than socialist feminism, cultural feminism highlights how women have a particular standpoint or perspective different from that of men. However, while socialist feminism focuses on women's economic standpoint, cultural feminism focuses on women's cultural standpoint.

Cultural feminism is best illustrated by the Entwives, and Treebeard's long-lost wife, Wandlimb. Reminiscent of cultural feminists, who argue that "women's ways" are better than "men's ways," the Entwives and Ent-maidens (who love gardens) argue with the Ents (who love the wild' woods) in song over who is right about their land being best (II: 466). Similarly, cultural feminism reverses traditional masculine-over-feminine dominance relationships in arguing that femininity is different from and better than masculinity, that feminine traits should be valued more highly, and that women should create women-centered, empowering so-cial communities. Such communities are illustrated by those the Ent-wives create, far from the Ents, because both Ents and Entwives are too stubborn to recognize the positive elements of the other's interests and priorities. Although the Entwives gain the freedom to live as they choose, retaining dichotomous thinking—sticking with feminine-only instead of masculine-only approaches—restricts them. This is shown by Tree-beard's comment that Ents and Entwives "shall find somewhere land where we can live together and both be content . . . [only] when we both [have] lost all that we now have" (II: 465).

As this illustrates, cultural feminism's argument that women can ad-vance by reversing the current gender hierarchy is mythologized as al-lowing this advancement only in a limited way; this is because—although cultural feminism compensates for previously devalued feminine char-acteristics—it *over*compensates by simply reversing a (still problemati-cally zero-sum) hierarchical relationship between men's and women's traditional roles. This illustration also highlights how early standpoint approaches, including radical-cultural feminism, are mythologized as limited by defining women's ways as superior to men's. Related perspec-tives include World War I feminist peace activists and current, more tra-ditional IR scholars who have argued that women are "more peaceful" and men "more aggressive" (e.g., Fukyuama 1998).

As noted previously, current standpoint approaches have moved be-yond this kind of focus. However, the story of Wandlimb and the other Entwives usefully corrects a common misinterpretation by traditional IR scholars that assumes that feminist arguments aim to simply reverse hier-archical gendered relationships (e.g., having women "rule the world"). Counter to this assumption, feminist scholarship instead suggests that re-versing gendered hierarchies is not enough to solve problems of gender and international relations. Instead, it observes that this kind of approach oversimplifies understandings of actors in global politics, restricts creative options, and perpetuates hierarchical relationships (Tickner 1999). In Wandlimb's case, she gave up the opportunity to be with her partner,

Treebeard, so she could live in an Entwife community but was unable to find a way to be with both her friends and her partner.

Third-wave ideal type approaches such as *postcolonial feminism* and *postmodern feminism* critique first- and second-wave assumptions that all women experience the same kind of oppression and focus on how gender norms affect both men and women in different ways, depending on other elements of their context, including ethnicity, class, postcolonial status, religion, or disability. These feminisms hold that women's oppression is inextricable from the oppression of nondominant groups of all kinds, and consequently address how to improve the status of all marginalized populations, not just women. Postcolonial and postmodern feminisms redefine assumptions of existence (i.e., ontology) and knowledge (i.e., epistemology) in different ways, as discussed below.

Postcolonial feminism, like socialist and radical feminism, assumes that hierarchical gender relations are created, rather than arising naturally, through individual and social experience (a constructivist ontology). It also assumes that more can be learned about overcoming women's oppression by drawing on the experience of people on "the bottom rungs" of society (including but not limited to women)—for example, through fieldwork, narrative analysis, or interviews (a modified standpoint epistemology) (Hansen 2010: 25). However, rather than assuming a homogeneous "woman's" perspective, postcolonial feminism suggests that women's perspectives and concerns vary, depending on their particular experience within these systems (see Crenshaw 1991; and Collins 1990). Particularly, it argues that people are oppressed in multiple, intersecting ways (e.g., ethnicity, class, postcolonial or neocolonial status, religion, and disability, as well as gender) and suggests that all forms of domination, not just those experienced by at least some members of elites, must be combated (Agathangelou and Turcotte 2010). Postcolonial feminism often also highlights the importance of language in constructing certain kinds of experience as dominant, while excluding and subordinating other kinds of experience.

Within this framework, the almost invisible Dwarf Dís can illustrate *postcolonial feminism.* Postcolonial feminism as an ideal type suggests that Dís's experience of gendered oppression—for example, being a woman and a Dwarf—gives her a unique standpoint vis-à-vis other women of Middle-earth in both burdens and opportunities. Thus her life involves multiple kinds of domination, which must be combated. Dís is a Dwarf princess—the daughter of King Thráin II, sister of Thorin Oakenshield (who headed the earlier quest to the Lonely Mountain, detailed in *The Hobbit*, during which the Hobbit Bilbo found the Ring of Power) and the mother of Fíli and Kíli (scouts on this earlier quest). Tolkien only mentions her in a footnote and notes that she "is the only dwarf-woman named in these histories" (III: appendix A, 1053). However, he does not say why, and most evidence of her life must be inferred.

As a Dwarf woman, Dís is part of a group of other Dwarf females who "seldom walk abroad except at great need" (III: appendix A, 1053). This reclusiveness could be the result of restrictions imposed by jealous Dwarf males on being seen by other races. (Tolkien observes that both sexes exhibit jealousy toward each other.) This makes Dís particularly dependent on the imperfect men in her life, who may not always stand up to the task and who can abuse their positions of power. As a Dwarf woman, she is also a significant minority: according to Gimli, Dwarf women make up "probably no more than a third of the whole [Dwarf] people" (III: appendix A, 1053). However, despite this strongly disproportionate sex ratio, Tolkien notes, "The number of dwarf-men that marry is actually less than one-third. For not all the women take husbands: some desire none; some desire one that they cannot get, and so will have no other. As for the men, very many also do not desire marriage, being engrossed in their crafts" (III: appendix A, 1053). This suggests a very different set of social experiences for Dwarf women relative to women of other races.

Despite such common traits, Dís's situation is also particular among Dwarf women. This is most clear because she is a princess but also because she is a member of the house (or clan) of Durin (rather than one of the other six Dwarf houses) and lives during a time of community displacement: her family fled their home under the Lonely Mountain when it was taken over by the dragon Smaug, and, after years of exile, her brother (Thorin Oakenshield) and sons (Fíli and Kíli) died in a quest to reclaim it (see Tolkien 1996). Like Wandlimb and Lobelia, Dís clearly takes some control over her own life, as Tolkien suggests when he states that Dwarf women make their own decisions over whether or not to marry. Consequently, she is not just a victim but an active shaper of her destiny. Despite this, her life is constrained in many ways.

Tolkien's limited discussion of Dís's situation raises many questions about both Dís and other Dwarf women. For example, how can the dramatically disproportionate sex ratio be explained, especially given that Dwarf males—but probably not restricted Dwarf females—are regularly killed in battle? Perhaps the sex ratio explains the eventual extinction of Dwarves, who disappear from Middle-earth after the Third Age, an evolutionarily, as well as socially, dysfunctional outcome. Why do some Dwarf females decide not to marry, despite the (over)abundance of available males? (Are social and institutional disincentives so much greater than incentives? Does Dwarf leadership, unlike European governments in our world, fail to create incentives to reverse declining population growth?) What does it mean for Dís to be royalty, an exile, and a member of a broader Dwarf diaspora—as a woman? Postcolonial feminism would highlight the importance of understanding the effects of these intersecting, interacting traits. Many other questions could also be raised.

Dís's standpoint at the intersection of these various experiences, even if we are unsure of how they all play out, illustrates the standpoint argument that focusing on simplistic, homogenized understandings about "universal" experience—whether they be about people, states, humans, women, or whoever—is profoundly limited in capturing the complexity of different sets of experience. The relegation of Dís's experience to a footnote also illustrates the standpoint argument that language is critical to constructing certain kinds of experience as dominant and other kinds as subordinate. However, it also cautions against focusing on any particular set of experiences (or "intersections of oppression") because no particular set can be exhaustive. Consequently, focusing only on particular kinds of backgrounds, even if they do improve our understanding, remains limited. In Dís's case, categorizing her simply as a woman—without understanding that she is also a Dwarf, a princess, and an exile—is inadequate to understanding or explaining her interests, insecurities, and goals. It also is inadequate to understanding or explaining her role in Frodo's quest for the Ring of Power—such as her support or lack thereof for her brother's or sons' decision to engage in the earlier quest, which brought the Ring of Power to light in the first place.

Finally, *postmodern feminism* as an ideal type assumes that hierarchical gender relations are created through language rather than being interpreted or arising directly from biological characteristics (a poststructuralist ontology). It also assumes that we can learn more about women's oppression and international relations by analyzing discourse to see how hierarchical gender norms are defined through language and how they then act to critically constrain behavior (a discursive epistemology) (Hansen 2010: 25). Unlike earlier feminist approaches, postmodern feminist scholarship rejects "modernist" narratives that assume that "progress" in IR is inevitable or unidirectional. One popular culture illustration of this approach is *Wicked*—a book and musical that reinterprets the classic *Wizard of Oz* story. In this interpretation, the "Wonderful Wizard of Oz" is a brutal dictator while the "Wicked Witch of the West" is a heroic freedom fighter. This highlights how stories and the actors in them are more complex than first appears. Similarly, postmodern feminism suggests that all "truth" is imbued with power (Zalewski 2000). As part of this, "The crucial project is to investigate the mechanisms of power that have forged female identities in order to resist identity itself" (27). Consequently "deconstructing" or taking apart the stories that are told, and their assumptions about relationships of power, is in itself political activism. Even a term like *gender* should be used carefully because of the way language powerfully restricts understandings of reality.

Galadriel, the Elven Lady of Lothlórien, best illustrates this worldview. Galadriel recognizes that success is not inevitable for the quest and questions the individuals within the Fellowship to help them navigate their journey. When the Fellowship confers with her in Lothlórien, she tells them that their quest "stands upon the edge of a knife. Stray but a little and it will fail, to the ruin of all" (I: 348). So, too, postmodern feminism rejects the modernist assumption that progress is inevitable or linear: there may be two steps back for every step forward on the same path, and completely different paths can be taken to different endpoints— whether of development or otherwise. At the same meeting, Galadriel also recognizes that each member of the Fellowship has his own journey to take, even if he is part of the Fellowship at the same time. She "held them with her eyes," and each felt that he had been questioned long and deeply—though it was in their minds and hearts and without any words spoken (I: 348). This later enables her to perfectly tailor her parting gifts to each, from Sam Gamgee's box of blessed earth (perfect for a Hobbit gardener) to Frodo's light of Eärendil's star (crucial for his later survival) (I: 366–67). Because of this period of questioning and outcome in thoughtful gifts, each member is better able to redefine his path and more freely pursue his journey both on his own and in conjunction with others. Similarly, postmodern feminists suggest that reconsidering stories in terms of their relations of power creates the opportunity to redefine traditionally told stories in more flexible and creative ways.

Galadriel's story also illustrates how the wave myth tends to define postmodern IR feminism as unable to craft practical solutions. Like other Elves, Galadriel refuses to advise Frodo or the others on what course of action to pursue. This remains true even though she is the bearer of Nenya, one of the three Elven Rings of Power, which makes her one of the most powerful inhabitants of Middle-earth, and even though Frodo is in desperate need. Galadriel's story also illustrates how the wave myth obscures the utility of postmodern IR feminism. Particularly, Galadriel is very effective in giving a thoughtful gift to each individual after effectively questioning him—a gift that ends up being a critical aid in navigating his journey. So, too, postmodern IR feminism enables new directions to be taken by interrogating old stories.

IMPLICATIONS: IMPORTANCE OF RAINBOW-COLORED LENSES

What does this mean for studying global politics today? Feminist IR scholarship suggests that traditional ways of looking at things are just the view of one narrow lens on a much more colorful world and a narrow way of explaining and understanding international relations. Because mainstream IR applies gender-blind rather than gender-sensitive lenses to global politics, it customarily misses how gender is both a causal and a constitutive (or proximate and ultimately causal) factor in international politics: In other words, it misses how political processes are indirectly enabled by gendered institutions, which are organized based on principles defining masculine traits as more valuable than feminine traits; it also misses how particular political processes (e.g., state decisions to engage in war) are directly caused by particular gendered influences (e.g., overestimating the likelihood that victory will be "short and easy" because "we" are defined as masculine and dominant while "they" are defined as feminized and subordinate).

As part of this line of reasoning, traditional IR theory misses how the way international politics is currently conducted also has causal and constitutive implications for personal politics. For example, traditional frameworks such as levels of analysis tend to ignore or minimize how different levels are interrelated. This misses how both "the personal is international" and "the international is personal." As a result, traditional concerns

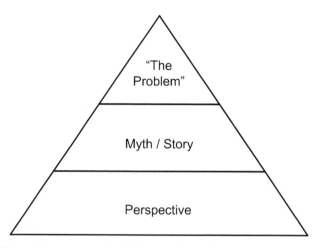

Fig. 5. How perspective influences definition of "the problem"

also promote particular kinds of stable orders that disproportionately benefit elite, dominant groups and disproportionately limit subordinate groups and their calls for alternative, more just forms of Order.

Furthermore, when traditional approaches do promote more just forms of Order, the kind of Justice envisioned is too often a "thin" kind that assumes people are isolated (rather than relational) individuals and minimizes the priorities and experience of women and minorities. However, feminist scholarship suggests that learning from women's experience changes guidelines for ethical behavior and promotes a "thicker" kind that is defined based on a broader set of concerns: because people are embedded in caring relationships, ethical judgments require identifying with and taking responsibility for the needs of others involved. This kind of approach supports creative problem solving and restricts violent exchanges between those involved (Hutchings 2010).

Why, from the viewpoint of feminist theorists, is traditional IR so off the mark? As figure 5 illustrates, mainstream concerns (such as state security) are based on myths and stories rooted in particular subsets of human experience. However, these stories are frequently portrayed in a way that values knowledge from dominant kinds of experience as valid but assesses knowledge from other kinds of experience as invalid. Thinking about rainbows, this is like wearing blue-colored glasses and not recognizing that some things in the world are green or yellow or pink. The

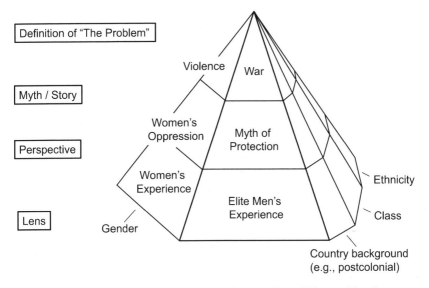

Fig. 6. Different lenses highlight different sides of "the problem"

figure illustrates this tendency by showing how any particular lens, used alone, obscures the existence or importance of other lenses or other ways of seeing the world. Thus perspective, at the base of the pyramid, rises to the level of mythologized storytelling and ultimately reaches up to problem definition.

Despite the value of this problem-solving approach in coping with the constraints of the global system as it is traditionally understood, it falls short of meeting the transformative needs of critical IR scholarship and is also limited in its ability to meet its own problem-solving goals because of its narrow vision. Feminists have argued that objective knowledge re- ally represents *subjective* knowledge of privileged voices disguised as neu- tral (Sjoberg 2009, 192). Thinking about perspectives as lenses that bring out certain "truths" or colors but not others illustrates how taking dominant stories at face value is a limited and biased way of thinking about the world—like seeing a world that is entirely blue or entirely or- ange or entirely green (see fig. 6, explored at greater length in the next chapter). Although such stories are one part of the world, they rely on, influence, and are influenced by other stories (often minimized, dele- gitimized ones) and other kinds of experience. They are only one part of the rainbow. This matters because seeing the world through a single color of glasses fails to recognize how colorful the world is, cannot shed as bright a light on the world as would be possible with a full rainbow, and does not recognize how the presence of the other colors makes the patterns originally found possible.

As the preceding line of reasoning suggests, focusing on "war stories" from a dominant, elite, masculine perspective provides just one (limited) picture of what is going on. Changing the focus and taking the perspectives of people on the bottom rungs due to a variety of sources of oppression—including gender, ethnicity, class, postcolonial status, religion, or disability—shows how dominant stories are limited and biased and reliant on large numbers of people accepting (rather than questioning) masculinized and feminized ways of being in the variety of ways that they play out from individual lives to institutional structures. Feminist theorists argue that it sheds a stronger light by bringing in other colors from the rainbow. This suggests, for example, that destabilizing exploitative social hierarchies (e.g, due to gender, race, or class) can destabilize exploitative inter- and intrastate hierarchies. Destabilizing state hierarchies can destabilize "personal" hierarchies as well. As such, traditional "power politics" is blind to critical kinds of power in global affairs. The next chapter applies a gender-sensitive lens to the "problem of war" to illustrate more concretely what feminist scholarship, which applies a gender-sensitive lens to politics, means for international politics and political theory.

CHAPTER 6

Middle-earth and Feminist Analysis of Conflict

[T]heir coming was like the falling of small stones
that starts an avalanche in the mountains.
—*Gandalf*

Gandalf points out in the epigraph that in Middle-earth Hobbits have a huge impact on political affairs, despite their small stature. This ranges from Frodo, the Ring Bearer, who is critical to the outcome of the quest; to Sam, who supports him from the very beginning to the very end; to Merry and Pippin, who stimulate an uprising of the Ents that plays a key role in the downfall of Saruman. So, too, feminists argue that women and gender critically both influence and are a part of global politics in our world.

In this chapter, we apply a gender-sensitive lens to *LOTR* and compare this to feminist analyses of World War I and the US War in Iraq. In that way we go beyond the problem-solving approach to these events of chapter 4 and apply one kind of critical approach to IR. This chapter refers to conflict, as well as war, because of the concern within feminist theory about underlying power structures that contribute to conflict beyond mainstream definitions of war as organized interstate violence. We conclude by reviewing how feminist analyses that bring to bear a gender-sensitive lens on politics create a stronger, more inclusive basis for understanding and explaining Order and Justice from the personal to the international.

WHAT DO GENDER-SENSITIVE LENSES SAY ABOUT WAR?

Feminist scholarship argues that gendered masculine and feminine relations of power imbue politics. As discussed in the previous chapter, *gender* is not just a politically correct term for male or female (sex); instead, in feminist theory *gender* refers to a system of meaning that creates unequal relationships of power based in associated masculine (dominant) and feminine (subordinate) relationships. Feminist scholarship argues that gendered relationships (e.g., those involving men and women or even different states) are not "normal" but are created and constantly changing. It suggests that changes in these relationships must be examined closely both because they are important in their own right and because they provide the foundation for what orthodox scholarship defines as "real" politics. Just as not counting cases of racial profiling would not stop profiling from happening, feminist scholarship argues that ignoring gender does not make it go away. Paying attention to gender by using a gender-sensitive—rather than gender-blind—analysis is critical to both recognizing and rectifying gendered problems.

Scholarship that has applied a gender-sensitive lens to war suggests that war depends on telling gendered "war stories" based in a "logic of protection" and silencing or delegitimizing stories that challenge them (Hunt 2010; Tickner 2008; Goldstein 2001). The logic of protection is characterized by a "gallantly masculine man [who] can only appear in their goodness if we assume that lurking outside the warm familial walls are aggressors, the 'bad' men, who wish to attack them" (Young 2003: 4, quoted in Hunt 2010: 117). This kind of story "serves to reinforce patriarchal power and justify violence abroad to a frightened and uncritical public 'at home'" (Hunt 2010: 117). It also silences or delegitimizes challenging alternative narratives that question the story or key elements of it—such as its heroic men, dependent women, dangerous public sphere, or secure private sphere. Figure 6 in the previous chapter illustrated how different lenses highlight different sides of what is seen as the problem—in this case, of war—and suggested why it is critical to apply a gender-sensitive (rather than gender-blind) lens to such problems in order to have a stronger basis for analysis. In other words, assessment takes place in three rather than two dimensions, as per figure 5.

Applying a gender-sensitive lens to global politics can be guided by asking two questions: first, where are the women; and second, what work is masculinity and femininity doing (Zalewski 2010)?

While feminist scholarship addresses these kinds of questions across a broad range of areas, the subfield of feminist security studies applies this approach to issues of war, peace, and security. It argues first that security should be defined broadly rather than narrowly; second, that current understandings of security award unequal weight to values associated with femininity rather than masculinity; and third, that gender is critical to conceptually understanding security, analyzing causes and predicting outcomes, and developing solutions and positive change (Sjoberg 2009: 186, 198–200; Blanchard 2003).

This kind of approach complements but goes beyond certain orthodox constructivist and critical IR scholarship by highlighting, rather than ignoring, the role of gender in politics. First, feminist scholarship supports constructivist scholarship, which suggests that perceptions are important in international politics. Second, feminist scholarship supports critical scholarship, which contends, against strictly rational actor models, that social institutions are very important. And third, feminist scholarship supports postmodern and poststructuralist IR scholarship, which highlights the importance of discourse in international politics. However, in each of these areas, feminist analysis contends that it is critical to pay attention to how politics is *gendered*, whether that means gendered perceptions, gendered institutions, gendered narratives, or otherwise. Such feminist contributions add value to the study of global politics, by enabling a fresh look to be taken at old problems, and consequently create the opportunity for more accurate analysis and creative problem solving.

The following sections apply a gender-sensitive lens to the War of the Ring, World War I, and the American War in Iraq in order to demonstrate feminist IR contributions more concretely. The final section of the chapter revisits the implications for Order and Justice of feminist IR contributions to IR theory and reviews how applying a gender-sensitive lens can facilitate more accurate, rigorous, and ethical scholarship.

WAR OF THE RING THROUGH A GENDER-SENSITIVE LENS

Applying a gender-sensitive lens to *LOTR* suggests that an uncritical reading of it may lend itself to a triumphal "hero story" interpretation of the quest; however, highlighting the experience of women, Hobbits, and people on "the bottom rungs" suggests a more complicated story and a more mixed set of results. Particularly, taking other points of view highlights how there are myriad other stories that make the quest possible and influence and interact with the buildup, conduct, and aftereffects of the War of the Ring. These stories are also political, and if they had played out differently, they could have—like small stones starting an avalanche, as noted in this chapter's epigraph—completely changed the main story about the Fellowship of the Ring. Furthermore, even if they had played out in the same way, these other stories suggest that focusing on a "successful" Quest abroad can restrict other political quests for more equal and less patriarchal relationships. We will now apply a gender-sensitive lens to *LOTR* to develop these kinds of implications.

First, where are the women? Although the preceding chapter's review of the different feminist movement waves behind existing feminist IR theory highlighted the roles of particular women in *LOTR,* the immediate answer is that women are, with certain notable exceptions, largely absent or hidden. Of course, Galadriel plays an important and powerful role, and the stories of Éowyn (in the book and movies) and Arwen (especially in the movies) do appear. Yet they are clearly exceptions to the rule. This trend is supported by an overall focus on the quest, which takes the heroes to the "front lines" of conflict and minimizes attention to the "home front" until the very end of the story when the war is declared to be "over." As in our world, this way of telling stories in Middle-earth emphasizes masculine war action by heroic men and minimizes action at home by women and other men. It also allows us to imagine that those at home are "protected" and safe due to the diligence of the men at the front lines— even when, as we will discuss later, this is not necessarily the case.

Second, what work is masculinity doing? A close look suggests that the answer is "a lot." For one thing, each race in Middle-earth is individually organized in ways that support the domination of masculine actors and institutions over feminized ones. This is most evident in the overwhelming composition and leadership of the groups that we see: the Fellowship appears to be made up entirely of, at least as yet, unmarried men; the Orc hordes are depicted as almost entirely male; and in general, depictions of women are exceptional. So, too, leadership within groups is highly masculinized. Galadriel and Éowyn are exceptions to the rule of male rule across all races: whether Hobbit thains or Dwarf or Human kings, leadership within groups tends to be dominated by men.

For another thing, relationships between and among groups are organized in ways that support disproportionately greater privilege for members of groups that are closer to globally dominant "hegemonic" forms of masculinity relative to those members of groups characterized by femininity and subordinate forms masculinity (e.g., masculinity associated with denigrated races or classes). The Fellowship itself is hierarchically structured. In the Council of Elrond, among elite males of each race, Elves and Men are closer to the global Middle-earth dominant or "hegemonic masculinity" than are Hobbits and Dwarves. This is demonstrated by their dominance in leadership at the Council of Elrond and their description of the (unusually brave) Hobbits both as "Halflings" and as being like "children" (Ho 1983). Outside of the Fellowship, alternative violent forms of masculinity (or what being a 'real man' entails) are also apparent in descriptions of Orcs (who are depicted as an almost entirely male force of formidably tough, fierce soldiers) and Southrons (who are depicted in the movie version of *The Return of the King* as ethnic warriors who ride elephantlike creatures into battle). These kinds of masculinity are depicted as inferior to dominant masculinity among the Free Peoples; for example, Orcs are depicted as hypermasculine and aggressive, but this is not regarded as desirable because it is seen as neither chivalrous nor good. So, too, the Southrons are depicted as less pure than the noble, whiter-skinned Elves and Dúnedain—described critically as having dark skin and bringing into battle giant elephantlike beasts (múmakil). As this suggests, not only is each society within Middle-earth organized based on gendered assumptions about masculinity and femininity, but all societies in this world are also organized in relationship to each other as part of a global social hierarchy supporting dominant masculinity over both femininity and subordinate alternative masculinities.

Gendered global structuring of relations between races in Middle-earth is centrally important to understanding why the quest succeeded to the extent that it did. The reason why Frodo and Sam are able to go as far as they do is because Sauron underestimates them, and a major reason he underestimates them is because of their minimized and feminized status: what threat could these small, "wimpy" creatures—only interested in eating, drinking, and making merry, with little regard for warcraft—be to him? In his proud and thoughtless way, Sauron dismisses the feminized, "childlike" Hobbits as unworthy of his attention. However, it is this very dismissal that creates a chink in his armor. Because he does not believe that Hobbits have what it takes to engage him and because he cannot imagine that anyone would want to destroy the Ring (rather than controlling it for themselves), he leaves himself vulnerable. This is a central and ultimately fatal flaw in his plans. So, too, in our world, feminists suggest that assuming ceteris paribus conditions apply to gender—or assuming that gendered relationships of domination are normal, stable, and unchanging—is a central flaw in traditional approaches to IR, which renders them unable to adequately understand either global politics today or opportunities for more just change. Feminist theorists argue that such approaches can achieve problem solving in the areas they focus on but must be complemented by other frames of reference to engage different normative concerns.

Insights from the Bottom Rungs

Focusing on the experience of women and others on the bottom rungs helps us improve our understanding and explanation of the stories that are center stage and backstage in *LOTR*, and the relationship between the two. On one hand, spotlighting Sauron highlights how dominating relationships *between* groups are often paralleled by dominating relationships *within* groups. Particularly, the dictatorial and dominating internal hierarchies on which Sauron bases his reign of terror provide the basis for the nightmare that would have been Middle-earth if he had succeeded in his goal of world domination. On the other hand, the relationship between personal politics and international politics among the "good guys" is less apparent: The myth assumed in *LOTR* about this connection says that it is up to the Fellowship to protect the Free Peoples from malevolent Sauron and his armies, and at the completion of their quest, Aragorn's crowning as King Elessar signals the beginning of a new and peaceful era of safety and prosperity for all. However, this story is described from the perspective of Frodo—an elite hero himself (among others), in spite of being a Hobbit—and does not incorporate other narratives, which suggest that the story may be more complex than it appears. This parallels the benignly patriarchal "just war story" discussed by feminists in our world, where "just warriors" protect "beautiful souls" from "bad guys" in theory but where this narrative obscures a much messier practice. As such, the story of the quest obscures the extent to which relations of domination, such as those between the good guys and the victims at home, support unequal and unjust relationships, despite being described in overall positive terms.

Although readers of *LOTR* have few glimpses into the experiences of people with such alternative perspectives, the previous chapter's discussion of Éowyn, Lobelia Sackville-Baggins, Wandlimb, Dís, and Galadriel suggests a few ways in which the hero story might be challenged. First, those narratives suggest that the private sphere the heroic Fellowship goes to defend may actually make some people *in*secure—this is particularly evident for Dís, whose security is highly compromised by the tradition of male Dwarves acting to restrict female Dwarves' movements. Second, the experiences of these characters suggest that actions taken for the "community's" good (i.e., saving Middle-earth from Sauron) may in fact support harm against certain members of the population. For example, increased support for masculinized heroes may reduce women's domestic security, limit their opportunities for public engagement or work because of reinvigorated gender roles, or support exploitative relationships among different races by projecting naturalized assumptions about gender hierarchy onto international interactions. Third, these experiences reveal that the War of the Ring was a part of a continuum of violence—on the part of the Free Peoples as well as the evil Sauron—that included personal as well as public forms. Fourth, by focusing on the costs borne by the Fellowship rather than those on the "home front," they suggest that Frodo probably underestimated the costs involved in the War of the Ring. Finally, they suggest that the quest's pursuit of a more peaceful and just world defined that peace and Justice in a "thin" way—and from a particular, masculine, and elite perspective—rather than a "thicker" way, which would allow for a positive peace involving "domestic" Justice, not just a "negative" peace involving the absence of war or threat of war as a preferred Order.

Thus even a war in pursuit of Justice can reinforce sexist and oppressive violence in many forms, especially for those in vulnerable positions, such as Hobbits in the Shire. Consequently, any war or violence proposed to overturn existing social violence must be evaluated carefully with an empathetic ethic that recognizes human connectedness (Sjoberg 2006). This point becomes evident by examining the lives of other members of subordinated groups as well as the women in *LOTR*.

First, focusing on the experience of Hobbits, who frequently are seen as being "like children" (e.g., Merry and Pippin), illustrates how gendered and hierarchical relationships can perpetuate insecurity for feminized "dependents" through unequal and vulnerable relationships, whether such dependents are male or female. In *LOTR*, the Hobbit Pippin illustrates such vulnerability when he and his friend Merry are captured by Orcs and then must fend for themselves without the great warriors of their Fellowship. While strapped to the back of a retreating Orc, Pippin "wished now that he had learned more in Rivendell . . . but in those days the plans for the journey seemed to be in more competent hands, and he had never reckoned with being cut off from Gandalf" (II: 443). As this episode illustrates, dependency, based in unequal relationships that assume that some kind of hero will save the day, puts people at risk because of their attendant, more vulnerable position. However, consider the significant later accomplishments of Pippin and Merry: Merry helps vanquish the Ringwraith; Merry and Pippin work through Treebeard to convince the Ents to contribute to the alliance of Free Peoples against Saruman; and Merry and Pippin lead efforts to eject the ruffians who were wreaking havoc in the Shire on their return from the quest. These actions contradict the assumption that certain kinds of people are inherently dependent. Instead, they demonstrate how such people are dependent because they are *treated as* less capable.

Second, although the story of *LOTR* itself consistently omits and minimizes the experiences of women, a major theme throughout the text is how people who are *not* recognized as important actually *do* influence key events in significant ways. As Elrond notes at his Council, "Yet such is oft the course of deeds that move the wheels of the world. Small hands do them because they must, while the eyes of the great are elsewhere" (I: 262). Later, discussing the Hobbits Merry and Pippin in relation to the rise of the Ents, Gandalf also comments, "Their coming was like the falling of small stones that starts an avalanche in the mountains" (II: 485). Similarly, it is Éowyn and Merry, a woman and a Hobbit, who emerge as unexpected heroes "excluded from the affairs of men" and "vindicate themselves in the great Battle of Pelennor Fields, dispatching together the fearful Ringwraith whom 'no living man may hinder'; yet another example of the weak and the despised succeeding where the strongest would fail" (Ho 1983: 7; Chance 2001: 72). Just so, feminists in our world have demonstrated how individual women have been able to impact the political process in ways beyond men. Consider, for example, Sacajawea's presence as the wife of an interpreter in Lewis and Clark's expedition. She redefined initial contact between the explorers and native tribes as peaceful because the tribes assumed a woman's presence meant it was not a war party (Tickner 1992: 62–63). We also see how women's devalued reproductive and productive work sustains current economic institutions (e.g., Waring 1988).

Third, a critical reading of *LOTR* highlights how private politics are foundational to the practice and understanding of public politics. Examples of the intersection of personal friendships in personal and public politics abound. For one thing, despite Elvish norms restricting strangers from entry, all of the members of the Fellowship ultimately are allowed to enter the Elvish forest of Lothlórien (even Gimli the Dwarf, whose people long had been barred) because they are friends of Aragorn (I: 334). All members of the Fellowship ultimately are permitted to walk free, removing blindfolds that had been required initially, once approval had come from Galadriel a short time later (I: 341). For another, even after the formal Fellowship is broken when Frodo tries to set out alone, Aragorn remains determined to help his abducted friends, declaring, "[W]e that remain cannot forsake our companions while we have strength left" (II: 409). For a third, at their initial meeting, Pippin joins Lord Denethor's service because of his friendship with his fallen comrade Boromir (son of Denethor) (III: 739). And probably most impressively, completion of the quest is not possible without both the support of Frodo's friend and servant Sam Gamgee and his pitying/disgusted relationship with Gollum: Sam, for example, both saves Frodo from being consumed by the giant spider Shelob and carries him physically up the cliffs of Mount Doom. Meanwhile, it is Gollum's knowledge of evil Mordor that guides Frodo through otherwise impassible geographical obstacles, and whose betrayal at Mount Doom ironically stops the quest from failing.

In each of these instances, the public politics of the quest intersect with and rely on the private politics of personal relationships. This is consistent with feminist arguments that highlight how private lives sustain public politics (e.g., participation in "old boy" networks and women's role as diplomatic wives support official state diplomacy and internal politics in our world).

Fourth, a critical reading of *LOTR* also points to nondominant perspectives as having important, even if underrecognized, sources of wisdom. For example, when Boromir scorns the "'old wives' tales' of Fangorn" (of the Ents), Celeborn of Lothlórien cautions him, "[D]o not despise the lore that has come down from distant years; for oft it may chance that old wives keep in memory word of things that were once needful for the wise to know" (I: 365). The same theme is repeated later in the story by a doctor who wrongly rejects the utility of the powerfully medicinal herb athelas: "It is but doggerel, I fear, garbled in the memory of old wives" (III: 847). Yet Aragorn uses athelas to save Frodo's life when he is stabbed by the evil blade of the Ringwraith and to save Faramir's life when he is pierced by a Southron arrow at the battle of Pelennor Fields

(I: 193; III: 846–48). (Women who work in the Houses of Healing are also charged with important related responsibilities.) And without Frodo, what would have happened to the quest?

Fifth, although he does not apply a gender-sensitive lens to his story, Tolkien repeatedly makes reference to how history is both selective and imbued with myth. As such, "legend among the Hobbits first becomes history with a reckoning of years" (I: 4), books of Hobbit history "contained much that was later omitted or lost" (I: 14), and for other races, Hobbits "passed once more out of the History of Men and of Elves" (I: 4). Although Tolkien does not explicitly recognize it, the same principle applies to women's experience in *LOTR*, with "much . . . [being] later omitted or lost." This provides a useful caution against reading *LOTR* through gender-blind rather than gender-sensitive lenses.

Finally, the implications of these different points are drawn out even more extensively in a late chapter in *LOTR* entitled "The Scouring of the Shire." In this dark chapter, the heroic Hobbits who fought in the War of the Ring return to their home in the Shire expecting to find it safe and saved. They are shocked to find devastation instead: the inhabitants of the Shire are essentially under constant house arrest because of a military curfew; the inns have all been closed; food is rationed (a major hardship for Hobbits, who eat six meals a day if they can get it); houses are burned, closed, and abandoned; Hobbits who complain risk imprisonment, beating, or death; and a group of armed "ruffians," the only ones allowed to drink the Hobbits' beer or smoke the Hobbits' pipeweed, patrol the streets in a reign of terror over the Shire, punishing any who get too "uppish."

This state of affairs clashes strongly with the hero story bound up in the narrative of *LOTR* and assumed by the Hobbits in the Fellowship, where heroes (the Fellowship) go out to protect feminized victims (the people the Fellowship left at home, away from the "front lines"), defeat the villain (Sauron), and return to a safe and secure home to live happily ever after. As Sam comments on their return, "No welcome, no beer, no smoke, and a lot of rules and orc-talk instead. I hoped to have a rest, but I can see there's work and trouble ahead" (III: 977). Rather than picking up in the idyllically described home where they had left off (as in the film version), on their return, Frodo, Sam, Merry, and Pippin instead confront the bullying ruffians, organize resistance by the Shire-folk, and fight the Battle of Bywater, in which nineteen Hobbits are killed. And afterward they still face the hard task of community reconstruction: "I shan't call it the end, till we've cleaned up the mess," said Sam gloomily. "And that'll take a lot of time and work" (III: 997). Description of the Shire as being its own "front" within the War of the Ring highlights a different set of experiences (that of those who were left at home) and consequently tells a different story.

First, the Shire-folk's experience highlights the War of the Ring as a continuum of violence in terms of both space and time: even though it is not on the front lines, the Shire is still devastated by the war because of the militarized ruffians who exploit it. Furthermore, the impact of the War on the Shire extends beyond its formal duration: in terms of aftereffects, its devastation is clearly not resolved when the war is officially over—fixing the infrastructure, reopening the inns, and replanting the trees will take time. However, even before the war's start, growing militarization had increased the fear and levels of violence experienced by the population—the climate of rising fear due to rumors of unusual Elf and Dwarf migration and the multiplication of Orcs, trolls, and other evil creatures (I: 42–43). As such, this suggests that the assumption by Frodo and other members of the Fellowship—that their quest would involve engaging in a dangerous public sphere while leaving a secure private sphere at home—was wrong: violence at home was interlinked with violence abroad.

Second, the Shire-folk's experience highlights how such violence builds on assumptions about relational hierarchy. When the returning Hobbits arrive at Bywater, the ruffians accost them: "Where d'you think you're going? . . . You little folk are getting too *uppish*" (III: 981, emphasis added). The militarized structure of the Shire as influenced by war supports this bullying and aggressive domination by ruffians of Hobbits, who were expected to stay in their subordinated "place." Years of naive dependence by Hobbits (on Rangers and Men of Gondor) also facilitated this domination, by limiting the experience and ability of Hobbits at home to take care of themselves. As Merry says, "Shire-folk have been so comfortable for so long they don't know what to do. They just want a match, though, and they'll go up in fire" (III: 983). When the returning members of the Fellowship provide that match by using the Horn-cry of Buckland to raise the Shire, Merry turns out to be right: Hobbits have been underestimated by their foes (once again) and are able to take back their country from the ruffians. As such, these events highlight how hierarchy enables corruption and suggests that those who are seen as dependent or weak (e.g., the Hobbits) often are weakened by their lack of familiarity with protecting themselves, and at least have the capacity to stand strong.

Overall, looking at the War of the Ring through a gender-sensitive lens suggests that focusing on one hero story and experience while ignoring or minimizing the lives, influence, and insights of others in the story, whether they be women (for *LOTR* readers) or Hobbits (for Sauron and the ruffians), distorts our understanding of what occurred and limits our ability to predict or plan for the future. As such, retaining a feminist curiosity that averts intellectual laziness promotes a clearer, more accurate, and more useful understanding of the context, duration, and aftereffects of the War of the Ring.

WORLD WAR I THROUGH A GENDER-SENSITIVE LENS

Scholarship analyzing World War I is far and away predominated by traditional, gender-blind (not gender-sensitive) analysis. Feminist IR scholarship only became part of the field relatively recently, with many citing *Millennium*'s 1988 special issue on women and IR as a crucial starting point. Because of this, IR scholarship of politics before the 1990s and 2000s is characterized by an "absence of systematic gender analysis in the tool kits" of researchers (Enloe 2010: 8). This makes it difficult to answer questions like "Where are the women?" and "What work is masculinity doing?" As a result, this section will highlight one of the few feminist analyses of World War I, authored by Lauren Wilcox, to provide one example of how applying a gender-sensitive lens contributes to explaining and understanding World War I, and will suggest how beneficial this kind of analysis can be if applied elsewhere.

As discussed in chapter 4, World War I is characterized by the "cult of the offensive," in which all major powers believed that they needed to exercise offensive dominance. Wilcox (2009) argues that a gender-blind analysis cannot on its own explain why state actors regularly overestimate offensive dominance capabilities. She suggests that a feminist analysis addresses this "missing link" in offense-defense theory by showing how gendered institutions constitute or create the foundation for global political processes. In this case, that means investigating "what assumptions about gender (and race, class, nationality, and sexuality) make it possible for belligerents to consistently exaggerate offensive capabilities and therefore engage in counterproductive offensive military strategies" (218). Gender creates the foundation for the "illusions" behind misperceptions of offense-defense balance in three different ways: "gendered perceptions of technology, gendered nationalism, and definitions of citizenship and honor based on the gendered concept of protection" (216).

Gendered Perceptions

First, the overestimation of offensive capabilities is facilitated by the combination of an "overwhelming" tendency to interpret developments in military technology as offensive, combined with a tendency—when military technology *is* interpreted as defensive—"to downplay the role of technology and overestimate the importance of the spirit and honor of offensive warfighting" (Wilcox 2009: 222). On one hand, the illusion of offensive dominance occurs because technology is interpreted as "offensive" or "defensive" not "objectively" but instead based in how it is perceived—which, in many cases, involves whether inventions are *seen* as "masculine" or "feminine" (220–21). On the other hand, the cult occurs because "the values associated with the hegemonic masculinity of heroic combat overwhelmingly favor aggressiveness and offense (bravery, strength, courage and control) and rarely favor military restraint" (225). Consequently, "offensive capabilities" are not evaluated on a consistent basis because of gendered perceptions valuing dominant masculinity over subordinate masculinities and femininity.

World War I demonstrates this dynamic in a number of ways. For one thing, the use of airplanes—involving leading technological advancements—was circumscribed by gendered assumptions. Planes were little used for dropping missiles because that was considered "unchivalrous"; instead British and French planes were prominently used for single-combat attacks against the Germans, whose (less risky and more effective) method of flying in squadrons was seen by British and French military leaders as cowardly, bullying, and essentially less manly (Wilcox 2009: 223–24). For another, although World War I involved military technologies that favored defense, such as barbed wire and machine guns (as a consensus of offense-defense theorists recognize), military leaders "dealt with those technologies much like they dealt with airplanes—by valuing boldness, bravery, strength, and chivalry over defensive positioning, patience, balancing, and calculation" (224). As such, World War I demonstrates how gendered assumptions influence how war is conducted, as well as how likely "success" is estimated in decisions of whether or not to go to war.

Gendered Institutions

Second, the "inappropriately aggressive military strategies" involved in the cult of the offensive are made possible by a militarized masculinity intertwined with military culture and nationalism rather than any "rational" calculation of interests. This does *not* mean that men are more disposed than women to go to war because they are inherently aggressive (Fukuyama 1998: 26; Steans and Pettiford 2005, 175). That relationship is too simply and clearly wrong: "If maleness, masculinity and militarism were inevitably bound together, militaries would always have all the soldiers they believed they required" (Wilcox 2009: 227, quoting Enloe 2000b: 245). The relationship of gender with aggression therefore is more complex.

Rather than biological sex, feminists in IR identify aggressive policies as based in military training and martial values. Particularly, militarized nationalism makes it possible for military planners to assume that their soldiers are superior to the others, so conquest will be "easy" (Wilcox 2009: 229). In this masculinized nationalism, enemies are dehumanized or feminized in relation to "our" soldiers, whose masculinity is valorized (230). In the process, overly aggressive military strategies are facilitated by projecting dominating relationships between men and women (interpreted as "natural") onto international relations between groups (Wilcox 2009: 233).

During World War I, this played out in variety of ways. For one thing, state leaders at the time saw war as counteracting 'emasculation' of society, a crucial test of ethnic/racial groups, and generally promoting and protecting masculine identity and values (Wilcox 2009: 228; Enloe 2000b: 212). This was evident in British government efforts to promote "traditional" gender roles in order to maintain its colonial empire and Germany's official and intellectual commitment to engaging in war so as to "fulfill its destiny of superiority over the inferior peoples of Europe" (Wilcox 2009: 228). For another, in the buildup to World War I, (militarized) nationalism was "at a highpoint," which supported a belief that conquest would be easy over the (feminized) German opponent (230–31). This was evident in discourses about Germany's "barbarism," in which British, French, and Americans characterized Germany using a subordinated or lower form of masculinity of "uncontrolled aggression," which "is to be feared and tamed" by our dominating or higher form of masculinity of "civilized values and accomplishments" (230). (This may also have supported the belief that Kaiser Wilhelm II of Germany and his advisers were "evil"; see chapter 4.)

As the preceding examples illustrate, naturalized, dominating "domestic" relationships between men and women in Britain, France, and the United States legitimized the dehumanization and feminization of Germany through discourses of "barbarism." In addition, high levels of masculinized, militarized nationalism promoted the belief that "our men" were superior to theirs across the board and thus victory in war would be easy and quickly obtained (Wilcox 2009: 230; see also chapter 4). Such ill-considered notions then promoted inappropriately aggressive military strategies. To sum up, constructions of different kinds of masculinity influence both "us" and "them": like the Orcs, Germany was defined by the British, French, and Americans as dangerously out of control. This story about "them" created a parallel (though also highly questionable) story about "us": it meant that feminized groups and individuals were interpreted to be at risk and needing protection from men who live up to ("our") masculine standards but do not slip over the edge into ("their") barbarism.

Gendered Narratives

Third, offensive military policies are encouraged by a "protection racket"—a gendered Just War narrative in which "Just Warriors" protect "Beautiful Souls" from malevolent "bad guys" (Wilcox 2009: 239, 236, 238; Elshtain 1987). Despite the apparent defensiveness of this war story, Wilcox argues that "the protection racket encourages offensive military policies even when it is couched in the language of defense and protection" (2009: 238). On one hand, this is because it encourages states to "value offense in order to be the best possible protectors" for those in need both within and outside of their borders. On the other, this is because it "brings [greater] attention to the protecting which is being done" and the boldness and bravery involved (236).

In World War I, protection racket war stories included British just warriors called to defend defenseless women and children (beautiful souls) from barbaric Germans: chivalric codes in vogue at the turn of the century identified the vulnerable female body as the main cause for war"—from sensationalized accounts of the 1914 "Rape of Belgium" to military recruiting posters framing Germans as racialized brutes abducting fainting, half-naked women (Wilcox 2009: 236). They also framed the decision of potential recruits whether or not to enlist as determined by their manliness (e.g., "There Are Three Types of Men: Those who heard the call and Obey, Those who Delay, and—The Others") (Wilcox 2009: 237; Goldstein 2001: 73–75). It is hard to imagine this type of war in the absence of the gender identities that escalated and legitimated it (Wilcox 2009: 238).

Overall, Wilcox's analysis illustrates how scholarship that addresses the causes of war would be strengthened and would address some of its major limitations by considering how gender shapes the outbreak and conduct of war. Such feminist scholarship explains how inaccurate perceptions of the offense-defense balance are supported by gendered perceptions of technology, gendered discourses of nationalism, and the protection racket. More broadly, this shows how "gender discourses and the production of gender identities are not confined to individuals and the private realm but rather are a pervasive fact of social life on an international scale" (Wilcox 2009: 240). Traditional IR approaches may consider contexts such as multipolarity under anarchy, low levels of institutions, or dynastic systems prone to producing weak leadership (see chapter 4). However, according to feminist principles, because they do so in a gender-blind way, their analyses are limited in accuracy and rigor, and the ethics of their application are also questionable. The preceding analysis of World War I illustrates how applying a gender-sensitive lens, which recognizes gender as a social system of power, can help to rectify these limitations.

US WAR IN IRAQ THROUGH A GENDER-SENSITIVE LENS

Feminist analyses of the US War in Iraq by Enloe (2010) and Sjoberg (2006) demonstrate two other ways in which applying gender-sensitive lenses facilitates more accurate, rigorous, and ethical scholarship. This section will highlight Enloe's work to provide some background for considering feminist contributions to militarization and security and then review how Sjoberg has built on these kinds of insights in the realm of Just War doctrine. Highlighting specific authors instead of linking with textbooks reflects the marginalization of feminist scholarship in the majority of introductory IR texts: with some notable exceptions (e.g., Baylis,

Smith, and Owens 2008; Edkins and Zehfuss 2009; and Tétreault and Lipschutz 2009), traditional texts typically only minimally refer (if at all) to feminist scholarship on global conflict processes, and thus do so in highly rudimentary ways. We provide a counterweight to this tendency by focusing on particular contributions in greater depth.

Masculinity and Learning from the Bottom Rungs

Enloe's body of work on gender and militarism incisively and engagingly explores the stories of people on the "bottom rungs" of society in order to analyze how "the personal is international" (e.g., Enloe 1993, 2000a, 2000b, 2004, 2007a, 2007b, 2010). It shows how people from military officials to civilians engage in strategic maneuvers that perpetuate gendered, militarized cultures (evident from camouflage-patterned condoms and tomato soup with Star Wars pasta weapons to missile factory executives). These actions, in turn, rely on and support militarized versions of masculinities and the subordinated femininities they are defined against. As a whole, gendered militarization has an enormous (though often ignored or minimized) impact on society (Enloe 2010; Cockburn 2010; Hunt 2010).

In *Nimo's War, Emma's War,* Enloe (2010) follows the stories of four Iraqi and four American ordinary women during the US War in Iraq. She shows how "unexpected theaters of operation," including marriage, sexual assault, prostitution, ethnic politics, and sexist economies, more accurately and clearly illuminate the causes, consequences, costs, and meanings of war. For one thing, despite official claims that wars will make women and other vulnerable people more safe (e.g., supporting a war story in which wars involve heroic men saving dependent women from villains), each of these stories highlights war as part of a continuum of militarized violence—rather than an occurrence separate and isolated from its context. As such, they turn war stories on their heads and suggest that the militarized culture that leads to and includes war actually exploits and reduces the security of women while also increasing their need to save *themselves* from increasingly difficult situations.

While discussions of a (concrete, isolatable) "Iraq War" catch only a glimpse of "war" violence, the experiences of women in Enloe's book highlight how violence exists in a spectrum and includes "prewar" and "postwar" as well as "war" time periods. For example, the experience of Maha, a displaced Sunni Iraqi widow, highlights the costs to personal security of militarization (Enloe 2010). Many women in positions like Maha's engaged in prostitution or "survival sex" (58) in order to "make a living in desperate circumstances"—and Enloe argues that following prostitution trends is "one way to chart escalating pressures on women" (213). Trends in Iraq indicate that prostitution and militarization were interrelated, with prostitution growing during international economic sanctions, and then even more during wartime (along with sexual assault and kidnapping [32]), and then to some extent becoming normalized "postwar" due to gendered assumptions in a joint Washington-Baghdad Status of Forces Agreement (SOFA) on women's roles as sexual servicers for American military "security" forces (60, 214; Moon 1997). (Despite a return to "normal" circumstances, Enloe asks "whether these young Iraqi women shared the view that in early 2009 Iraq's 'dark era' was over" [2010: 212].) Maha's experience also highlights how wars "can revive the 'old-fashioned' ways . . . [and] make 'uncivilized' relationships between women and men seem reasonable" (52)—in this case by reinstituting previously antiquated bans on interracial marriage, increasing domestic violence, and increasing restrictions on women's movement, education, and opportunities. These insights parallel those of American women Kim and Danielle—an American military wife and a member of the army—for whom increased militarization went hand in hand with increased levels of sexual harassment and domestic violence.

The stories Enloe draws on also highlight how state officials consistently and strategically underestimate the costs of militarization and war—essentially assuming that a "free ride" (or at least a reduced-cost ride) will be possible—because women and men will make a huge number of (little recognized, supported, or counted) sacrifices. For example, estimates of War in Iraq costs did not include many costs (emotional to financial) paid by Kim, the American wife of a National Guard member. However, the way it was conducted entailed many additional costs: Kim's experience highlighted her opportunity costs of sustaining morale among the families of her husband's unit rather than spending that time on real estate studies and consequently delaying entry into the paid labor force; the financial and emotional costs of credit card debt while her husband was forced to stay in the military with comparatively little military pay under the "stop-loss" policy; and the physical, emotional, financial, and health costs of dealing or being expected to deal with increased marital stress, instability, or domestic violence "quietly." Neither did they include the costs highlighted by Charlene, the American primary breadwinner of a three-generation household and the mother of a veteran amputee, who took several weeks off from paid work to help care for her son at Walter Reed Army Medical Center while her friends covered her hours and forwarded her paycheck, and who then supported him physically, emotionally, and financially through multiple operations and physical and mental health rehabilitation. These insights also parallel those of Iraqi women such as Nimo—a Baghdad beauty salon owner—whose uncounted war costs included the risk of bombing by militarized groups concerned that "beauty was subverting the country's wartime civic order" in the war's second (but not earlier or later) gendered phase (2010: 5), or other Iraqi women, Maha, Safah, and Shatha, whose war costs included decreased personal security (though at times increased political awareness and activism).

As this suggests, calculating the costs of war consistently relies on particular social expectations of masculinity and femininity that shift a significant burden of war costs to little-recognized and minimally supported women and men. In turn, these expectations of masculinity and femininity themselves circumscribe the extent to which states are able to "free ride" on such devalued emotional, physical, financial, and other forms of work.

Overall, *Nimo's War, Emma's War* shows how the occurrence of the War in Iraq "at a distinctive point in the national and international histories of women and patriarchy has shaped its causes, its winding course, and its aftermath" (Enloe 2010: 4) and how gendered political changes such as the "politics of marriage, of property, of women's paid work, of parenting—each changed in the midst of each war . . . [and] altered the dynamics of war—who were the key players, what were their resources and their rationalizations" (5). As such, Enloe's work underlines the importance of incorporating the experience of women and people on the bottom rungs of society to create a more accurate, rigorous, and ethical scholarship.

Just War through a Gender-Sensitive Lens

Laura Sjoberg's *Gender, Justice, and the Wars in Iraq* (2006) builds on feminist research highlighting women's experience as a stronger basis for understanding and analysis and offers a feminist critique and reconstruction of the Just War doctrine. The plural term in the title, *Wars,* introduces the idea that more than one conflict is entailed, and the text actually focuses on three: the First Gulf War (1991), the Second Gulf War (2003), and the war of sanctions, which seamlessly linked the two using other means. To briefly review, Just War doctrine identifies "the moral criteria identifying when a just war may be undertaken and how it should be fought once it begins" (Kegley and Blanton 2010, 503).[1] This traditionally refers to two main principles: "jus ad bellum" (just reasons) and "jus in bello" (just conduct). In brief, jus ad bellum requires that war be fought only for reasons characterized by right intention, just cause, right authority, proportionality of ends, and as a last resort. Jus in bello requires that war be conducted only when noncombatants are ensured immunity and the war will do more good than harm (proportionality).

Despite the laudable premise behind them, Just War principles have been defined and interpreted in a gendered way that limits their moral weight and practical utility. Sjoberg's analysis highlights how women are invisible and subordinated in the construction and application of Just War doctrine and how just war stories support insidiously abstract understandings of gruesome wars by casting men and women in gendered heroic or dependent roles. Instead of drawing on knowledge based in elite male experience (the Just War tradition is rooted in arguments by Saint Augustine and Saint Thomas Aquinas as developed by Hugo Grotius), Sjoberg draws on knowledge based in female experience and an international feminist ethics of care that assumes that people are connected (not just autonomous) to critique and reformulate what counts as "just" war (see also Hutchings 2010: 65). Feminist care ethics is the idea that the moral worth of an action should be determined by identifying with and taking responsibility for others within the context of caring relationships. Unlike traditional ethical approaches, such as utilitarianism, which assume that individuals are independent and autonomous, feminist care ethics draws on women's experience as caregivers and cared for in recognizing that people are related to and responsible for each other (65–67).

Drawing on the concept of "empathetic cooperation" (Sylvester 1994a), ad bellum standards are reformulated in support of "gender

---

1. As the Just War tradition is addressed broadly in most introductory textbooks, only a brief review of the major points will be mentioned here. See Shapcott 2008: 201–2; Reus-Smit 2008: 288–89; D'Anieri 2010: 366; Inayutullah 2010: 355; Goldstein and Pevehouse 2009: 262–63; Kegley and Blanton 2010: 502–7; Mansbach and Rafferty 2008: 399–403; Mingst 2008: 229–30; Ray and Kaarbo 2008: 324–26; Rourke and Boyer 2010: 218–22; Russett, Starr, and Kinsella 2010: 263–66; and Viotti and Kauppi 2009: 176–83.

emancipation" (Sjoberg 2006). *Empathetic war-fighting* is proposed as a principle to guide feminist in bello ethics (Sjoberg 2006). This brings the emotional experience of war—which is left out in the traditional masculine articulation of the Just War tradition—back into it (50). For the ad bellum rationale, it does so by reformulating concepts in a way that validates interpretations of identity as emotional and connected (traits traditionally gendered feminine) rather than just rational and autonomous (traits traditionally gendered masculine). For one example, this includes defining *right authority* not as a state *entitlement* (as traditional interpretations tend to assume) but as based in an open and participatory *process* of empathetic dialogue (communication with feelings as well as words) within and among groups (71–72). For another, it includes defining *reasonable chance of success* as including success in achieving Justice in the long term *after* the war (rather than as just "winning" the war in the short term) with a conception of Justice based in dialogue between victor and vanquished and "not immediately repulsive to the basic moral understandings of those on whom they are being imposed" (80).

For in bello standards of conduct, Sjoberg's reformulation brings in the emotional experience of war by requiring that belligerents attempt to empathetically understand (emotionally identify with) opposing positions while taking an "impact-on" approach. Such an approach asks who war-targeting strategies will affect and how—unlike traditionally articulated Just War doctrine—it does not allow belligerents to avoid responsibility for the effects of war making on noncombatants simply because they are not specifically targeted. This reformulation offers a "more realistic, more responsible, and less gendered way to answer just war questions about the morality of targeting" (2006: 104).

Sjoberg (2006) applies her feminist reformulation of Just War doctrine to the wars in Iraq in a way that further illustrates the practical utility of gender-sensitive lenses.[2] Her reformulation highlights how the United States "told a story of heroism and rescue" (133) about the 2003 Iraq War—a war story not atypical compared to other gendered war stories, which generally involve "a hero, a bad guy, and a woman to be res-

---

2. For textbook references to the US War in Iraq as seen through the Just War tradition, see Zehfuss 2009: 487–90; Kegley and Blanton 2010: 506–7; Mansbach and Rafferty 2008: 401; Mingst 2008: 230; Rourke and Boyer 2010: 219–22; and Russett, Starr, and Kinsella 2010: 268–71.

cued. The hero goes to amazing lengths to defeat the bad guy and rescue the woman. The bad guy dies, the woman is safe, and everyone lives happily ever after" (133). President Bush's belief that Saddam Hussein had an inherently evil and irrational nature, his "neocon" advisers' support of militarized solutions, and the militarized discourse of the War on Terror following 9/11 all can be understood as playing into this story. In doing so, they also contributed to an inability of US leaders to empathetically communicate with the Iraqi regime or pursue alternative courses of action.

Despite this, Sjoberg (2006) asserts that the "Iraq War" is both longer and messier than this gendered story suggests, for "the political context that constructed and sustained Iraq was in itself both gendered and unjust," and that the sanctions regime before the 2003 war should be defined as a war in itself, one unjustly aimed at civilian targets. More broadly, historical injustices here were abundant and overlapping, between Iraq and Kuwait, Iraq and the United States, and Iraq and its people—including, but not limited to the Saddam Hussein administration (Sjoberg 2006). Iraq's "postwar" large-scale civil strife is largely the opposite of what a feminist understanding of "success" in Iraq would look like: "A success in Iraq would be an Iraq where the tense and diverse groups of the population lived together in peace, not because of the threat of violence or the presence of US troops but because they put together a government that could serve their needs." Economic prosperity restored, rebuilt hospitals, schools, and transportation infrastructures, and job opportunities for women, also would be part of success defined in feminist terms. "A success in Iraq," furthermore, "would be the United States' ability to withdraw from a peaceful Iraq and apologize for the war," with "the 'old' gendered state being replaced by a new, empathetic state, despite the change being prompted by a gendered and unjust war" (231). In sum, feminist reformulation of Just War doctrine highlights the problems of pursuing a supposedly "just" war in an unjust context and suggests that a feminist "Just War" must deal with those injustices "on the ground."

Beyond this, Sjoberg suggests that while the formal War in Iraq may be on rocky ground even in terms of traditional interpretations of the Just War doctrine, it was undoubtedly unjust under her feminist reformulation of Just War principles. In terms of the ad bellum rationale, it is clear, for example, that the United States did not prioritize the assumption of a "reasonable chance of success," which focused on long-term stability over short-term military victory or which defined *justice* based on dialogue between victor and vanquished. Instead, the Bush administration's focus on nation building in Iraq supported goals defined largely in one-sided terms—for example, promoting the first Arab democratic regime (a goal of certain US leaders, defined in US terms), rather than defining goals mutually based on broad-based dialogue with (not just elite) Iraqi people. In terms of in bello standards of conduct, it seems clear that the United States and the "Coalition of the Willing" avoided empathetic dialogue with the Iraqi regime and took the opposite of an "impact-on" approach: demonizing Saddam Hussein as "evil" certainly cut off opportunities for emotionally identified dialogue with others in the regime. Furthermore, focusing on assumptions of a fast win with light casualties created a self-centered focus on US and coalition (rather than Iraqi) casualties. This allowed the United States to avoid broader responsibility for its actions by minimizing other effects of war making (nonfatal injuries, infrastructure destruction, etc.).

Overall, Sjoberg's application of gender-sensitive lenses to Just War doctrine enables more accurate and rigorous scholarship by recognizing previously minimized or ignored costs of war, especially due to a weak formulation of the noncombatant immunity principle. It also enables more ethical scholarship by promoting a thicker, rather than thinner, kind of ethics based in a feminist ethics of care (Sjoberg 2006; Hutchings 2010: 65–67).

ASSESSING WAR AS A CONTINUUM OF VIOLENCE

What emerges from a comparison of conflict periods in our world and that in *LOTR* is the need to question *everything:* to exchange our gender-blind lenses for gender-sensitive ones. This does not just mean simplistically focusing on a "gender variable" (e.g., Should women rule the world if we want peace?). Instead, it means being less narrow in our assumptions and language (e.g., about "war," "states," "people," or "power") and asking how traditional gendered assumptions—which define dominating, hierarchical relationships as "natural"—permeate and influence our social world. Asking where the women are and why can be first steps in this process, which aims to "distinguish 'reality' from the world as *men* know it" (Peterson and True 1998: 23). By demanding this more critical assessment, it becomes possible to conduct more accurate, rigorous, and ethical scholarship on a variety of issues in global affairs, including the gendered conditions that make war possible, and the multiple ways gender influences and interacts with war's buildup, conduct, and aftereffects.

In thinking about IR, a feminist approach suggests that multiple paradigms and levels of analysis are interlinked: "the personal is international" and "the international is personal." This is relevant throughout issues of international affairs, from the belief systems of leaders that lead them to war to plans of strategic interaction to understandings of Justice. This chapter's unique contribution is to introduce *LOTR* to complement what can be learned from our world about war as part of a spectrum of violence and its gendered facilitating conditions, causes, occurrences, and consequences. Comparative analysis suggests that gendered assumptions in Middle-earth are different from those in our world (just as they are, depending on context, within our world). However, it further confirms that in both worlds gendered assumptions influence the context, causes, conduct, and consequences for war.

This chapter has used *LOTR* to illuminate the discussion and application of gender-sensitive lenses to IR. It is now time to shift back to *LOTR* as a mirror and take another look at what we believe we know about IR as a body of scholarship.

CHAPTER 7

Middle-earth as a Source of Inspiration and Enrichment

We now move from using *LOTR* to illustrate existing **IR** discussions to using it as a mirror to challenge existing perspectives and raise new and interesting questions. Chapter 1 relied on the literary technique of following a theme to gain insight into the implications for Order and Justice of the quest to destroy the Ring. The present chapter uses two other literary techniques—*comparison* and *tracing,* defined momentarily—to reassess scholarly approaches associated with different *LOTR* characters in the quest for understanding of IR. In the first part of this chapter, we reassess the Great Debates and feminist approaches, illuminated in chapters 3 and 5, respectively. We compare ideas associated with male and female characters from the same race in order to explore parallels and divergences in assumptions and highlight how different kinds of experience encourage different kinds of assumptions, goals, insecurities, and concerns. This suggests that building on a broad range of experience (women's as well as men's) creates a stronger basis for understanding. In the next part of this chapter, we illustrate this point by drawing on experience from Middle-earth and our world regarding key issues: security and preemptive war, global health, state and human security, learning and international institutions, and global ethics. The final section sets the stage for the concluding chapter.

TAKE STORIES WITH A GRAIN OF SALT

Reexamining the connections made in earlier chapters can produce additional insight about the relationship of theories to our world. Consider earlier observations about characters and races from Middle-earth in relation to IR's Great Debates in IR theory and feminist approaches. It quickly becomes apparent that it is sometimes simpler to use a character to illustrate an IR approach but other times easier to use the stereotype of an entire race. For example, it is more evident that Hobbit communities illustrate constructivist insights about the social creation of (in)security than it is that Frodo, Pippin, or some other Hobbit is a particularly good exemplar. Put differently, theories can explain aspects of characters as opposed to individuals being held up as *illustrating* any given point of view from IR.

This illustrates how systems manifest "emergent properties" from the interactions of individuals (Mansbach and Rafferty 2008: 12). Individual action can have unintended consequences for the system as a whole. For example, the belief systems of individuals—including (gendered) stereotypes and enemy images—may have a precipitating influence on causing war; however, the institutionalization of those kinds of belief systems in the structures of states and international society may provide a broader understanding of the basis for conflict and cooperation. As this suggests, any particular analytical framework should be taken with a grain of salt. Illustrations in many cases work better in certain frameworks or levels than others; this includes levels of analysis (introduced in chapter 2), as well as multilevel gendered institutions, as highlighted by gender-sensitive lenses (introduced in chapter 5). As with Hobbits in the Shire, the central tendency among members of the system is evident when their behavior is viewed as a collective. In Middle-earth, outliers, such as Lotho Sackville-Baggins (who joins the ruffians occupying the Shire) and Bilbo (a confirmed eccentric), are to be expected but do not alter the group norm.

Similarly, although different characters are associated with different approaches, there is significant overlap among them. For example, different feminist approaches would agree that public work, assumed to be performed principally by men, relies on and is interconnected with private work, disproportionately performed by women. This is made clear by the experiences of multiple women in Middle-earth that we have highlighted—including those of Lobelia, Dís, Wandlimb, Éowyn, and

Galadriel, as well as others not discussed such as Arwen, Rosie Cotton, and Goldberry. The position of each of these women highlights a division of labor in their societies, which, as in our world, defines public work and public life as more valuable than but separate from (while reliant on) private and informal work.

While multiple characters can highlight similar insights, any particular character can also illustrate multiple sets of insights. The Dwarf Gimli's change of heart about the Elves is one case in point. His shift to a favorable view may be taken to illustrate relationship building, which enhances the prospects of international society (a concept emphasized by the English School) through increasing institutionalization (emphasized by neoliberal institutionalists) (see chapter 3). In terms of level of analysis, change in this instance starts at the individual level. This, in turn, catalyzes a system-level improvement in trust that extinguishes the mind-set of the security dilemma among Dwarves and Elves. In tales of Middle-earth after *LOTR*, Gimli and Legolas travel together, with their friendship serving as an exemplar for cooperation between their races.

A second example is the shift in how the Hobbit Lobelia Sackville-Baggins is viewed from the start to the finish of the story. At the outset she is seen as an annoying, grasping person—a member of Bilbo and Frodo's extended family but hardly in their favor. However, when the Shire is occupied by ruffians during the war, Lobelia is among the very few who stand up to them directly. She is put in jail and, upon her release, is transformed into someone admired by her fellow Hobbits for being assertive and strong in the face of coercion. This illustrates how certain perspectives can be seen as more valuable under some circumstances than others and how different worldviews or perspectives can be interpreted more positively or negatively, depending on the situation.

We must ask ourselves in instances such as those just noted why this is the case and what the implications are. In answering, it becomes obvious that the world of *LOTR* is not perfectly related to the IR theory we have associated it with and no one theory has a monopoly on fictive or actual history. White light is made up of rainbows. This answer facilitates understanding: the world is not always perfectly explained by our theories. Ambiguities and rough edges frequently exist and should be considered, both in our world and in Middle-earth. So, too, historical accounts of IR's Great Debates and feminist theory are frequently caricatured and only roughly approximate the more complicated historical reality (Hewitt 2010; Rupp 1997; Schmidt 1998; Springer 2002). Waves in IR and feminist theory are like different-colored waves of light: they must be put together through the prism of comparison in order to produce the greatest clarity. This becomes a useful reminder to guard against assuming that any interpretation is infallible. All should be questioned.

REVISITING MILES' LAW: COMPARING IR'S GREAT DEBATES AND FEMINIST WAVES

Reexamining story dynamics from *LOTR* in terms of implications for the real world of IR (rather than vice versa) provides another useful basis for comparison. What do relationships between and among *LOTR* characters suggest about our understanding of international politics? One way of investigating this is to compare theoretical perspectives based on the shared race of their associated male and female characters in *LOTR*. Table 6 does this by integrating tables 1 and 3. Each row lists the IR and feminist approaches associated with each race and the *LOTR* characters used to illustrate them in past chapters. The far right-hand column summarizes the relationship between the IR and feminist approaches linked by race: this can be positive (+), which signifies limited parallels, negative (-), which signifies limited divergences, or "no relationship" if neither positive nor negative associations are clear. Note that Table 6 should not be interpreted as saying that characters actually think about or believe in IR theories. Instead, the point of the table is to communicate how their actions can be regarded as consistent with one theory or another.

One major lesson to be drawn from this table is that, although characters from each race can provide interesting insights into IR, the ideas gleaned from male and female characters of the same race can be very different. This illustrates how diverse contexts inhabited by different characters create varied insecurities and assumptions with different concerns and goals. For example, IR approaches illustrated by male characters in *LOTR* (Elves, Orcs, Humans, Hobbits, and Dwarves) generally prioritize the problems of states as most important. Feminist approaches illustrated by female characters in *LOTR*, by contrast, prioritize the individual and collective problems of women and other nondominant groups as both most important and inadequately addressed by state security. The connection with IR's concepts of state (national) versus human (individual) security is straightforward here. Insights between male and female characters of each race diverge in other, variegated ways as well. In problem-solving words, Miles' Law (or *where you stand depends on where you sit*) comes to the fore again. This appears accurate not only for the explanation of how bureaucratic roles affect foreign policy positions (what this statement usually means in traditional IR discussions) but also for how positions, including gender, race, class, sexuality, and development, influence one's point of view, as standpoint feminists suggest, and the narrative one tells, as postmodern IR and postmodern feminists suggest. These relationships now will be explored.

Table 6 lists characters we have used to illustrate both IR and feminist theory, each of which evolves over time. A side-by-side listing illustrates how women's experience is minimized or excluded in *LOTR*, just as in orthodox IR theory. For one thing, named females exist in the Elf, Human, Hobbit, Dwarf, and Ent races. However, there is no named female Wizard, Orc, or Huorn. For another, with the exception of Galadriel, female characters in *LOTR* are less powerful and important than their male counterparts, just as feminist theorizing has had a relatively weaker impact on IR than traditional theorizing has. Despite these broad similarities, the theoretical traditions illustrated by the male and female counterparts of each race offer a range of worldviews, some more similar than others.

Humans, Hobbits, and Ents can be linked to approaches that exhibit limited parallels in terms of how to think about IR. Human behavior is consistent with assumptions about the causes of problems at the system level, in line with variants of IR theory: the neorealist tradition illustrated by Boromir and the Ringwraith leader assumes that it is the international system's anarchic structure that perpetuates the problem of international conflict. The neoliberal feminist tradition assumes that it is the patriarchal system's legal inequalities that perpetuate the problem of women's oppression, with Éowyn as a principal instance of being on the wrong end of such things.

Hobbits act in a manner consistent with assumptions at the individual level as the cause of problems: the constructivist tradition linked to Frodo Baggins argues that assumptions based in perceptions undergird the problem of international conflict. The socialist feminist tradition connected with Lobelia Sackville-Baggins argues that assumptions relying on and diminishing the value of "reproductive" labor (as the basis for "productive" labor) are the source of the problem of women's oppression.

Ents act in ways consistent with assumptions as the cause of problems (although they look at a different set of assumptions): the Frankfurt

TABLE 6. Quasi Relationships of Similarity (+) or Dissimilarity (−) between Approaches Based on the Race Their Associated Characters Share in *LOTR*

Race	Male Character	IR Approach	Female Character	Feminist Approach	Relationship between IR and Feminist approach
Wizard	Gandalf	Rational choice	(Galadriel)	(emotional intelligence [EQ])	−: Autonomous/relational view of actors (IQ/EQ)
	Saruman	Postmodernism	Galadriel	Postmodern feminism (3rd wave: antiessentialist, i.e., gendered oppression manifests in diverse ways)	+: (Ungendered/gendered) "truth" is imbued with power
Elf	Elrond	Classical liberalism (1st debate: positive future)	Galadriel	Postmodern feminism (3rd wave: antiessentialist)	−: Actors are/are not inherently similar (good/oppressed in similar ways)
	Legolas	English School (2nd debate: historical)			
Orc	Uglúk, led by Saruman	Classical realism (1st debate: negative future)	—[a] (Shelob)	(Non-existent [not critical: Iron Ladies])	No relationship (no progressive version)
Men	Boromir / Ringwraith leader	Neorealism (2nd debate: scientific method)	Éowyn	Liberal feminism (1st wave: de jure, i.e., legal inequality)	+: The system (anarchy/legal inequality) is the problem
Wild Men	Ghân-buri-Ghân	World Systems Theory	—[a]		

	Character	IR theory	Female character	Feminist theory	Assumptions
Hobbit	Frodo Baggins	Constructivism (3rd debate: problem-solving and critical versions)	Lobelia Sackville-Baggins	Socialist feminism (2nd wave: de facto i.e., substantive inequality)	+: Assumptions (perceptions / reliance on reproductive for productive labor) are the problem
	Smeagol/Gollum[b]	Postcolonialism	—[a]		
Dwarf	Gimli	Neoliberal Institutionalism (2nd debate: scientific method)	Dís	Postcolonial feminism (3rd wave: antiessentialist)	-: The problem is the same/different for everyone (need increased institutionalization everywhere/need particularized solutions)
Ent	Treebeard	Frankfurt School Critical Theory (Marxist roots) (3rd debate: postpositivist)	Wandlimb	Radical (cultural) feminism(2nd wave: de facto inequality)	+: Assumptions (focus on states and order/dominance of masculinity) are the problem
Huorn	Old Man Willow	Marxism (1st debate: positive future)	—[a]		

[a]No female character named in *LOTR.*
[b]Of a people related to Hobbis.

School Critical Theory tradition illustrated by Treebeard suggests that assumptions focusing on states' security and Order, as opposed to individual security and Justice, are the important problem, while the radical cultural feminist tradition illustrated by Wandlimb argues that assumptions about dominant masculinity and subordinate femininity are the problem and should be reversed.

While Humans, Hobbits, and Ents show limited positive associations, Elves and Dwarves reveal limited negative associations. This also comes out in table 6. Assumptions linked to Elves diverge over how similar actors are: classical liberalism (Elrond) assumes that actors are inherently similar in their good nature, while postmodern feminism (Galadriel) instead assumes that actors are inherently dissimilar in that they are oppressed in varied and particular ways. Dwarves diverge in suggestions of whether problems have universal or particular solutions: the neoliberal institutionalist tradition, with which Gimli's actions are consistent, assumes that the problem of international conflict can be addressed by increasing institutionalization everywhere, whereas the postcolonial feminist tradition, which explores the life of Dís, assumes that diverse kinds of women's oppression call for diverse solutions tailored to a given context. Each of these comparisons suggests that despite limited similarities, positions in different contexts are associated with very different assumptions and goals.

Four rows in table 6 (Wizards, Orcs, Huorns, and Wildmen) lack obvious male and female counterparts. Two of them can be filled in by a broad interpretation of their race: Huorns are related to Ents, and even the male Huorns are not explicitly named in LOTR (Old Man Willow appears to be one but is not definitely so categorized). Relatedly, Wild Men are one of the branches of Men and could be stretched to relate to Éowyn; they are also related to the people of Haleth, one of whom is a female, Amazon-like character whose leadership of her people is discussed in The Silmarillion and Unfinished Tales. We will not focus on these, as they are hardly referenced at all in LOTR and are members of races minimized in LOTR discourse, which makes analysis based on them difficult. What we can say is that they do support the gendered trend, already discussed, of minimizing women's and minority experiences in the story of LOTR. We also do not focus on a comparison for the creature alternatively known as Sméagol or Gollum; his over five-hundred-year stint with the Ring warped him into a creature eventually unrecognizable as a relation of the Stoor Hobbits (as he once was), which makes him a unique case. The other two absences—of a female Wizard and female Orc—stand out more because of the centrality those races have to the *LOTR* story and provide a better basis for discussion. As such, we will focus on them.

First, this table highlights the absence of a female Wizard in *LOTR*, which illustrates a similar lack of women in powerful roles in our world. The Elf Galadriel is the closest female character to having Wizard status, as she initiates and participates in the meeting of the White Council in order to contest the rising power of evil. Although the rational choice tradition assumes individual, autonomous choice, Galadriel embodies a more embedded kind of decision making, which bases identity in social relationships (Hall 1993). This alternative kind of being and decision making seems to draw much more on emotional intelligence (EQ), which includes emotional self-awareness, assertiveness, independence, self-regard, and self-actualization, as well as interpersonal empathy, social responsibility, and adaptability (Stein and Book 2006). This is different from the rational choice behavior exemplified in different ways by Gandalf and Sauron. It values community-oriented ideas of power as "power with" rather than traditional coercive ideas of "power over" (e.g., Allen 2008).[1]

Galadriel exists within ambiguous dimensions and must cope with a complex reality that includes cooperation and conflict. This is illustrated by her gifts to the individual members of the Fellowship, which range from weapons to a box of earth and a seed. Galadriel must deal with the challenges of both war and peace (Scott 1972: 28).

Consider, in the context of dealing with ambiguity, Galadriel's initial encounter with the Fellowship. She reveals extraordinary empathy. Galadriel knows the prayers of Aragorn and fulfills them. She also detects the torment experienced by Boromir, who wants to remain loyal to his comrades but experiences an ultimately overpowering urge to take the Ring for Gondor, if necessary, by force. Galadriel also reveals a high level of emotional self-awareness and control when she refuses an offer of the Ring of Power from a very troubled Frodo. She can dwell in the world without accepting the common mind-set regarding the exercise of power

---

1. The emphasis on EQ-related characteristics related to Galadriel is not meant to imply that other characters do not display empathy and associated traits. Gandalf, for instance, is quite understanding toward Frodo, along with other Hobbits and even Gollum. The traits are emphasized in relation to Galadriel instead to bring out her overall connection with one particular type of theorizing.

over others. This is true despite her position of power on the White Council itself and as the leader among Elves in Lothlórien. As such, here she demonstrates the added value to IR theorizing of considering alternative feminist assumptions regarding the kind of emotionally, as well as cognitively intelligent, actors and the assumed basis of their behavior in relational, as well as autonomous, kinds of identities.

Depending on how the race of Wizards is analyzed, comparisons and contrasts in this category vary. On one hand, Gandalf and Galadriel illustrate differences regarding how individualistic or relational people are assumed to be: the rational choice tradition (Gandalf) assumes that agents are autonomous individuals, while the feminist tradition (Galadriel) assumes that everyone is embedded in relationships and acts within that context. On the other hand, Saruman and a different interpretation of Galadriel illustrate similarities regarding assumptions about what exists: both the postmodern tradition (Saruman) and the postmodern feminist tradition (Galadriel) agree that definitions of *truth* are all imbued with power, and that truth claims must consequently be evaluated for how they contribute to structurally unequal power relations—whether that be along the lines of gender, race, class, or otherwise.

Second, table 6 highlights the absence of a female Orc character in *LOTR*.[2] The closest thing to this that is explicitly referenced is Shelob, the evil giant spider described as Sauron's "cat" (II: 708), who (like her master) is ruthlessly murderous toward other living creatures. (Shelob just as readily consumes Orcs as others not allied with Sauron.) Shelob illustrates the important principle that simply being female does not entail a feminist or "pro-woman" agenda. What is more, there can be no "feminist" parallel to Machiavellianism, as feminism assumes that progressive change toward equality is possible, though not inevitable (Fraser 1989). Machiavellianism, by contrast, assumes continuation of the structural status quo, with an ongoing effort to turn it to one's advantage.

Shelob, however, shows how some women adopt traditional values to succeed in masculinist systems. These values are particularly evident in the historical case of the "Iron Lady," Margaret Thatcher, who, for example, led Great Britain to victory in war against Argentina in 1982. Other female leaders, such Golda Meir of Israel and Indira Gandhi of India, also beat the masculinist system on its own terms.[3] Once in power,

---

2. Tolkien's publications do not reference female Orcs directly. However, *The Silmarillion* suggests that they do exist, since Orcs "breed after the manner of Elves and Men."

3. For an analysis of these women's leadership styles, see Steinberg 2008; a broader review of gender and leadership roles appears in Kauppinen and Aaltio 2003.

however, these leaders gave a female face to the patriarchal status quo rather than trying to change it so more women could succeed as well. Taking this to the level of caricature, Shelob pursues her gluttonous self-interest in a way that ensures her own success in independent prosperity and support by Sauron by using whatever tactics necessary, including eating trespassers, to stay at the top of a hierarchy of dominance from which only she benefits. As such, Shelob is an important reminder of the problems of assuming that sex or other "biological traits" define interests or behavior (biological essentialism) and the importance of considering how prioritized goals impact broader groups of minorities, not just the few who crack but do not destroy glass ceilings.

Shelob also usefully illustrates the feminist point that women who act counter to social standards of femininity—especially those who commit violence—are seen as having made a "double transgression": the norm against violence in general, and the norm against *women* being capable of being violent in particular (Sjoberg and Gentry 2008: 15). Here Shelob is portrayed as particularly gruesome: not only is she a giant, all-devouring monster but because monsters are expected to be male, not female, she is even more of a monstrosity.

Overall, the preceding comparative exercises in feminist analysis support the inference from Miles' Law that where you stand depends on where you sit: concerns, goals, and understandings of problems and insecurities are influenced, though not determined, by context, including gender, race, class, sexuality, and postcolonial position. Other discussions of experience could be added as well.

In addition, the preceding discussion illustrates how failing to include a broad range of experience limits our scholarly ability to understand the world. Not having female counterparts for Wizards, Orcs, Huorns, and Wildmen, as well as the creature Gollum, limited our ability in this chapter to explore the assumptions associated with characters from each of these races and created a select (skewed to elite male experience) basis for our analysis. Furthermore, the limited material available on the female characters who are mentioned in *LOTR* makes the comparisons and contrasts we can do less rich. The blank spaces in table 6 suggest that IR scholarship that does not build on a broad range of women's as well as men's experience can fail to make accurate predictions, especially about political change, just as Sauron's dismissal of Hobbits and failure to consider alternative preferences of the Free Peoples meant that he could not predict the goals of and participants in the Fellowship (Enloe 2004: 23–24). Put differently, while extraordinarily com-

plex and nuanced, Tolkien's depiction of Middle-earth skews and trun-
cates our understanding of the politics of this fantastical world because
of using lenses that inadequately recognize gender.

Using *LOTR* as a mirror both reminds us that our theories are imperfect representations of the world and suggests that the stories we tell are
not completely "objective" but are instead influenced by a variety of different contexts. To return momentarily to figure 2, on thinking about
IR, recall that the box regarding individual perspective on evidence appeared in two sizes: smaller and larger for how problem-solving and critical IR see their world as influenced by perspective. The preceding analysis would tend to support critical IR in the sense that individual
perspective may matter more frequently and with greater magnitude
than anticipated. Advocates of problem-solving paradigms might reply
that the analysis encourages efforts to assess empirically how personal
outlooks impact the interpretation of what is observed. Further dialogue
on this issue is to be expected, but at the very least the analysis here
draws attention to a neglected issue in orthodox IR scholarship.

ILLUSTRATION: DRAWING ON BROADER EXPERIENCE
BROADENS UNDERSTANDING

The first part of this chapter suggests that drawing on broader kinds of
experience (especially from women, as well as men) encourages better
understanding. In this next part of the chapter, we illustrate this point by
drawing on experience from Middle-earth in conjunction with experience from our world to address key issues of global politics: preemptive
foreign policy, global health, state and human security, learning and institutions, and global ethics. Each case highlights how comparing stories
based in different worlds enables a richer, stronger basis for understanding global politics.

Foreign Policy Decision Making

Foreign policy decision making involves issues of both Order and Justice,
which is especially apparent when we step back to consider the big picture. Reflecting on decisions made in Middle-earth will reveal how limited thinking can be when it focuses on only the apparent immediate results. A longer view of events, which neither elites nor publics tend to

favor, can be more appropriate than generally assumed. This is made evident by considering events both in Middle-earth and in our world.

First, recall the failure of the White Council to act against Sauron in a timely manner because of Saruman, its treacherous leader. With dreams of his own power at the forefront, Saruman successfully blocked Gandalf's call for an attack on Sauron's sanctuary at Dol Guldur. Hundreds of years before the War of the Ring, the Dark Lord occupied this inconspicuous place, in Mirkwood and distant from Mordor, and began to rebuild his forces. Failure by the White Council to take action permitted him to build the enormous military machine that nearly overwhelms the Free Peoples of Middle-earth, who manage to stop him only by destroying the Ring against heavy odds.

Second, compare that scenario with the situation faced by the George W. Bush administration in the spring of 2003 regarding Iraq. Over the previous twenty-five years, Saddam Hussein had gone to war with two of his neighbors, Iran and Kuwait. The war against Iran in the 1980s ended with mutual exhaustion from over one million casualties, while Saddam's occupation of Kuwait in 1990–91 resulted in forceful ejection by a US-led coalition. Saddam also had used WMDs against his own citizens and claimed to still have them. With all of this background, the United States went to war preventively against the Iraqi dictator, with one key argument being that failure to do so could result in many more lost lives later on because Saddam's regime intended to inflict great harm on both the United States and others.

Let us consider these parallel cases in more depth from a utilitarian ethical perspective based in the rational choice tradition. Doing so will help us elaborate how time perspective, like other perspectives, influences interpretations of foreign policy and IR more generally.[4] Utilitarian ethics uses cost-benefit analysis to decide how different courses of action should be evaluated in comparison to the status quo. According to this approach, a just action is one that results in the greatest good for the greatest number of people.

From this perspective, probability estimates play an essential role in each decision. Consider the White Council's estimate five hundred years before the War of the Ring, based on Saruman's assurances, that Dol Guldur should not be attacked. As pointed out earlier, this act of re-

---

4. For elaboration, see especially the textbook by Bueno de Mesquita (2010: 70–78).

straint turned out to be an error. Sauron not only resided at Dol Guldur but did so to draw less attention to himself while he prepared for eventual war against the Free Peoples. This choice of location also made it easier for Saruman, who hoped to gain from the rise of Sauron, to mislead others about his intentions. Thus Sauron acted to shift downward the White Council's probability estimate regarding the danger he posed to the Free Peoples. This, in turn, pushed upward the relative value assigned by the White Council to the status quo.

Given the subsequent loss of life and material damage, it seems clear from this particular moral point of view that the Council should have acted against Saruman's advice. This point is instructive because, when it comes to preventive war, the decision must be made with information available *at the time*. What if Saruman had been right? Then the Council would have been seen as acting in an imperious and unjust way. Only long after did its erroneous judgment become clear.

What about Bush and Iraq? The key probability estimate here pertains to Saddam and WMDs. His possession and potential use of such weapons, along with a track record of ignoring UN sanctions and obstructing inspections, served as the principal justification for the war. Interestingly enough, in spite of Saddam's prior misconduct and even his claim to have such capabilities, the US-led occupation forces discovered no significant capacity to use WMDs. Thus the dictator's prior behavior and current assertions, along with intelligence failures on the part of the world community, combined to produce the belief that Saddam had WMDs.

Right now it would be tempting to adopt the easy conclusion that the preceding examples from Middle-earth and recent US foreign policy both represent errors: Sauron continued to gather strength and inflicted a horrible war on the Free Peoples, while the US assault on Iraq eventually became very costly in terms of human life, with attendant political losses from a falling out with significant allies when no WMDs turned up. Consider, however, a key difference that emerges from this comparison and impacts judgments about what happened: the perspective on time. It took hundreds of years for the error of the White Council to be recognized. Judgment against the Bush administration, by contrast, looks quite rapid, given that the war began in 2003.

Could this suggest that our own, real world time frame is simply too myopic? The answer obviously is yes, at least in the initial sense. President Bush rather embarrassingly declared "mission accomplished" right after the quick and easy victory of the United States in the conventional war that unfolded in the spring of 2003. No one agrees with that assessment now. Nine years later Iraq still is experiencing civil strife, and its democracy remains frail. However, the verdict could change yet again. If this state turns out to be a role model for democratization and greater respect for human rights, Iraq could influence others to follow the same path. Whether that will occur is a question that might not be answered for decades. Human beings, however, do not reach the life spans essential to know how such large-scale changes will work out; unlike Gandalf or Galadriel, it is rare for anyone to see the consequences of actions even a century after their birth.

One way to react to this discussion, as per the famous dictum from economist Lord Keynes, is simply to observe, "In the long run we are all dead." So what if a day comes, perhaps far away, when the War in Iraq starts to look like a good idea after all? Not so fast, however—what about other matters we might care about beyond our lifetime? A long-term perspective is required, for example, in order for anyone to become concerned about the environment and act accordingly. Millions of people already do. With that in mind, perhaps we all should be encouraged to take a more gradual view of the outcomes from decision making in IR with regard to Order and Justice. Acknowledge our temporal bias. In terms of citizenship this even could promote more cooperation and lower levels of extremism brought on by disappointment and anger at the moment from those who are on the losing side of one issue or another. In sum, we could learn a lesson here from the Ents: As Treebeard would say, "Don't be hasty."

What does all of this mean for IR theory? It would appear to once again support Miles' Law: where you stand depends on where you sit. This includes temporal as well as other kinds of context and perspective. Foreign policy decision making can be interpreted as a success or failure depending on who is interpreting, what standard is being used, and how long after the fact the interpretation tales place. The examples just considered point to one improvement that could be made across the board in foreign policy analysis: resisting the urge to allow one's own personal position and immediate context to produce a rush to judgment. Events in both Middle-earth and our world suggest that reversals in judgment as time progresses are not only possible but likely in at least some instances.

Global Health

With regard to making the world a safer and better place, global health stands out as an issue that spans both concerns. This topic increasingly finds its way into the pages of IR textbooks, as well as featured status with news media. Highlighting issues of global health in the world of IR and Middle-earth suggests that things are not always as rosy as they appear and that increased integration brings challenges as well as benefits.

How does Middle-earth compare to our world? On the surface, the Shire appears idyllic. Hobbits live a long time compared to people in our world. Life spans of a century appear not that uncommon, so the difference is about 20 percent compared to developed states and even more in contrast to the developing world. One obvious advantage of the Hobbits would seem to be the cleanliness of their environment, a by-product of a preindustrial economy. Other positive traits include a much less sedentary lifestyle than ours—only a few wealthy or lazy Hobbits avoid manual labor—and perhaps lower levels of stress because of a slower pace.

Consider, however, the prevalence of smoking in the Shire. One of the most unhealthy activities among those legal in our world, smoking is associated authoritatively with cancer and heart disease, among other maladies. However, it appears to do no harm to Hobbits, who seem to favor the use of pipeweed across the board. In fact, smoking is a habit favored by virtually all members of the Fellowship, who are the principal heroes of the story.

No evidence exists in *LOTR*, moreover, of infectious disease. Just one example exists in the history of Middle-earth: the plague created by Melkor in the First Age of Middle-earth (Tolkien 1977). Thus the Shire in particular emerges as a happy place indeed, but not just because of its political culture, which stresses peace and cooperation. Instead, it also is out of touch with the unpleasant aspects of global health issues in our world. Smoking persists without consequences, and no need seems to exist for medical care.

Despite this, appearances of a global health utopia may be misleading. Just as early descriptions of the Shire are idyllic whereas later ones highlight its vulnerabilities and imperfections when overtaken by ruffians, so, too, the rosy description in *LOTR* may mask an underlying set of problems that remain unaddressed in the story of the quest. A less utopian version of the Shire would entail public health challenges, which open the door to the need for more extensive infrastructure and governance. Such changes, in turn, could alter the basic character of the Shire itself, or our rosy understanding of it.

In our world, health challenges can seek out any society and have become more intense as globalization picks up. Examples such as severe acute respiratory syndrome (SARS), acquired immunodeficiency syndrome (AIDS) and potential pandemics, such as influenza come to mind immediately (Mingst 2008: 288–95; D'Anieri 2010: 406–15; Kegley and Blanton 2010: 319–22). Consider the fate of native Americans in North America, who perished in huge numbers from diseases for which they had no immunity. They had existed in relative isolation, but contact with Europeans brought disease along with new health technologies—the bad and the good. Epidemics since then have picked up in geographic expanse as a by-product of more extensive contacts among far-flung peoples. A place like the Shire seems very vulnerable indeed when considered in the context of our contemporary world, in which millions of people travel around the globe on an ongoing basis. Accompanying effects from high levels of travel over significant distances and other dimensions of globalization can be expected to include both positive and negative elements. Interdependence may promote cooperation while producing additional challenges.

Two implications arise from comparing IR theory with the story of public health in Middle-earth. First, things are not always as rosy as they appear: when perfect health is assumed despite widespread smoking, it is likely that stories that highlight the problems involved with this are not being heard. Second, globalization is a mixed blessing. Neither its advocates nor its opponents can point to unequivocal outcomes. More contact with the outside world, with resulting technological advancement, could make the world more connected for Hobbits but might also increase their exposure to foreign diseases and other detrimental effects. The same applies to our world, as well as Middle-earth.

State and Human Security

What does security mean? As IR continues to evolve as a field, there is increasing scholarly divergence about what this concept involves. People might be safe from other states because of what their government does but in harm's way precisely because of what that same government is doing otherwise. Thus state security—securing the survival of countries—

and human security—securing freedom from fear and want for people—emerge as two overlapping but separate components within an overall conception of safety. Highlighting issues of security in the world of IR and Middle-earth highlights how a meaningful analysis of security requires that the relationship between state and human security be addressed and that any focus on one or the other is limited and insufficient for adequate understanding. Both must be considered to obtain a full picture of Order and Justice.

State and human security intersect in a dark episode that takes place in the Shire during the War of the Ring and continues until shortly after the four Hobbits of the Fellowship return home. Frodo and his companions are confronted with the reality of war in their own home when they return to find a cabal of Men and corrupted Hobbits inflicting a reign of terror on the Shire. The four Hobbits also see a Shire hideously disfigured by wartime mobilization, with significant environmental and other kinds of damage (III: 993). They soon discover that the occupation's leader, named "Sharkey," is really Saruman, who was released from the custody of the Ents. Led by Merry and Pippin, a force of Hobbits succeeds in overthrowing the regime, with Saruman dying in the aftermath following a murder attempt against Frodo.

These events bring home the interconnectedness between wars as state- and individual-level phenomena. While major battles unfolded in Gondor and Rohan, the Shire, far behind the front lines, still could not escape the evil of war. Hobbits under the occupation witnessed the natural beauty of the Shire damaged and nearly destroyed. They lost freedom of expression and freedom from fear, experienced reduced freedom from want, and found themselves unjustly put in jail if they complained. These increased insecurities for Hobbit males parallel the insecurities frequently experienced by many females in Middle-earth—for example, the Dwarf Dís's physical confinement, Éowyn's ordered curtailment from military service, restricted opportunities for political participation at home or in the quest as experienced by all but Galadriel, and above-average levels of insecurity due to dependence on male counterparts by most. However, these injustices are *in this context* (though not previously, when they only applied to women) recognized as insufferable violations and used as a rallying point for defensive action.

Reduction of *human* security in the Shire came about as a result of the removal of *state* security and remained for a time even in postconflict conditions when the War of the Ring was over. Unknown to residents of the Shire who distrusted the Rangers, these Men—led by Aragorn—had played a key role in keeping the Shire safe. Only with their departure to fight directly in the War of the Ring did Hobbits come to understand the invaluable role the Rangers had played in protecting them. In a larger sense, Gondor's resistance to Mordor enabled the Shire to exist in blissful ignorance of its peril for a very long time—a point made by Boromir to representatives of the Free Peoples in general during the Council of Elrond. As Boromir and others understand, however, the waning power of Gondor relative to Mordor meant that protection could not last much longer.

For our world, these events reflect back on the destructive side effects of war on even those not directly involved as combatants. Among the harmful aspects of involvement in war are loss of personal freedom, a reduced standard of living, and misconduct by military personnel when carrying out an occupation. The problems created by modern war beyond loss of life in battle itself are truly staggering (Tétreault and Lipschutz 2009: 117–36). Although war is often made in the name of protecting civilians at home, women are particularly vulnerable during war and in its aftermath: increased prostitution and trafficking, systematic rape, a combination of reduced resources but increased responsibility to maintain families (especially for refugees), and deliberate targeting of civilians (especially in civil wars) all contribute to this vulnerability (Seager 2003: 98–99). Even women who serve in the military face harassment, rape (even by men on their own "side"), and restricted career opportunities because of being excluded from certain (e.g., front-line) military posts (see Seager 2003: 100–101; Cockburn 2010; and Pankhurst 2010).

War's aftermath can also include long-term environmental damage, as with the burning of oil wells by Saddam Hussein's troops during their retreat from Kuwait. With WMDs the impact is much worse, as witnessed by the lingering radiation effects in the Japanese cities of Hiroshima and Nagasaki after the atomic bombings of August 1945. As this suggests, human and state security are interrelated, but one does not always guarantee the other.

Looking back on the Shire, it becomes clear that state or national security is not a sufficient condition for human security. The Free Peoples of Middle-earth won the war against Sauron, but at least one society, that of the Shire, experienced deep personal insecurity as a by-product of that conflict. It is also the case that human security cannot guarantee state security. Even Elvish society, which is portrayed as more equitable and Just than others, must enlist participants in the quest because the success that they have found within their ranks does not stop Sauron from being a rising threat. Thus addressing either human or state security alone by IR as a field is clearly insufficient: the interrelationship of both must be addressed for a meaningful understanding of "security" to be understood in broad terms that consider both Order and Justice.

Learning and Institutions

One basic point of division in IR is between realists and virtually all others about whether learning can happen and, by implication, whether institutions are worth constructing. Realists have said that flawed human nature guarantees that war will recur and institutions cannot change that fact. Critics of various kinds, starting with classical liberals, have claimed that learning is possible and thus institutions may be developed to hold collective wisdom and apply it to stave off future warfare. Highlighting issues of institutions and learning in the world of IR and Middle-earth reveals how institutional learning is evident and possible but also how it is difficult to accomplish and therefore not a panacea.

Can we do better in meeting global challenges through learning from past mistakes and creating institutions to facilitate peaceful resolution of conflicts? Classical liberalism (chapter 3) would suggest that we can. Middle-earth shows evidence of learning, as manifested in Aragorn's creation (as King Elessar) of the Council of the North-kingdom. Recall that all three of the wars studied in chapter 4—the Ring, Iraq, and the Great War—featured institutional weakness as a cause. Early in the Fourth Age of Middle-earth, the king reveals awareness of this problem for his new realm by creating "a group of advisors enrolled to give counsel concerning the reconstituted realm of Arnor [formerly the northern kingdom of Men]. Included in this Body were the Mayor and Thain of the Shire and the Master of Buckland" (Tyler 1976: 94). This represents the beginning of a potentially more extensive institutional network that could be an agent of peace in Middle-earth.

Creation of the Council also illustrates the increased institutionalization of learning. First, the Council's intended role is as an advisory body to the king. This shows recognition of the dangers of "going it alone" with regard to decision making, identified in chapter 4 as a significant factor contributing to the outbreak of war. Second, in contrast to the

White Council, the Council of the North-kingdom's membership is not restricted to the old elite. Instead, given the presence of Hobbits among its representatives, the Council of the North-kingdom clearly represents a commitment to hearing a wider range of voices than in the past. Overall, the creation of the Council of the North-kingdom is a favorable departure from the past as opposed to a "reinvention of the faulty wheel" from an institutional point of view.

Middle-earth looks remarkably like our own vis-à-vis conclusions that might be reached about learning and institutions. Learning seems to take place rather slowly and painfully. Great loss of life appears necessary in order to encourage the creation of institutional memory. While the effectiveness of the Council of the North-kingdom in Middle-earth is unknown, realist critics in our world can point to the relative weakness of the UN and regional analogues in conflict management. Great powers still call the shots when it matters the most. Thus the insight of Middle-earth reflecting on our world is that realists have a reason to be skeptical about the overall impact of learning and institutions while their critics are on target to say that at least some progress has been made.

GLOBAL ETHICS

Understanding Order and Justice in global politics highlights how different approaches to international ethics support different kinds of political action. Focusing on the concept of mercy—which is traditionally juxtaposed to Justice and is a strong theme in *LOTR*—can produce insight in this regard. Here we discuss the case of mercy in Middle-earth and our world in order to compare and contrast two different approaches to international ethics: utilitarianism and feminist care ethics. In *LOTR* we focus on the villainous characters: Gollum, Wormtongue, and Saruman. In our world we focus on the 2009 release of Abdel Baset al-Megrahi after the 1988 bombing of Pan Am Flight 103 over Lockerbie, Scotland.

Early in *The Fellowship of the Ring*, Gandalf explains the story of the Ring to Frodo, focusing on the part played by Bilbo. This produces an intense exchange on the subject of mercy. Frodo expresses disgust and a sense of assurance that the world would be a better place without Gollum. Gandalf points out, however, that Bilbo's initial act of mercy made his possession of the Ring less damaging. Even after sixty years the Ring's evil had but a mild effect on Bilbo. In addition, Gollum's survival also

could not be judged easily as something with ultimately good or bad consequences. Gandalf observes that Gollum's fate is tied to the Ring (I: 58)..
As we know, Gollum went on to commit evil acts, but he also unintentionally played a crucial role as a guide for Frodo and Sam in the quest to destroy the Ring. Mercy, in this case, ends up having unequivocally positive consequences because a substitute for the role ultimately played by Gollum is impossible to imagine.

Gríma the Wormtongue emerges as a more vile character than Gollum, perhaps, because there is no sense that, like Gollum, he is compelled to evil. Instead, it seems to be his choice to betray Rohan in order to obtain rewards from Saruman. After Saruman's spell is broken by Gandalf, a decision must be made regarding the disposition of Wormtongue. In spite of his treachery, Wormtongue receives mercy from Théoden and Gandalf. The king, now restored to health and alertness, gives Wormtongue the choice of riding with him into battle or leaving forever, with the latter being the result (II: 509).

What is the result of this generous act? Wormtongue flees to Isengard and continues to assist Saruman in preparing for war against Rohan. His evil ways persist even when Saruman is defeated and must look to the Shire as his new realm to exploit. After Saruman is once more defeated during the battle of the Shire, Frodo urges Wormtongue to leave Saruman and go his own way. Wormtongue's final act, however, after one too many abusive treatments from Saruman, is to fatally stab his master. Wormtongue then falls dead from three Hobbit arrows. In this case, mercy does not ensure redemption.

Finally comes Saruman himself, perhaps the worst character of the three discussed here because of his choice in favor of evil combined with the magnitude of the harm he causes. He is shown mercy even after attempting to kill Frodo. As noted, he is murdered by his one remaining follower—a grim ending but one that seems suitable. In this instance mercy plays the role of keeping Frodo's conscience clear because he does not have to order the death of someone who once had been a leading force for good and a much greater figure than himself. This action, treated with scorn by its recipient, reveals how much Frodo has grown as a result of his experiences with Gollum.

Now we turn to an instance of mercy in our world, ask ourselves how it will work out, and look for guidance from Middle-earth. In 1988 a bomb exploded in the cargo hold of Pan Am Flight 103 over Lockerbie,

Scotland. It killed all 259 people on board and another 11 on the ground. A Libyan, Abdel Baset al-Megrahi, was convicted of this heinous act. Now comes the exercise of mercy and accompanying controversy: Under protest from various quarters, the Scottish government released al-Megrahi in August 2009, citing his imminent death from terminal cancer as the reason for doing so. (Releasing prisoners in that condition is consistent with the Scottish legal system.) This action, which the Scottish government defended on compassionate grounds, produced immediate outrage from the families of those killed in the attack, as well as leading political figures, including President Barack Obama. Families of victims cited al-Megrahi as a poor choice for any kind of compassionate treatment, while Western political leaders expressed concerns about the message being sent regarding commitment to antiterrorism. To compound matters, the Libyan government gave al-Megrahi a hero's welcome when he arrived home.

Did the Scottish government do the right thing? This question can be addressed by drawing on the experiences, also involving dreadful characters, with the exercise of mercy in Middle-earth. Things worked out well regarding Gollum and the opposite with Wormtongue. Frodo's mercy toward Saruman came almost at the end of the Wizard's life, so it is more difficult to assess this act in terms of costs and benefits beyond how it might have influenced the Hobbit's conscience.

Implications of Utilitarian Ethics

Applying a utilitarian ethical approach rooted in rational choice suggests that what is "right" can be determined by calculating the costs and benefits involved so as to make the best choice under constraints of time and resources. From this perspective, were these merciful actions the right thing to do?

Let us first consider the cases in Middle-earth. First, it could be said that Gandalf had strong intuition about preserving Gollum due to his fate being tied to the Ring. In the language of expected utility theory, Gandalf could not metaphorically calculate the balance between Gollum's anticipated contribution to good versus evil. Under such conditions, execution of Gollum would seem inappropriate on moral grounds. With regard to Wormtongue, however, there is near certainty about his future role after rejecting Théoden's offer to stay and serve with renewed honor. Perhaps a more appropriate response, assuming available resources, would have been confinement rather than release, which permitted Wormtongue to do more harm.

What, then, of al-Megrahi in our world? First, note the similarity with Saruman: He might have lived a very short time after receiving this act of mercy. Thus arguments easily could be made back and forth regarding the expected (dis)utility of his release in the short to medium term. On one hand, the release could impact public opinion in generally anti-Western states in a favorable way, with the Scottish government seen as acting in accordance with principles of mercy that are prominent in all major religions. On the other hand, his release unfortunately could be seen as an act of weakness—a concession toward terrorism that might encourage more of this activity. It would not be difficult to raise other aspects as well, with debate going back and forth.

This raises a point brought up earlier in this chapter: the need to learn from Middle-earth's more extended time frame the value of a longer perspective on current events. In other words, this may not be the time to draw conclusions about whether the Scottish government's act of mercy was a good or bad thing—yet we leap to do so. Perhaps the tendency to rapid and heated argument itself is a harmful thing in the world of IR and reserving judgment is a neglected virtue. The overall normative implication of the example may be that all judgments are fraught with even more uncertainty than we would have believed at the discussion's outset.

Implications of Feminist Care Ethics

Applying a feminist care ethics approach rooted in the assumption that people are embedded in relationships provides a very different framework for ethical evaluation. Particularly, it suggests that ethical action can be determined by identifying with and taking responsibility for others within the context of caring relationships. This means that ethical action does not simply "judge" people, but it must also take their perspective and "judge with" them, preferring "merciful mitigation" over "strict judgment" because of seeing things from their point of view (e.g., Nussbaum 1999: 161). Like Sjoberg's (2006) application of feminist care ethics to Just War Theory suggests in chapter 6, this approach emphasizes empathetic dialogue over any judge's "right authority," long-term over short-term outcomes, and "on the ground" context for the decisions' impact.

From this kind of perspective, were these merciful actions the ethical thing to do? As a whole, it appears that the answer is yes, but it also seems that they were not enough and should have gone even further.

Let us first consider the cases in Middle-earth. In Gollum's case, merciful action seems to particularly qualify as ethical conduct because Gollum is compelled by the Ring to evil regardless of his personal desires otherwise. Emotionally identifying with Gollum here highlights his heavy constraints in rejecting evil: even Gandalf and Galadriel, the most powerful members of the "good guys," reject Frodo's offer to give them the Ring because they know that they will not be able to resist its corruption. This does not mean that Gollum has no responsibility for his actions. However, it does mean that he was dealt an incredibly difficult hand in the game of life and that judging "with" him would particularly encourage merciful action about past wrongs. Beyond this, however, this also suggests that because of the lingering effects of the Ring, even more ethical action would work toward the rehabilitation of his positive original self, the character once known as Sméagol. In their journey through Mordor, this would support Frodo's kind treatment of Gollum, which brings out the best in him, but would not support Sam's suspicious behavior, which brings out the worst.

In Wormtongue's case, a merciful approach remains supported, but greater malintent must be mitigated. Unlike Gollum, Wormtongue is not corrupted by force to anywhere near the same degree: he, much more than Gollum, must take responsibility for his own bad actions. Despite this, Gandalf points out to King Théoden that, although killing Wormtongue would be just because of the "snake" he has become, he was not always so corrupted and once did serve the king. As such, identifying with Wormtongue looks for the better man that he once was. Doing so would give him a chance to live up to his former self, but would recognize that he is particularly vulnerable to corruption, such as by listening to Saruman's beguiling words. Consequently, ethical action would again seem to go beyond what occurs in *LOTR*: not only would it involve not killing Wormtongue, but it would also involve separating him from Saruman and giving him the opportunity to benefit from a positive influence instead. One possible interpretation of this would be requiring him to perform "community service" under the mentorship of someone like Gandalf so that he can begin to repay the wrongs he has committed while participating in freeing rather than destructive relationships and seeing how a more positive path can be followed.

Of the three cases in Middle-earth, Saruman's case is the most difficult to address here because he is the most difficult of the three with whom to identify. Like Wormtongue, he has actively chosen his corrupt path. However, because he is a Wizard like Gandalf, he is culpable in an even greater corruption and breach of trust: with the other Wizards, or Istari, he was sent by the godlike Valar to Middle-earth in order to protect it and "contest the power of Sauron" while being "forbidden to . . . seek to dominate Elves or Men by force and fear" (III: appendix B, 1059). As such, becoming Sauron's right-hand man is a monumental violation of trust. Empathetic dialogue seems even more difficult because of Saruman's deviousness: his voice appears to be almost always seductive but full of lies.

Despite this, a feminist care ethics approach requires emotional identification as a first step in pursuing ethical action. Focusing on the part of Saruman that remains, if any, from before he became corrupted is one way of making this identification. Focusing on this part of his identity highlights how he was too weak to be able to engage in the difficult task he was given of being a caretaker of Middle-earth. He instead succumbed to corruption. What would it look like to allow him to "move on" in a way that promotes liberating rather than dominating actions? Taking away his authority, as Gandalf does, is one important part of the solution: he is clearly unable to handle it responsibly. However, as with Gollum and Wormtongue, this is only one part of the project. A more ethical action from this perspective would be to address Saruman as someone who has become defined by destructive relationships: all his known relationships in *LOTR* appear to be either exploitative (as with those under him) or exploited (as with his overlord, Sauron); none appears to be genuinely caring or freeing. More ethical action would support Saruman's ability to rebuild his relationships in caring and egalitarian rather than dominating and corrupt ways.

In practical terms, this would provide yet another reason not to let Wormtongue continue to follow Saruman around as his minion. Allowing this to continue, as occurs in *LOTR*, perpetuates (even if in small scale) Saruman's problematic and corrupted style of relationships. Instead, trying to take the very difficult step of standing in Saruman's shoes suggests that ethical action would put him in a situation with greater constraint and greater opportunity for rehabilitation in the long term. For example this might involve sending Saruman back to the Far West from where he came; there he could do his community service as a relatively weak character among the strong and relatively beneficent Valar and would have less ability and temptation to dominate and corrupt those around him and more opportunity for freeing rather than dominating relationships.

Moving back to our world, what about al-Megrahi? Emotionally identifying with him highlights possible injustices of his original arrest and supports merciful action within what may have been an unjust context. Although al-Megrahi spent seven years in house arrest and nine years in prison following his 2001 conviction by Scottish judges of the Pan Am Flight 103 bombing, in 2003 his lawyers argued that there had been a "miscarriage of justice" and demanded that the case be reviewed. By 2007, some Scottish legal experts said that they believed al-Megrahi's unwavering argument of his innocence, based on new information indicating, for example, that witnesses had been offered money or had actually been paid off to testify against him.

Emotionally identifying with al-Megrahi highlights the problems of his trial and confinement given these ambiguous circumstances. It also suggests that even if he was guilty, twenty-one years of house arrest and detention and his infection with terminal cancer could have given him time to ponder his actions and maybe even change. Even if he had not done so, it would suggest that such rehabilitation should be encouraged. A feminist care ethics approach in this case would therefore support mercy as a right action. However, like with the cases in *LOTR*, it would support even further action: Particularly, supporting something like the "truth tribunals" in Africa in this case might be appropriate. There al-Megrahi should have been given the opportunity to state his story truthfully and apologize to the victims' families under the promise of not being reincarcerated. It might also have been appropriate to support mediation between al-Megrahi and family members of those bombed to bring closure to the families of those killed and help everyone move on with their lives.

Stepping Back

Reflecting on the concept of mercy helps us compare different—utilitarian or feminist care—approaches to global ethics. Overall, a utilitarian ethical approach supports merciful solutions over strict Justice *if* it seems that the benefits of this kind of action would outweigh the costs. This treats the person as an isolated individual whose actions should be impartially judged by a separate authority. A feminist care ethics approach provides a very different way of approaching the situation. Overall, a feminist care ethics approach tends to support merciful solutions over strict Justice because it requires identifying with the difficulties each actor faces in these situations, despite their failings. However, it also suggests that responses must go beyond what typically occurs in *LOTR*. It is not enough to *not destroy* culpable actors; instead, emotionally identifying with them also requires that they be supported so that they can take better actions in the future and not continue on the same path of evil or injustice. As such, a feminist care ethics approach gives greater priority to action that supports possible long-term rehabilitation of individuals, whereas a utilitarian ethics approach gives greater priority to retribution.

OF PRISMS AND RAINBOWS

In this chapter, we stepped back and tried to obtain new insight about global politics. Instead of illustrating existing perspectives, we used comparison and tracing of characters and concepts to apply *LOTR* as a mirror to challenge assumptions and stimulate creative thinking. This highlights how the stories IR scholars tell about our world highlight just one array of colors in a broader rainbow and suggests that richer and more complete understanding of global politics requires drawing on a broad set of colorful experiences and a variety of different kinds of stories. It illustrates how doing so promotes creativity and new insight and helps avoid leaving gaping holes in knowledge and risking inappropriate generalizations or a weak ability to make useful predictions.

Our first exercise in comparison integrated our previous use of characters from *LOTR* to illuminate Great Debates and waves of feminist theory by exploring what kind of relationship—parallels, divergences, or no relationship—existed between traditions illustrated by male and female characters of the same race. Stepping back illustrated how certain approaches work better or are seen as more valuable in some contexts than others, and how theories of global politics only tell a simplified story that cannot fully capture historical experience in either Middle-earth or our world. Beyond this, the comparison highlighted how different kinds of experiences encourage different kinds of assumptions, insecurities, concerns, and goals. This was illustrated by a tendency for feminist approaches, which are illustrated by female characters, to prioritize gender-sensitive understandings of human security and for traditional IR approaches, illustrated by male characters, to prioritize traditional approaches to state security. However, sex is not destiny: other experiences (such as race, class, sexuality, and development) also influence experience, perspective, and the stories that are told as well. Finally, the blank spaces in our review table jumped out as highlighting how IR scholarship that does not build on a broad range of (women's as well as men's) experience risks bias in its foundation and generalizations and is limited in richness. To avoid a failure to adequately understand and anticipate important political actions—as Sauron did in Middle-earth—this suggests that a broader range of experience must be recognized, valued, and included.

Our second exercise in comparison illustrated this first point, by showing how drawing on broader kinds of experience (in this case, that of Middle-earth, as well as our world) encourages better understanding. We focused on five concepts from IR: preemptive foreign policy, global health, state and human security, learning and institutions, and global ethics. In each case, drawing on experience from both Middle-earth and our world created a richer, stronger basis for understanding the political concerns at hand, and comparing stories from one world to the other stimulated creative thinking. For one example, experience in our world highlights challenges regarding global health that are abstracted away from the Shire. Comparing the two worlds suggests that experience "on the ground" may not be as rosy as stories make it appear and that increased global integration brings challenges as well as benefits. For another example, comparing merciful actions toward villains in our world and Middle-earth highlights how different approaches to global ethics— such as utilitarian or feminist care ethics—support different kinds of political action because they are based in different kinds of assumptions. We explored whether the merciful action taken was "right" in regard to the 1988 Pam Am 103 bomber in our world and Gollum, Wormtongue, and Saruman in Middle-earth. These cases illustrate how traditional masculine assumptions about Justice support action prioritizing retribution and restriction, while feminist care assumptions about Justice support action prioritizing rehabilitation. Overall, this exercise in comparison illustrated how drawing on a broader range of colorful experiences (in this case, from Middle-earth) creates a clearer, stronger, and richer understanding of global politics.

Conclusion:
International Relations and
Our Many Worlds

When Iranian government central television put on a marathon of *The Lord of the Rings* after disputed elections in June 2009, the intention was to quell riots—to reinstitute a more stable social Order. What this plan failed to recognize is that because *LOTR* highlights issues of both Order and Justice within an imagination-grabbing and fantastical epic context, the *LOTR* marathon drew popular attention to the very issues that the government sought to suppress. Rather than promote general apathy and submission, the films encouraged critical engagement and determination to continue the resistance, whether in the present or future. It highlighted how Order and Justice are interlinked, how the Iranian Order was unjust, and how quests for more Just social Orders were possible in Middle-earth and beyond.

This book's introduction to IR and its analysis of Order and Justice in global politics has emphasized the interlinkage of Order and Justice: first, how different kinds of social Orders are characterized by different levels of social Justice for different groups; and second, how some kind of Justice is required to sustain any kind of Order. As a citizen of the world, it is now up to you to decide what actions you will take to make your world more stable and more safe—from personal steps in your home or with your family to international steps on the global stage.

We hope that as you pursue your own journey, you take with you the idea that—like the different colors of a rainbow—different perspectives shed different kinds of light on our many worlds. We have argued that the strongest, clearest, and richest understanding of our world requires conjoining different perspectives. White light is made up of rainbows.

Building on this idea, this book has undertaken the task of being a form of a prism. We have combined worlds, and have highlighted different perspectives, which focus on different patterns or colors. Because juxtaposing different perspectives allows each one to illuminate and critique the other, we hope that combining these worlds has facilitated stronger understandings of all of them.

Now that we have enriched our understanding of the discipline and practice of international relations by comparing Middle-earth with our world, what next steps should we take, and how should we engage with other students and scholars of IR who are engaged in quests for Order and Justice? We begin with a discussion of what insight *LOTR* provides for quests for more Just forms of Order. We continue by reviewing how different approaches to IR are associated with different kinds of goals. Finally, we conclude by emphasizing the interlinkage between Order and Justice, and encouraging the practice of engaging with other worlds and other perspectives in order to enable a richer, more colorful understanding of global politics.

JUSTICE AS RIGHT ACTION:
THE QUEST FOR A MORE JUST ORDER

How can we make the world a safer and more stable place? Both through the characters and quest in *LOTR*, Tolkien highlights how creating more Justice in societal Order is extremely important. Despite this, he also usefully points out obstacles that we should be prepared for on the journey, which include difficulty in taking action, divergent perspectives on Justice, and imperfectly conceived solutions.

Obstacle #1: Pursuing Justice Requires Taking Action

As the wise Wizard who shepherds the Fellowship, Gandalf repeatedly uses his position to affirm just action rather than inaction or unjust action. This theme is set up early on, when Frodo discovers that the seemingly ordinary trinket he has inherited from Bilbo is the One Ring of Sauron, made for domination and enslavement. He asks Gandalf, "How, how did it come to me? . . . I wish it need not have happened in my time." And Gandalf replies, "So do I . . . and so do all who live to see such times. But that is not for them to decide. All we have to decide is what to do with the time that is given us" (I: 50). Later Frodo reiterates his question: "Why did it come to me? Why was I chosen?" Gandalf emphasizes Frodo's responsibility to act: "Such questions cannot be answered. . . . But you have been chosen, and you must therefore use such strength and heart and wits as you have" (I: 60). Authors such as Skoble (2003) and West (2002) have recognized a theme within *LOTR* about our moral accountability for our choices. This is particularly evident at the Council of Elrond, where it is clear that the Ring *can* be destroyed in Mount Doom but the question is whether or not it *should* be destroyed (Skoble 2003: 112).

As this implies, a first step in pursuing a just Order is accepting responsibility to take just action. This applies to both the great and the small, the likely and the unlikely heroes. At his Council, Elrond states, "This quest may be attempted by the weak with as much hope as the strong. Yet such is oft the course of deeds that move the wheels of the world: small hands do them because they must, while the eyes of the great are elsewhere" (I: 262). Similarly, Gandalf tells Aragorn about the arrival of the Hobbits Merry and Pippin at the Forest of Fangorn and says, "Their coming was like the falling of small stones that starts an avalanche in the mountains" (II: 485).

Throughout the quest, the choice of Hobbits as unlikely heroes on whom the fate of the world depends reiterates the theme that the small and unlikely can make the world a more fair and safe place. This parallels an observation popularly attributed to the distinguished anthropologist Margaret Mead: "Never doubt that a small group of thoughtful, committed citizens can change the world. Indeed, it is the only thing that ever has." While this is a fair statement, change impacts different people in different ways and usually includes elements of both "good" and "bad."

Obstacle #2: What Counts as "Just" Action Depends on Perspective

Because change brings mixed blessings, determining what action is just can be difficult. *The Lord of the Rings* demonstrates that there are different interpretations about what constitutes just or ethical action. This is made evident by comparing the position of the Man Boromir with those of other members of the Fellowship of the Ring. At the Council of Elrond, where representatives of the Free Peoples from the races of Elves, Dwarves, Men, and Hobbits gather with the Wizard Gandalf to discuss the history of and future plans for the Ring of Power, a division is made clear between what different members of the Council would like to do. Most members agree with Elrond, who asserts that the Ruling Ring cannot be used because anyone who tried "would then set himself on Sauron's throne, and yet another Dark Lord would appear" (I: 260–61). Boromir, however, is doubtful, and says, "Valour needs first strength, and then a weapon. Let the Ring be your weapon, if it has such power as you say. Take it and go forth to victory!" (I: 261).

Although Boromir eventually submits to the Council's decision to try to destroy the Ring by dropping it into Mount Doom, he remains unconvinced in his heart. Just before the breaking of the Fellowship, he debates their direction with Frodo, again, claiming that the Ring's use could extend to good as well as evil. Frodo responds, "Were you not at the Council? . . . Because we cannot use it, and what is done with it turns to evil." Boromir defends his position: "True-hearted Men, they will not be corrupted. . . . It is mad not to use it, to use the power of the Enemy against him. The fearless, the ruthless, these alone will achieve victory" (I: 389). Boromir then tries to seize the Ring from Frodo by force. He fails but compels the Hobbit to desert the Fellowship and pursue the rest of the quest alone. Frodo ends up going with his stalwart companion Sam; however, this occurs only because of Sam's swift intuition about Frodo's plan and his determination to stay with Frodo, as he had promised Gandalf at the journey's outset.

Boromir's juxtaposition with the other members of the Fellowship demonstrates that there are different conceptions of just action. It is not enough to say that one must act (or "use such strength and heart and wits as you have") rather than remain on the sidelines. Different kinds of action seem just from different perspectives. According to Gandalf and Elrond (both of whom are much, much older than anyone else at the Council—Elrond has been estimated to be over six thousand years old, and Gandalf has been in Middle-earth for almost two thousand years and existed before then as well), the Ring of Power would corrupt anyone who used it; consequently, it has to be destroyed. Both of them draw on their long memories about the Ring of Power and its context in coming to this conclusion. In his discussion of the history of the Ring, Elrond remembers back to the end of the Second Age when Isildur cut the Ring from Sauron's hand at the Battle of Dagorlad and took it for his own; Elrond says that Isildur "took it to treasure it. But soon he was betrayed by it to his death; and so it is named in the North Isildur's Bane" (I: 237). *The Silmarillion,* which chronicles the history of Middle-earth, suggests that Elrond also had previous experience with Sauron's treachery and the Ring's dominating power; it also suggests that Gandalf (who is of the same Order as Saruman, a Maia or lesser Valar [i.e., angelic power]) had similar experience with the dominating and treacherous power embodied in the Ring, although this may have been with Sauron's evil superior and predecessor, Morgoth (see especially "Of the Rings of Power and the Third Age" in Tolkien 1977).

However, Boromir has a different perspective. He has not seen the Ring misused and does not believe that his "true-hearted" Men could be corrupted. Furthermore, he is also frustrated with having to use the blood and treasure of his people to defend the West. At the Council of Elrond, he declares, "By our valour the wild folk of the East are still restrained, and the terror of [Sauron's] Morgul kept at bay; and thus alone are peace and freedom maintained in the lands behind us, bulwark of the West" (I: 239); he also acknowledges that, despite such valor, "we are hard pressed" (I: 241). Consequently, he sees the Ring as a potential savior—something that would enable evil to be kept at bay without further dependence on the lives and livelihoods of his people in Gondor. For Gandalf and Elrond, and the rest of the Council, whose peoples gain from Gondor's sacrifices with less cost to themselves, the destruction of the Ring is a more clear-cut case. But for Boromir, who sees the guarding of Mordor as paid for either by his people (if the quest to destroy the Ring fails) or by the apparently miraculous Ring, the need for its destruction remains doubtful.

Difficulty in determining which kind of action is most just is further developed by repeated references in *LOTR* to judgment versus mercy. When Gandalf first tells Frodo that he possesses the One Ring of Power, the Hobbit is informed that Gollum was tortured into telling Sauron that the Ring was with a Hobbit called Baggins in the Shire. Frodo responds, "What a pity that Bilbo did not stab the vile creature, when he had the chance!" Gandalf responds, "Pity? It was pity that stayed his hand. Pity, and Mercy: not to strike without need." Frodo remains distraught: "He deserves death." But Gandalf cautions, "Deserves it! I daresay he does. Many that live deserve death. And some that die deserve life. Can you give it to them? Then do not be too eager to deal out death in judgment. For even the very wise cannot see all ends" (I: 58).

Later in the story, when Frodo and Sam are trekking toward Mordor and encounter Gollum, Frodo flashes back to this conversation. Frodo accepts Gandalf's remembered caution and expresses pity for Gollum

(II: 601). And at the end of the book, this turns out for the best: without Gollum at Mount Doom, the quest almost certainly would have failed (see III: 924). Appendix 2 tells this part of the story.

Right or just action as mercy rather than judgment is an idea repeated elsewhere in *LOTR* as well. A memorable instance occurs after the end of the quest; Frodo returns to the Shire to find Saruman causing conflict and refuses to kill him despite popular demand. Here Frodo says, "I will not have him slain" and denounces revenge (I: 995). And then again, even when Saruman has tried to kill him, Frodo says, "Do not kill him even now. For he has not hurt me . . . his cure is beyond us; but I would still spare him, in the hope that he may find it" (I: 996). Based on these kinds of passages, it can be argued that Tolkien transforms the concept of justice into mercy in *LOTR* (Wood 2003). The material from *LOTR* also demonstrates how different kinds of action appear to be just from different perspectives. Moreover, what is most appropriate for a particular case is not always immediately clear.

Obstacle #3: Justice Is a Journey— There Is No Perfect Solution

Even when a plan for just action is determined, no plan is perfect or will solve all of the world's woes. Justice and injustice in the world are dynamic and evolving characteristics. Consequently, pursuing a better world must be an ongoing practice, rather than a one-shot deal. This is made clear by considering the impact of a "just war" of the Ring in *LOTR*.

Since the *LOTR* story ends soon after the quest, readers only have a brief glimpse at what life looks like for the Free Peoples in the postwar world. Despite this, hints emerge about the impact on social hierarchies of the War of the Ring. On one hand, with the elimination of major threats, societies may have the "luxury" of thinking about other social issues. War can bring about social change. For example, in Middle-earth, Sam Gamgee, an extraordinary hero because of his role in the Fellowship, is elected mayor for multiple terms after the war is over, despite being from the working class. In addition, Merry and Pippin become honored guests in the king's court who have roles in the new security regime created by the king for the postwar world. It seems unlikely that this would have been possible before the war. Similarly, in our world, women in World War II worked in factories and that had an impact over the course of decades on what could be included as acceptable employment, that is, activities outside of a home setting. Consequently, it is possible that pursuing one overarching goal (e.g., winning a war) can facilitate broader social change.

However, the conclusion of a war is not a perfect solution for other social problems. For example, in Middle-earth, Sam's heroism does not change his immediate economic need to be Frodo's servant, although he eventually inherits Bag End and rises far above his prewar station in life. Neither does Sam, Merry, and Pippin's increased status immediately seem to translate into increased upward mobility or diplomatic connections for Hobbits other than themselves. In our world, women's increased opportunities during war are also often limited in impact after the war: "women's issues" are often deprioritized, increased paid work opportunities are rarely complemented by adequate institutional support for women's traditional familial roles, and women rarely attain the same rate of political leadership as men in postconflict settings (see, e.g., Waylen 1996, chapter 4). Consequently, because minority concerns may be assumed to be relatively unimportant, compared to other concerns at hand (such as those raised by Sauron's expansionism or the need for "peace" afterward), there is a risk that such concerns may be deferred or ignored indefinitely. As this suggests, no plan is a panacea: Justice is a journey. Consequently, making the world a better place must be an ongoing endeavor.

The Importance of Creating Justice, Despite Obstacles

Despite all of these obstacles, Tolkien makes it clear that there is a difference between what we *can* do and what we *should* do. Kraue (2003) quotes a letter from Tolkien that states, "If there is any contemporary reference in my story at all it is to what seems to me the most widespread assumption of our time: that if a thing can be done, it must be done." Tolkien wrote *LOTR*, according to Kraue, "in part, as a protest against the sense that the past no longer had any relevance, that humans could act, in the absence of God, however they wished" (140).

In *LOTR*, this is made clear by the repeated refusal by most members of the Fellowship and their allies to use the power of the Ring, even though it was in their possession. This is contrasted with Sauron's absolute determination to find and use the Ring's power to conquer all. Despite the difficulty of taking the high road—especially as illustrated by

Boromir's quandary over the Fellowship's decision not to use the Ring—it is very clear that pursuing this quest for Justice is worth it. The slavery and domination under Sauron's rule is too awful, and the opportunity for freedom and joy without him too wonderful to reject the dangers and thrills of the quest. Frodo takes up the challenge that he is presented and ends up a hero. So, too, *LOTR* suggests that, despite the obstacles, pursuing the journey for Justice is a critically important endeavor.

WHERE HAVE WE BEEN?

This book has aimed to enable students of IR to clarify their understanding of existing interpretations of world politics and to suggest alternative meanings by using *LOTR* in two ways: first, to shed light on existing debate; and second, to step back and provide unique inspiration and different perspectives on our world. In doing so, we have sought to provide a prism that recognizes the strength of white light as being rooted in its rainbow colors and to integrate a rainbow of perspectives in creating a stronger light of understanding. We have used different characters within *LOTR* to illustrate different ideal types of approaches to IR, with the hope that this would clarify their major differences and similarities, despite simplifying them in the process. We also sought to gain unique inspiration for IR from *LOTR* by tracing themes of Order and Justice using images of Mordor, the Shire, and Rivendell; by comparing and contrasting theoretical insights illustrated using male and female characters of each race; and by analyzing topical issues of concern to IR today within the world of Middle-earth. By taking this approach, we hope that we have provided some tools for students to use both in navigating the sometimes complicated academic discourse of IR and in engaging critically and imaginatively with issues of concern.

We focused on questions of Order (How can the world be made a more stable place?) and Justice (How can the world be made a more fair place?). At the outset, we pointed out that these respective questions have been primarily associated with different approaches to explaining and understanding IR: from the traditional perspective, "problem-solving" approaches tend to take the world as it is and search for explanations of what goes on (focusing on issues of Order), while "critical" approaches tend to focus on perceptions of what ought to be and how things might be changed (focusing on issues of Justice). Furthermore, each question, along with the (problem-solving or critical) perspective associated with it, tends to be associated more with some issues than with others: For example, problem-solving approaches focusing on issues of Order often prioritize issues, including WMDs, conventional war, and terrorism, while critical approaches focusing on issues of Justice often prioritize issues of inequality and development, environmental degradation, or human rights.

Despite this simplified framing, using *LOTR* as a mirror, as well as a light, to explain and understand global politics highlights how (1) Order and Justice are interlinked and (2) any particular issue area involves both questions (of stability and fairness). This may not always be apparent on face value, but comparing experiences from different worlds makes it much more clear than is apparent by focusing on any one world or any one perspective. Table 7 outlines points discussed in the previous chapter that demonstrate the connection between Order and Justice. An interesting property of the table is that opposing effects are not only possible but even likely, depending on how a given policy is implemented. It is not difficult to think of further examples; consider freedom and democracy in the context of Order. Imposed democratization is unlikely to succeed, while democracies that arise naturally have the favorable by-product of staying at peace with each other. (As with most generalizations, exceptions exist, such as the regimes in Germany and Japan after World War II.) The table also encourages us to think about Order and Justice simultaneously when evaluating policy within a given issue area. For example, with regard to learning and institutions, increased institutionalization would appear to have good effects on both Order and Justice.

WHERE ARE WE GOING? (IMPLICATIONS FOR IR)

While drawing on *LOTR* may not always be the answer to providing insight into our world on issues of Order and Justice, our use of it in this book highlights how it is critical to draw on multiple perspectives and points of view to gain a stronger and more comprehensive understanding of global politics. In problem-solving words, this supports a broad interpretation of Miles' Law: where you stand depends on where you sit. In critical words, this supports a feminist argument that highlights how stories rooted in different kinds of experience—whether gender, race, class, sexuality, or development—all influence one's point of view and interpretation of the world. Both of these arguments support looking beyond face value of the stories that we tell ourselves about our worlds (fantastical or otherwise) to see how the experiences of other people in other positions (especially those marginalized and excluded) suggest alternative interpretations of the world. They also highlight issues of Order and Justice that are not apparent from existing or dominant perspectives. Both of them recognize the importance of integrating a rainbow of insights to achieve the clearest vision.

TABLE 7. Examples of Concerns about Order and Justice by Issue Area according to Various IR Paradigms

Issue Area	Order (stability)	Justice (fairness)
Foreign policy decision-making	Short-term views about the impact of foreign policy decisions on social stability are often different from long-term views	Foreign policy decisions which appear to be just in the short term may appear to be unjust in the long term
Global health	Formal and informal institutions provide care and support global health ($\uparrow$ Stability) Informalization of public health institutions strains households, communities, and "human capital" ($\downarrow$ Stability)	Informalization of public health institutions skews the burden of care between formal and informal care providers and reduces standards of living for providers and recipients of care ($\downarrow$ Justice)
State and human security	Militarized state security is meant to protect a population's human security (Military industrial complex: $\uparrow$ Stability) Militarized state security can reduce women's and others' human security ($\downarrow$ Stability)	Militarized state security can reduce women's and others' human security ($\downarrow$ Justice)
Learning and institutions	Increased institutionalization may reduce the recurrence of war ($\uparrow$ Stability)	Without moderating institutions, the international system may be guided strictly by (realist) assumptions of "might makes right" ($\downarrow$ Justice)
Mercy	Showing mercy to villains may encourage popular support of the mercy-granting actor ($\uparrow$ Stability) or risk encouraging more villainous or chaotic behavior ($\downarrow$ Stability)	Showing mercy to villains may contribute to future greater "good" ($\uparrow$ utilitarian Justice) or greater "evil" ($\downarrow$ utilitarian Justice) Creative solutions can mercifully try to do something about both the pain of villains and their victims ($\uparrow$ "ethics of care" Justice)

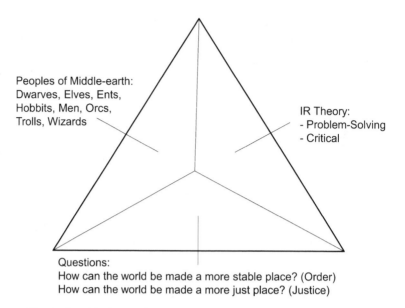

Peoples of Middle-earth:
Dwarves, Elves, Ents,
Hobbits, Men, Orcs,
Trolls, Wizards

IR Theory:
- Problem-Solving
- Critical

Questions:
How can the world be made a more stable place? (Order)
How can the world be made a more just place? (Justice)

Fig. 7. Considering multiple dimensions of International Relations:
Taking a broader view

Figure 7 illustrates this point by showing how different kinds of questions can be addressed in different ways, depending on perspective (e.g., different peoples or characters of Middle-earth) or paradigm (e.g., problem-solving or critical IR theory). Each approach provides a different angle on a prism and focuses on different colors and patterns in view. This figure also highlights how a richer understanding of these kinds of questions requires drawing on multiple perspectives—using the intersection of perspectives like a prism to bring out a rainbow. Without doing so, our theories lose their richness and predictive value, just as would occur if we assumed a monochromatic vision of the world.

FINAL THOUGHTS

Drawing on *LOTR* for illustration and critique provides one way of responding to Agathangelou's (2004: 21, 22) call for "poetic inspiration" in search of "multiple worlds" in IR. Simply drawing on the world of Middle-earth in comparison to our own world highlights how we make many worlds, whether through fictive and fantastical development (as with

Middle-earth) or through the stories we tell using the different paradigms and worldviews about IR. This can include telling stories about interstate war (as in the realist tradition), cooperation (as in the liberal tradition), class (as in the Marxist tradition), or women and disempowered groups (as in the feminist tradition). The richest and most colorful stories are the ones that recognize the intersection of the multiple worlds we live in and provide different ways to interpret and live within and between those worlds.

As a student of IR and a citizen of the world, it is now up to you to decide how you will act to promote greater stability and safety. We hope that by using *LOTR* as a light and a mirror, we have provided some tools that will help you understand and critically engage with efforts by IR scholarship and beyond to create greater Order and Justice in the worlds of which you are a part.

The War of the Ring
Up to Its Climax

This narrative combines the book and movie versions of *LOTR,* the story of the War of the Ring, which concludes the Third Age of Middle-earth. Its predecessor, *The Hobbit* (Tolkien 1996), does contain what later turns out to be a crucial part of the story, and that is recounted briefly here. Bilbo Baggins, a Hobbit who lives in the Shire (a quiet place, as described momentarily), has a taste for adventure. During his travels in *The Hobbit,* Bilbo obtains the Ring of Power from the demented but cunning Gollum (originally known as Sméagol and a tormented character who reappears, like Bilbo, in *LOTR*). While *The Hobbit* stands the test of time as a children's book, it does not develop in full the complexity of Middle-earth that is found in *LOTR* and facilitates analysis of problems from the real world. Thus the summary that follows focuses on the story of the Ring of Power, which reaches its point of culmination in *LOTR.* For interest's sake, the story's ending is saved for a second appendix.

Bilbo Baggins's birthday party is the unassuming starting point for *The Fellowship of the Ring,* the first volume in the trilogy. Bilbo, uncle of Frodo Baggins, resided at his home in the Shire for sixty years after obtaining the Ring. Think of a small, idyllic English village from medieval times, with eating, gardening, brewing of fine ale, and smoking of pipeweed as common preoccupations, and that gives a good sense of the Shire. The Shire is inhabited by Hobbits, as they call themselves—or Halflings as designated by others—with adults being less than four feet tall and somewhat longer in life span but otherwise typical of humans.

Bilbo did not understand the Ring's truly evil nature until many years after obtaining it from Gollum. However, he knows that the Ring is magical. When it is worn, for example, the bearer becomes invisible. Possession of the Ring also grants unusually long life—even centuries of existence. The Ring also causes an increasingly pernicious attachment to it. Made thousands of years earlier by the Dark Lord, Sauron, the story's principal villain, the Ring contains all of his malice and evil power. He lost the Ring during a battle with the Free Peoples, which marked the end of the Second Age of Middle-earth, long before *LOTR* takes place. (Sauron existed during the First Age as well and played an important but subordinate role on behalf of the equally evil Morgoth, ultimately defeated by the Free Peoples; this story is told in *The Silmarillion* (Tolkien 1977).) It should be noted that Sauron, along with several other characters in Middle-earth, is immortal unless destroyed in a particular way. Elves and Wizards also meet this description, that is, they can live for many thousands of years because they do not die of natural causes. Ents, introduced later in the story, also seem to meet this description.) At that time, Isildur, King of Gondor, the most powerful realm among Men, managed to cut the Ring from Sauron's hand even after the Dark Lord had broken his blade. This gave victory to the alliance of Men and Elves, led by Elendil, Isildur's father, and the Elven King Gil-galad, who fought Sauron and his minions, the Orcs. Loss of the Ring resulted in Sauron losing corporeal form and fading into obscurity for over two millennia.

Isildur had a golden opportunity at that time to cast the Ring into the place where Sauron made it: the fires of Mount Doom in the land of Mordor, which had provided the Dark Lord's base of operations. The evil of the Ring, however, overcame Isildur as he stood at the precipice of Mount Doom—the one place where this most evil creation could be unmade. In spite of Elrond of Rivendell's urgings, he decided not to destroy the Ring, allowing evil a new opportunity to flourish in Middle-earth. Two years later the Ring betrayed him; Isildur perished when ambushed by Orcs. He lost the Ring in a river, and it lay quiet for a very long time until it was discovered by Deagol, friend of Sméagol, members of a people related to Hobbits. Immediately overcome by a yearning for the Ring, Sméagol killed Deagol to obtain it. He learned about the Ring's magical power, including disappearance and the granting of unnaturally long life, but sank into evil under its influence. Sméagol committed heinous acts, and the people of his village cast him out. The evil of the Ring transformed him into Gollum. Living in darkness and seclusion, Gollum held the ring for five hundred years but then lost it to Bilbo.

Back to Bilbo's party, where *LOTR* begins. Exhausted by the Ring and increasingly under its influence for sixty years, Bilbo finally agrees to give it up after persuasive efforts by a Wizard, Gandalf the Grey. Known among Hobbits for his previous adventures and eccentricity, Bilbo believes that disappearing at his birthday party and going on an adventure once more will be just the thing to do. He comes up with this plan under counsel from Gandalf, although the Wizard disapproves of the attention-getting use of the Ring to disappear outright. One of just five Wizards, Gandalf possesses extraordinary power and serves as a de facto advocate and strategist for the Free Peoples. He has suspected for some time that Bilbo's Ring might be more than just one of many magical entities within Middle-earth. After some urging from Gandalf and even unpleasantness between these two old friends, Bilbo gives up the Ring to his nephew, Frodo Baggins, and literally disappears from the Shire.

Both Gandalf and Bilbo regard Frodo as the best Hobbit in the Shire. Gandalf, off to look further into the origins of the Ring, instructs Frodo to keep it both secret and safe. The Wizard suspects already that the Ring might be Sauron's master creation—even more so after the confrontation required for Bilbo to give it up—and knows that, as someone of already great stature, it would be extremely dangerous and corrupting for him to possess. The Ring, by its very nature, creates the potential for evil in proportion to the standing of its bearer.

Events pick up dramatically after emissaries of the Dark Lord, the Ringwraiths, capture Gollum and force out of him the secret that the Ring is held by a Hobbit in the Shire; they even learn the name Baggins. Recognizable as Black Riders, these wraiths, neither living nor dead, were once great kings of Men. Sauron long ago had given each a lesser ring, which enabled him to enslave them through his Ring of Power. The Black Riders, also known as Nazgûl, exist in a shadow world, obsessed with regaining the Ring for their master. At Sauron's command they leave Mordor for the Shire in great haste in the hope of seizing the Ring.

Gandalf returns to the Shire after confirming the true nature of the Ring. He advises Frodo to leave and make for the village of Bree. Located at the edge of the Shire, Bree will serve as a rendezvous point. The Wizard promises to meet Frodo there after going on an urgent side trip. Gandalf feels the need to seek advice immediately from the head of his order at the time, Saruman the White, greatest of all Wizards. But Saruman turns out to be a traitor in league with Sauron and imprisons Gandalf in the Tower of Orthanc at his stronghold at Isengard. Saruman had become corrupted after looking into one of the palantíri, ancient seeing stones from beyond Middle-earth. Sauron also possesses a palantír and by force of will gained power over the mind of Saruman.

Frodo is unaware of these events and, accompanied by three other Hobbits—his servant, Samwise (Sam) Gamgee, along with two younger friends, Perigrin (Pippin) Took and Meriadoc (Merry) Brandybuck—he departs the Shire. The Hobbits narrowly escape Sauron's Black Riders, who catch up to them at Bree. Fortunately for Frodo and his companions, Gandalf had advised Aragorn, the greatest huntsman and traveler of Middle-earth, to meet the Hobbits at the Inn of the Prancing Pony in Bree. Called "Strider" by the locals, it is learned later in the story that Aragorn is the rightful heir to the Kingdom of Gondor, still greatest among the Free Peoples of Middle-earth. After another close call with the Black Riders, the Hobbits, led by Aragorn, set out for Rivendell. Rivendell is one of the two remaining strongholds of the Elves, Middle-earth's oldest and wisest inhabitants and home to the powerful Elrond. Part of the way through the journey, the Black Riders manage to locate Aragorn and the Hobbits at Weathertop, an ancient lookout. Although Aragorn is able to fend off the Black Riders, Frodo is stabbed with a poisonous blade and sinks into a feverish state. He is in danger of turning into a wraith, that is, crossing over into the undead, shadow world of the Black Riders.

Just in time, Frodo is able to reach the protection of Rivendell. Elrond uses Elvish medicine to limit the effects of the wraith's sword. After a brief period of recovery, Frodo and Bilbo attend the Council of Elrond, at which representatives of the Free Peoples debate what to do with the Ring. After some controversy the Council decides that the Ring must be destroyed. With the principal exception of Boromir, a Man of high nobility from Gondor, those present agree that an attempt to use the Ring against Sauron would corrupt whoever wielded it, plunging the world into evil. A Fellowship is created to accompany Frodo, now the official Ring Bearer, in an attempt to eliminate the Ring in the only way possible: by casting it into the fires of Mount Doom. The Fellowship consists of the four Hobbits, Gandalf (who had escaped from Saruman), Boromir, Aragorn, Legolas (an Elf), and Gimli (a Dwarf). Thus the Fellowship starts its journey from Rivendell with at least one member from each of the Free Peoples of Middle-earth represented at the Council. This occurs in spite of long-standing suspicion and even hatred between Elves and Dwarves.

While attempting to climb around the mountain Caradhras, the Fellowship is thwarted by heavy snow, which causes it to turn back and change course. This overwhelming, snowy obstacle results from a spell cast by Saruman, who has become aware of the Fellowship's location. While he is in league with Sauron, Saruman hopes to take the Ring for himself. The Fellowship reluctantly takes an alternate route through the Mines of Moria. Rather than encountering the expected thriving city of Dwarves beneath the mountains, the Fellowship finds Moria to be in ruins. Moria is extremely dangerous—overrun with Orcs, Trolls, and one even more odious creature. Near the exit to Moria a fatal confrontation takes place with one such entity: Gandalf falls into darkness, locked in combat with a Balrog, an enormous fire-breathing demon of the ancient world. The Fellowship believes Gandalf to have perished and leaves Moria without him. Aragorn leads the way.

Soon after the Fellowship arrives in Lothlórien, the other stronghold of the Elves remaining in Middle-earth. They are greeted by Lady Galadriel, a powerful Elf gifted with the ability to see the minds of others. Galadriel permits Frodo to look into a special pool of water that reveals the horrific consequences if his mission to destroy the Ring is not fulfilled. (Sam also looks into the pool.) Frodo offers Galadriel the Ring, but she refuses, reminding him of its corrupting power, most notably in relation to the stature of the one holding it. This private meeting reaffirms in multiple ways the necessity of the quest to destroy the Ring. Galadriel also warns Frodo of the Ring's ability to corrupt even members of the Fellowship itself. Soon after her warning is confirmed. When the Fellowship leaves Lothlórien on a river journey and takes a rest near its bank, Frodo wanders away for reflection and is followed by Boromir, who now succumbs fully to the lure of the Ring. He initially tries to persuade Frodo to give him the Ring and, upon refusal, attempts to take it by force. Frodo puts on the Ring, becomes invisible, and manages to escape. The Fellowship is in disarray when attacked by Saruman's Uruk-hai, a well-armed and especially dangerous company of hybrid Orcs, along with Orcs from Moria. Boromir is killed by the Uruk-hai while defending Merry and Pippin. Sam and Frodo slip away together and cross the river, heading for Mordor.

The Two Towers, the second volume of the trilogy, begins with a brief conversation between Aragorn and the dying Boromir. Gimli, Legolas, and Aragorn learn that Boromir had tried to seize the Ring and then attempted, unsuccessfully, to prevent Merry and Pippin from being taken away by force. The three remaining members of the Fellowship set off in pursuit of the Uruk-hai, who are bringing Pippin and Merry to Isengard in great haste. Saruman hopes, mistakenly, that these Hobbits are the ones bearing the Ring. Near Fangorn Forest the Uruk-hai are overtaken by riders from the Kingdom of Rohan, who kill all of them. During the battle, Merry and Pippin escape into Fangorn Forest and encounter Treebeard the Ent. He is a sentient, treelike creature—a shepherd of the forest and one of the most ancient beings in Middle-earth. Treebeard befriends Pippin and Merry and is urged by them to bring the Ents, a potentially formidable ally for the Free Peoples, into the struggle. Treebeard is reluctant and consults with his peers in an Entmoot—a meeting of the minds conducted in the slow-paced, ancient language of the Ents. Pippin and Merry anxiously await a decision.

Revealed at this stage is a major twist in the story: Gandalf, thought to be dead, is resurrected. After a titanic struggle with the Balrog, he is reborn as Gandalf the White, now the most powerful Wizard in Middle-earth, exceeding even Saruman. He reveals himself in Fangorn Forest to Aragorn, Gimli, and Legolas. Gandalf informs them that Merry and Pippin are safe and that it is urgent to travel to the Kingdom of Rohan, which is poorly prepared for an imminent attack by Saruman, under instruction from Sauron.

Meanwhile, in Rohan, King Théoden, in serious decline and poor in judgment due to spells cast by Saruman, falls increasingly under the influence of Gríma the Wormtongue. A traitor in league with Saruman, Wormtongue is trying to weaken Rohan so it will fall when attacked by Isengard. Saruman, under orders from Sauron, is tasked with destroying Rohan and uses magical powers to breed an enormous army: tens of thousands of Uruk-hai. When Gandalf, Legolas, Aragorn, and Gimli arrive in Rohan, the Wizard successfully breaks Saruman's spell. King Théoden, now able to see the imminent danger, banishes Wormtongue and moves his people to Helm's Deep, an ancient stronghold that has never fallen to attackers. While heavily outnumbered, the people of Rohan have support from the members of the Fellowship to meet the assault from Saruman's army.

After deliberation, the Ents decide to attack Isengard. This action greatly assists the people of Rohan, who otherwise would have had even more threats with which to contend while holding out at Helm's Deep. The Ents succeed in destroying Saruman's war machine by flooding Isengard with water held back by dams. They confine him in the impenetrable Tower of Orthanc. The Ents render Isengard irrelevant to the further struggle. Against great odds, Helm's Deep is defended and the remaining Uruk-hai are driven into Fangorn. There they are destroyed by Huorns, Ents who have become extremely treelike and quite aggrieved at those who have been cutting down their brethren.

After the battle, Gandalf is aware that the next stage of the war will take the form of a full-scale attack on Gondor. Taking Pippin with him, he makes haste for Minas Tirith, Gondor's principal city and the home of Denethor the Steward (also the father of Boromir). The stewards have ruled Gondor for millennia, waiting for the return of the king after the line was broken with the fall of Isildur.

Alone in the wilderness and approaching Mordor, Frodo and Sam are pursued by Gollum. Sauron has turned him loose from the dungeons of Mordor, hoping that his obsession will create a path to the Ring. Gollum proves to be incredibly elusive and shadows the Fellowship for his own purposes, continuing to stalk Sam and Frodo after they leave the others. The Hobbits, however, manage to overpower him and extract a promise: Gollum swears by the Ring to serve Frodo.

Led by Gollum, a valuable guide to the wasteland ahead, Frodo and Sam negotiate the Dead Marshes and come to the Black Gate of Mordor. At that point, persuaded by Gollum—who seems unaware that Frodo intends to destroy the Ring—the Hobbits veer away from a futile attempt to enter Mordor directly. While pursuing a way around the Black Gate, they fall into the hands of a raiding party from Gondor, led by Boromir's younger brother, Faramir. Faramir becomes aware of Frodo's objective and ultimately, unlike Boromir, proves able to resist the lure of the Ring. He releases the two Hobbits and Gollum, who continue their journey into Mordor.

Near the dead city of Minas Morgul, home of the Nazgûl, Gollum's plan to betray Frodo and take the Ring for himself becomes apparent: He leads the Hobbits up the cliff stairs of Cirith Ungol, where an ancient terror awaits—an enormous spider, Shelob. Shelob stings Frodo, who then loses consciousness. However, Gollum is unable to obtain the Ring. Instead, Sam now believes Frodo to be dead and takes the Ring. He hides while Orcs happen suddenly upon Frodo. To his astonishment, Sam learns from listening to the Orcs that Frodo still lives and will regain consciousness in the near future. Hoping for a chance to rescue him, Sam follows the Orcs, who take Frodo to the Tower of Cirith Ungol.

The Return of the King, the third volume of the trilogy, begins with Gandalf's arrival at Minas Tirith. The city is bracing itself for a siege and suffers from low morale in light of the overwhelming forces Sauron is assembling against it. Like Saruman, Denethor possesses and uses a palantír, increasingly seduced under the Dark Lord's sway and weakened by a resulting defeatist mind-set.

Shortly before Sauron's forces lay siege to Minas Tirith, the city's beacons are lit to summon help from Rohan. Rohan's forces are reassembled after the great battle of Helm's Deep, with a long ride ahead to Gondor and time being of the essence. Unknown to Théoden, his niece Éowyn rides along in spite of his disapproval, disguised as a male warrior known as Dernhelm. Also uninvited is Merry, who is eager to fight and brought along by Éowyn, who identifies with his exclusion.

With the forces of Mordor turning out to be huge and powerful in comparison to the city's defenses, the siege takes its toll on Minas Tirith. Many thousands of Orcs, with siege towers, catapults, and a great battering ram, Grond, operated by enormous mountain Trolls, are arrayed at the gates and succeed in breaking into the city.

With the arrival of Rohan's army, skilled at fighting on horseback, the fortunes of Gondor rise. Éowyn and Merry combine to slay the Witch King of Angmar, greatest of the Nazgûl. However, the decisive element in the battle's favorable outcome comes about with the army brought by Aragorn, Isildur's heir, from the Paths of the Dead. The Army of the Dead, able to fight with invincibility, agrees to come to Minas Tirith. This support is provided in return for Aragorn's promise to release the Army of the Dead from a curse placed on them by Isildur for failing to help when summoned during the ancient time of greatest need in the fight against Sauron. After victory in the battle outside the gates of Minas Tirith, Aragorn fulfills his promise, and the Army of the Dead is allowed to rest in peace.

Denethor, ultimately driven mad by his viewing of the palantír and feeling certain of defeat, commits suicide at the height of the battle. He also attempts to burn Faramir, who had been seriously wounded, along with himself. Pippin, however, warns Gandalf, and the Wizard is able to intervene and save Faramir.

In spite of the recent success at Minas Tirith, Sauron's forces remain much more powerful. The leadership of the Free Peoples confers and decides to ride with whatever forces can be assembled to the Black Gate of Mordor. This tactic is known to be hopeless in and of itself but is intended as a diversion. The goal is to draw Sauron's eye outside of Mordor—away from Frodo and the quest to destroy the Ring—which represents the only hope for ultimate victory. Led by Aragorn, now in the open as the would-be King of Gondor, the armies of the Free Peoples reach the Black Gate of Mordor. Sauron unleashes vast hordes, and a battle ensues on the Field of Cormallen.

Meanwhile, aided by infighting among Orcs, Sam succeeds in rescuing Frodo. Together they leave the Tower of Cirith Ungol and, disguised as Orcs, make their way toward Mount Doom. Once again Gollum finds them, and Frodo warns him not to try to take the Ring. The situation is desperate, both for Frodo and Sam inside Mordor and for the Free Peoples at its gates. Sauron's army heavily outnumbers the forces led by Aragorn, the Ring is not yet destroyed, and its evil appears to be overwhelming Frodo.

This seems like a good point at which to interrupt the story. Middle-earth is in every imaginable kind of crisis. So what happens next? We will not spoil the ending! The account provided so far is sufficient for the purposes of this textbook, so the story's conclusion will be revealed in appendix B.

How the Story Ends

Frodo and Sam reach the opening of Mount Doom. They enter, but at the Crack of Doom, Frodo is unable to fulfill his mission, finally overtaken by the evil power of the Ring. He decides instead to claim the Ring for himself and puts it on. At that moment he is attacked by Gollum, who knocks Sam unconscious and then bites off Frodo's finger and takes the Ring for himself. Gollum, however, loses his balance and falls into the Crack of Doom, taking the Ring with him. At that moment the Ring is consumed in the flames, and Sauron and all of his works, are destroyed. The Dark Tower of Mordor falls, and Sauron's minions on the field of battle surrender or run off in terror. At long last, Middle-earth is free of the evil of Sauron.

Aragorn takes the throne of Gondor as King Elessar and enjoys a long and successful reign. He and Arwen, Elrond's daughter, are wed and rule over Gondor together. Faramir and Éowyn also are wed, which unites the kingdoms of Gondor and Rohan. Legolas and Gimli journey through Middle-earth together, each showing the other his favorite places. This put to rest the old animosity between Elves and Dwarves once and for all.

After a period of celebration, the Hobbits return from Gondor to the Shire. However, on their arrival, they are horrified to find the Shire under the rule of evil Men in the employ of Saruman, who was released by the Ents. Some Hobbits, out of fear or opportunism, have joined the new regime, which rules by terror. Any Hobbit who defies Saruman can expect to be mistreated and even put in jail or killed. Led by Merry and Pippin, now experienced warriors, the Hobbits mobilize and overthrow the dictatorship in the last battle ever fought in the Shire. Saruman, in total disgrace, attempts to stab Frodo, only to be stabbed to death by Worm-tongue, his last remaining follower.

For some time the Hobbits dwell peacefully in the Shire. The injury received by Frodo at Weathertop never fully heals, however, and he cannot be at peace in Middle-earth. With Gandalf, Bilbo, and others, he leaves Middle-earth to escape the legacy of the Ring. Merry and Pippin, after many happy years in the Shire, return to Gondor to live out their final years as honored guests. The now heroic Sam marries Rosie Cotton, has many children, and serves as the Shire's mayor for seven consecutive terms. As a widower, he finally crosses the sea as well—the last of the Ring Bearers to leave Middle-earth.

References

Agathangelou, Anna M. 2004. "The House of IR: From Family Power Politics to the *Poises* of Worldism." *International Studies Perspectives* 6:21–49.

Agathangelou, Anna M., and L. H. M. Ling. 2009. *Transforming World Politics: From Empire to Multiple Worlds.* London: Routledge.

Agathangelou, Anna M., and Heather Turcotte. 2010."Postcolonial Theories and Challenges to 'First World-ism.'" In *Gender Matters in Global Politics: A Feminist Introduction to International Relations,* edited by Laura J. Shepherd, 44–58. London: Routledge.

Alker, Hayward R. 1996a. "The Presumption of Anarchy in World Politics: On Recovering the Historicity of World Society." In *Rediscoveries and Reformulations: Humanistic Methodologies for International Studies,* 355–93. Cambridge: Cambridge University Press.

Alker, Hayward R. 1996b. *Rediscoveries and Reformulations: Humanistic Methodologies for International Studies.* Cambridge: Cambridge University Press.

Alker, Hayward R. 2005. "On Curricular Perestroika: Seven Principles of Methodological Pluralism." In *Perestroika! The Raucous Rebellion in Political Science,* edited by Kristen Renwick Monroe, 434–64. New Haven, CT: Yale University Press.

Allen, Amy, ed. 2005/2008. "Feminist Perspectives on Power." In *The Stanford Encyclopedia of Philosophy,* edited by Edward N. Zalta. http://plato.stanford.edu/archives/Spr2011/entries/feminist-power (accessed 18 October 2010).

Allen, Beverly. 1996. *Rape Warfare: The Hidden Genocide in Bosnia-Herzegovina and Croatia.* Minneapolis: University of Minnesota Press.

Allison, Graham. 1971. *Essence of Decision: Explaining the Cuban Missile Crisis.* Boston: Little, Brown.

Anderson, Joel. 2000. "The 'Third Generation' of the Frankfurt School." *Intellectual History Newsletter* 22. http://www.phil.uu.nl/~joel/research/publications/3rdGeneration.htm (accessed 18 October 2010).

Annan, Kofi. 2005. "Empowerment of Women the Most Effective Development

Tool, Secretary-General Tells Commission on Status of Women." United Nations Press Release SG/SM/9738 WOM/1489, 2 February. http://www.un .org/News/Press/docs/2005/sgsm9738.doc.htm (accessed 16 August 2006).

Ashworth, Lucian M. 2006. "Where Are the Idealists in Interwar International Relations?" *Review of International Studies* 32(2): 291–308.

Auden, W. H. 1967. "Good and Evil in the Lord of the Rings." *Tolkien Journal* 3(1): 5–8.

Badran, Margot. 2001. *Feminists, Islam, and Nation: Gender and the Making of Modern Egypt.* Princeton, NJ: Princeton University Press.

Barnett, M. J. 1969. "The Politics of Middle-earth." *Polity* 1(3): 383–87.

Baylis, John, Steve Smith, and Patricia Owens, eds. 2008. *The Globalization of World Politics: An Introduction to International Relations.* 4th ed. Oxford: Oxford University Press.

Bentham, Jeremy. 1789/2005. *An Introduction to the Principles of Morals and Legislation.* Whitefish, MT: Kessinger Publishing.

Blanchard, Eric. 2003. "Gender, International Relations, and the Development of Feminist Security Theory." *Signs* 28(4): 1289–1312.

Blount, Douglas K. 2003. "Überhobbits: Tolkien, Nietzsche, and the Will to Power." In *The Lord of the Rings and Philosophy,* edited by Gregory Bassham and Eric Bronson, 87–98. Peru, IL: Carus Publishing.

Boyer, Mark A., Vincent Kelly Pollard, Lynn M. Kuzma, and Patrick J. Haney. 2002. "At the Movies: A Continuing Dialogue on the Challenges of Teaching with Film." *International Studies Perspectives* 3(1): 89–94.

Bueno de Mesquita, Bruce. 2009. *The Predictioneer's Game: Using the Logic of Brazen Self-Interest to See and Shape the Future.* New York: Random House.

Bueno de Mesquita, Bruce. 2010. *Principles of International Politics.* 4th ed. Washington, DC: CQ Press.

Bull, Hedley. 2002. *The Anarchical Society: A Study of Order in World Politics.* 3rd ed. New York: Columbia University Press.

Bull, Hedley, and Adam Watson, eds. 1984. *The Expansion of International Society.* Oxford: Oxford University Press.

Butler, Judith. 1990. *Gender Trouble: Feminism and the Subversion of Identity.* New York: Routledge.

Caprioli, Mary. 2000. "Gendered Conflict." *Journal of Peace Research* 37(1): 51–68.

Carr, E. H. 2002. *The Twenty Years' Crisis, 1919–1939: An Introduction to the Study of International Relations.* New York: Palgrave.

Chance, Jane. 1992. "Power and Knowledge in Tolkien: The Problem of Difference in 'The Birthday Party.'" In *Proceedings of the J. R. R. Tolkien Centenary Conference, 1992,* edited by Patricia Reynolds and Glen GoodKnight, 115–20. Altadena, CA: Mythopoeic Press.

Chance, Jane. 2001. *The Lord of the Rings: The Mythology of Power.* Lexington: University Press of Kentucky.

Cockburn, Cynthia. 2010. "Militarism and War." In *Gender Matters in Global Politics: A Feminist Introduction to International Relations,* edited by Laura J. Shepherd, 105–15. London: Routledge.

Collins, Patricia Hill. 1990. *Black Feminist Thought: Knowledge, Consciousness, and the Politics of Empowerment*. Boston: Unwin Hyman.

Cox, Robert W. 1981. "Social Forces, States and World Orders." *Millennium: Journal of International Studies* 10(2): 126–55.

Crawford, Neta C. 2006. "Feminist Futures: Science Fiction, Utopia, and the Art of Possibilities in World Politics." In *To Seek Out New Worlds: Between Science Fiction and Politics*, edited by Jutta Weldes, 195–220. New York: Palgrave Macmillan.

Crenshaw, Kimberlé W. 1991. "Mapping the Margins: Intersectionality, Identity Politics, and Violence against Women of Color." *Stanford Law Review* 43(6): 1241–99.

D'Anieri, Paul. 2010. *International Politics: Power and Purpose in Global Affairs*. Belmont, CA: Wadsworth Cengage.

Davidson, Scott. 2003. "Tolkien and the Nature of Evil." In *The Lord of the Rings and Philosophy*, edited by Gregory Bassham and Eric Bronson, 99–109. Peru, IL: Carus Publishing.

De Gouges, Olympe. 1791. *Declaration of the Rights of Woman and the Female Citizen*. http://www.library.csi.cuny.edu/dept/americanstudies/lavender/decwom2.html (accessed 26 May 2011).

De Grazia, Sebastien. 1994. *Machiavelli in Hell*. New York: Vintage.

Dickerson, Matthew. 2003. *Following Gandalf*. Grand Rapids, MI: Brazos Press.

Dietz, Mary G. 2003. "Current Controversies in Feminist Theory." *Annual Review of Political Science* 6: 399–431.

Diez, Thomas, and Jill Steans. 2005. "A Useful Dialogue? Habermas and International Relations." *Review of International Studies* 31: 127–40.

Dougherty, Beth K. 2002. "Comic Relief: Using Political Cartoons in the Classroom." *International Studies Perspectives* 3(3): 258–70.

Drury, Roger M. 1980. "Providence at Elrond's Council." *Mythlore* 25: 8–9.

Edkins, Jenny, and Maja Zehfuss, eds. 2009. *Global Politics: A New Introduction*. New York: Routledge.

Ehrenreich, Barbara, and Arlie Russell Hochschild, eds. 2002. *Global Woman: Nannies, Maids, and Sex Workers in the New Economy*. New York: Henry Holt.

Elias, Juanita, and Lucy Ferguson. 2010. "Production, Employment, and Consumption." In *Gender Matters in Global Politics: A Feminist Introduction to International Relations*, edited by Laura J. Shepherd, 234–47. London: Routledge.

El-Saadawi, Nawal. 1977/1980. *The Hidden Face of Eve: Women in the Arab World*. Translated by Sherif Hetata. London; New York: Zed Books.

Elshtain, Jean Bethke. 1987. *Women and War*. New York: Basic Books.

Enloe, Cynthia. 1993. *The Morning After: Sexual Politics at the End of the Cold War*. Berkeley: University of California Press.

Enloe, Cynthia. 2000a. *Bananas, Beaches, and Bases: Making Feminist Sense of International Politics*. 2nd ed. Berkeley: University of California Press.

Enloe, Cynthia. 2000b. *Maneuvers: The International Politics of Militarizing Women's Lives*. Berkeley: University of California Press.

Enloe, Cynthia. 2004. *The Curious Feminist: Searching for Women in a New Age of Empire*. Berkeley: University of California Press.

Enloe, Cynthia. 2007a. *Does Khaki Become You? The Militarization of Women's Lives.* Berkeley: University of California Press.

Enloe, Cynthia. 2007b. *Globalization and Militarism: Feminists Make the Link.* Lanham, MD: Rowman & Littlefield.

Enloe, Cynthia. 2010. *Nimo's War, Emma's War: Making Feminist Sense of the Iraq War.* Berkeley: University of California Press.

Finnemore, Martha, and Kathryn Sikkink. 2001. "Taking Stock: The Constructivist Research Program in International Relations and Comparative Politics." *Annual Review of Political Science* 4(1): 391–416.

Fischer, Frank. 1998. "Beyond Empiricism: Policy Inquiry in Postpositivist Perspective." *Policy Studies Journal,* 26(1): 129–46.

Follett, Mary Parker. (1942) 2003. "Power." In *Dynamic Administration: The Collected Papers of Mary Parker Follett,* edited by Henry C. Metcalf and L. Urwick, 72–95. New York: Harper.

Fonstad, Karen Wynn. (1979) 1991. *The Atlas of Middle-earth.* Rev. ed. Boston: Houghton Mifflin.

Fraser, Nancy. 1989. *Unruly Practices: Power, Discourse, and Gender in Contemporary Social Theory.* Minneapolis: University of Minnesota Press.

Friedan, Betty. 1963. *The Feminine Mystique.* New York: W. W. Norton.

Fukuyama, Francis. 1998. "Women and the Evolution of World Politics." *Foreign Affairs* 77(5): 24–40.

Goldstein, Joshua S. 2001. *War and Gender: How Gender Shapes the War System and Vice Versa.* Cambridge: Cambridge University Press.

Goldstein, Joshua S., and Jon C. Pevehouse. 2009. *International Relations,* 2008–2009 Update. 8th ed. New York: Longman.

Gray, Thomas. 1980. "Bureaucratization in *The Lord of the Rings.*" *Mythlore* 24: 3–5.

Griffin, Penny. 2010. "Development Institutions and Neoliberal Globalization." In *Gender Matters in Global Politics: A Feminist Introduction to International Relations,* edited by Laura J. Shepherd, 218–33. London: Routledge.

Habermas, Jürgen. 1971. *Knowledge and Human Interests,* trans. Jeremy J. Shapiro. Boston: Beacon Press.

Hall, Lavina, ed. 1993. *Negotiation: Strategies for Mutual Gain: The Basic Seminar of the Harvard Program on Negotiation.* Newbury Park, CA: Sage.

Hall, Martin. 2006. "The Fantasy of Realism, or Mythology as Methodology." In *Harry Potter and International Relations,* edited by Daniel H. Nexon and Iver B. Neumann, 177–96. Oxford: Rowman & Littlefield.

Hansen, Lene. 2010. "Ontologies, Epistemologies, Methodologies." In *Gender Matters in Global Politics: A Feminist Introduction to International Relations,* edited by Laura J. Shepherd, 17–27. London: Routledge.

Harding, Sandra. 1986. *The Science Question in Feminism.* Ithaca: Cornell University Press.

Harding, Sandra. 1990. "Starting Thought from Women's Lives: Eight Resources for Maximizing Objectivity." *Journal of Social Philosophy* 21(2–3): 140–49.

Harding, Sandra, ed. 2004. *The Feminist Standpoint Theory Reader: Intellectual and Political Controversies.* New York: Routledge.

Hewitt, Nancy, ed. 2010. *No Permanent Waves: Recasting Histories of U.S. Feminism.* New Brunswick, NJ: Rutgers University Press.

Ho, T. 1983. "The Childlike Hobbit and *The Lord of the Rings*." *Mythlore* 9: 3–9.

Hollis, Martin, and Steve Smith. 1990. *Explaining and Understanding International Relations.* Oxford: Clarendon Press.

Hooker, Mark T. 2004. "Frodo's Batman." *Tolkien Studies* 1(1): 125–36.

Hooper, Charlotte. 1998. "Masculinist Practices and Gender Politics: The Operation of Multiple Masculinities in International Relations." In *The "Man" Question in International Relations,* edited by Marysia Zalewski and Jane Parpart, 28–53. Boulder, CO: Westview Press.

Howland, Courtney W., ed. 2001. *Religious Fundamentalisms and the Human Rights of Women.* 2nd ed.. New York: Palgrave.

Hunt, Krista. 2010. "The 'War on Terrorism.'" In *Gender Matters in Global Politics: A Feminist Introduction to International Relations,* edited by Laura J. Shepherd, 116–26. London: Routledge.

Hunt, Michael. 1987. *Ideology and US Foreign Policy.* New Haven: Yale University Press.

Hutchings, Kimberly. 2010. "Ethics." In *Gender Matters in Global Politics: A Feminist Introduction to International Relations,* edited by Laura J. Shepherd, 61–73. London: Routledge.

Inayatullah, Naeem. 2010. "Why Do Some People Think They Know What Is Good for Others?" In *Global Politics: A New Introduction,* edited by Jenny Edkins and Maja Zehfuss, 344–69. New York: Routledge.

James, Patrick. 2002. *International Relations and Scientific Progress: Structural Realism Reconsidered.* Columbus: Ohio State University Press.

Jang, Gyoung Sun. 2009. "The Sexual Politics of the Interwar Era Global Governance: Historicizing the Women's Transnational Movements With(in) the League of Nations, 1919–1940." PhD diss., Clark University.

Jayawardena, Kumari. 1986. *Feminism and Nationalism in the Third World.* New Delhi: Zed Books.

Jenkins, Lee. 2010. "Dynasty: Beginning or Ending?" *Sports Illustrated,* 28 June: 40–44.

Johnson, Allan G. 2005. *The Gender Knot: Unraveling Our Patriarchal Legacy.* Revised and Updated ed. Philadelphia: Temple University Press.

Kauppinen, Kaisa, and Iiris Aaltio. 2003. "Leadership, Power, and Gender." In *Encyclopedia of Sex and Gender: Men and Women in the World's Cultures,* edited by Carol R. Ember and Melvin Ember, 97–106. New York: Kluwer.

Kegley, Charles W., Jr., with Shannon L. Blanton. 2010. *World Politics: Trend and Transformation.* 2009–2010 Update ed., 12th ed. Boston: Wadsworth Publishing.

Keohane, Robert O. 1988. "International Institutions: Two Approaches." *International Studies Quarterly* 32(4): 379–96.

Keohane, Robert O. 1998. "Beyond Dichotomy: Conversations between International Relations and Feminist Theory." *International Studies Quarterly* 42(1): 193–97.

Kocher, Paul. 2004. "Middle-earth: An Imaginary World?" In *Understanding The*

Lord of the Rings: The Best of Tolkien Criticism, edited by Ross A. Zimbardo and Neil D. Isaacs, 142–62. Boston: Houghton Mifflin.

Kratochwil, Friedrich V. 1989. *Rules, Norms, and Decisions: On the Conditions of Practical and Legal Reasoning in International Relations and Domestic Affairs.* Cambridge: Cambridge University Press.

Kraue, Joe. 2003. "Tolkien, Modernism, and the Importance of Tradition." In *The Lord of the Rings and Philosophy*, edited by Gregory Bassham and Eric Bronson, 137–49. Peru, IL: Carus Publishing.

Krolokke, Charlotte, and Ann Scott Sorensen. 2005. *Gender Communication Theories and Analyses: From Silence to Performance.* Thousand Oaks, CA: Sage.

Kuzma, Lynn, and Patrick Haney. 2001. "And Action . . . ! Using Film to Learn about Foreign Policy." *International Studies Perspectives* 2(1): 33–50.

Lapid, Yosef. 1989. "The Third Debate." *International Studies Quarterly* 33: 235–54.

Lapid, Yosef, and Friedrich Kratochwil, eds. 1996. *The Return of Culture and Identity in IR Theory.* Boulder: Lynne Rienner Publishers.

Lense, E. 1976. "Sauron Is Watching You." *Mythlore* 13: 3–6.

Levitin, Alexis. 1969. "Power in *The Lord of the Rings.*" *Orcrist* 4: 11–14.

Lloyd, Paul M. 1976. "The Role of Warfare and Strategy in *The Lord of the Rings.*" *Mythlore* 11: 3–7.

Mansbach, Richard W., and Kirsten L. Rafferty. 2008. *Introduction to Global Politics.* New York: Routledge.

Mernissi, Fatema. 1975. *Beyond the Veil: Male-Female Dynamics in Modern Muslim Society.* London: Al Saqi Books.

Michaeli, Merav. 2011. "Exclusive: Now You See Them, Now You Don't." *Women's Media Center Exclusive*, 25 May. http://womensmediacenter.com/feature/entry/now-you-see-them-now-you-dont (accessed 26 May 2011).

Milbank, Alison. 2003. "'My Precious': Tolkien's Fetishized Ring." In *The Lord of the Rings and Philosophy*, edited by Gregory Bassham and Eric Bronson, 33–45. Peru, IL: Carus Publishing.

Miles, Rufus E. 1978. "The Origin and Meaning of Miles' Law." *Public Administration Review* 38: 399–403.

Mingst, Karen A. 2008. *Essentials of International Relations.* 4th ed. New York: W. W. Norton.

Mohanty, Chandra Talpade. 1988. "Under Western Eyes: Feminist Scholarship and Colonial Discourses." *boundary* 2 12(3): 333–58.

Moon, Katharine H. S. 1997. *Sex among Allies: Military Prostitution in U.S.-Korea Relations.* New York: Columbia University Press.

Morgan, April. 2006. "*The Poisonwood Bible:* An Antidote for What Ails International Relations?" *International Political Science Review* 27: 379–403.

Nau, Henry R. 2009. *Perspectives on International Relations: Power, Institutions, Ideas.* 2nd ed. Washington, DC: CQ Press.

Nau, Scott C. 1972. "War and Pacifism in *The Lord of the Rings.*" *Tolkien Journal* 15: 23–30.

Nexon, Daniel H., and Iver B. Neuman, eds. 2006. *Harry Potter and International Relations.* Lanham, MD: Rowman & Littlefield.

Nussbaum, Martha C. 1999. *Sex and Social Justice.* Oxford: Oxford University Press.

O'Brien, Tim. 1990. *The Things They Carried.* New York: Broadway Books.

O'Connor, Gerard. 1971. "Why Tolkien's *Lord of the Rings* Should *Not* Be Popular Culture." *Extrapolation* 13(1): 48–55.

Onuf, Nicholas G. 1989. *World of Our Making: Rules and Rule in Social Theory and International Relations.* Columbia: University of South Carolina Press.

Pankhurst, Donna. 2010. "Sexual Violence in War." In *Gender Matters in Global Politics: A Feminist Introduction to International Relations,* edited by Laura J. Shepherd. London: Routledge.

Peterson, V. Spike. 2003. *A Critical Rewriting of Global Political Economy: Integrating Reproductive, Productive, and Virtual Economies.* New York: Routledge.

Peterson, V. Spike. 2009. "How Is the World Organized Economically?" In *Global Politics: A New Introduction,* edited by Jenny Edkins and Maja Zehfuss, 271–93. New York: Routledge.

Peterson, V. Spike, and Anne Sisson Runyan. 1999. *Global Gender Issues.* 2nd ed. Boulder, CO: Westview Press.

Peterson, V. Spike, and Jacqui True. 1998. "New Times and New Conversations." In *The "Man Question" in International Relations,* edited by Marisa Zalewski and Jane Parpart, 14–27. Boulder, CO: Westview Press.

Pettman, Jan Jindy. 1996. *Worlding Women: A Feminist International Politics.* Sydney, Australia: Allen and Unwin.

Price, Richard, and Christian Reus-Smit. 1998. "Dangerous Liaisons? Critical International Theory and Constructivism." *European Journal of International Relations* 4: 259–94.

Ray, James Lee, and Juliet Kaarbo. 2008. *Global Politics.* 9th ed. Boston: Houghton Mifflin.

Reus-Smit, Christian. 2008. "International Law." In *The Globalization of World Politics: An Introduction to International Relations.* edited by John Baylis, Steve Smith, and Patricia Owens, 278–94. 4th ed. Oxford: Oxford University Press.

Richardson, William D., and Ronald L. McNinch. 1996. "Citizenship, Community, and Ethics: Forrest Gump as a Moral Exemplary." *Public Voices* 2(1): 82–96.

Roach, Steven C., ed. 2007. *Critical Theory and International Relations: A Reader.* New York: Routledge.

Rourke, John T., and Mark A. Boyer. 2010. *International Politics on the World Stage.* 8th ed. Boston: McGraw-Hill.

Rowley, Christina. 2007. "*Firefly/Serenity:* Gendered Space and Gendered Bodies." *British Journal of Politics and International Relations* 9(2): 318–25.

Ruane, Abigail E. 2006. "'Real Men' and Diplomats: Intercultural Diplomatic Negotiations and Masculinities in China and the United States." *International Studies Perspectives* 7(4): 342–59.

Ruane, Abigail E. 2010. "Pursuing Inclusive Interests, Both Deep and Wide: Women's Human Rights and the United Nations." PhD diss., University of Southern California, School of International Relations, May. Available at http://digitallibrary.usc.edu/assetserver/controller/item/etd-Ruane-3494.pdf (accessed 3 January 2011).

Ruggie, John Gerard. 1998. "What Makes the World Hang Together? Neo-utilitarianism and the Social Constructivist Challenge." *International Organization* 52(4): 855–85.

Rupp, Leila. 1997. *Worlds of Women: The Making of an International Women's Movement.* Princeton, NJ: Princeton University Press.

Russett, Bruce, Harvey Starr, and David Kinsella. 2010. *World Politics: The Menu for Choice.* 9th ed.. Boston: Wadsworth Cengage.

Schick, Theodore. 2003. "The Cracks of Doom: The Threat of Emerging Technologies and Tolkien's Rings of Power." In *The Lord of the Rings and Philosophy,* edited by Gregory Bassham and Eric Bronson, 21–32. Peru, IL: Carus Publishing.

Schmidt, Brian C. 1998. *The Political Discourse of Anarchy: A Disciplinary History.* Albany: State University of New York Press.

Scott, Nan C. 1972. "War and Pacifism in *The Lord of the Rings.*" *Tolkien Journal* 15: 23–25, 27–30.

Scull, Christina. 1992. "Open Minds, Closed Minds in *The Lord of the Rings.*" In *Proceedings of the J. R. R. Tolkien Centenary Conference, 1992,* edited by Patricia Reynolds and Glen GoodKnight, 151–56. Altadena, CA: Mythopoeic Press.

Seager, Joni. 2003. *The Penguin Atlas of Women in the World, Completely Revised and Updated.* New York: Penguin.

Shapcott, Richard. 2008. "International Ethics." In *The Globalization of World Politics: An Introduction to International Relations,* edited by John Baylis, Steve Smith, and Patricia Owens, 192–206. 4th ed. Oxford: Oxford University Press.

Sharma, Chandradhar. 2000. *A Critical Survey of Indian Philosophy.* Delhi: Motilal Banardsidass.

Shepherd, Laura J., ed. 2010a. *Gender Matters in Global Politics: A Feminist Introduction to International Relations.* London: Routledge.

Shepherd, Laura J. 2010b. "Sex or Gender? Bodies in World Politics and Why Gender Matters." In *Gender Matters in Global Politics: A Feminist Introduction to International Relations,* edited by Laura J. Shepherd, 3–16. London: Routledge.

Shippey, T. A. 2001. *J. R. R. Tolkien: Author of the Century.* New York: Houghton Mifflin.

Sjoberg, Laura. 2006. *Gender, Justice, and the Wars in Iraq: A Feminist Reformulation of Just War Theory.* Lanham, MD: Lexington Books.

Sjoberg, Laura. 2009. "Introduction to Security Studies: Feminist Contributions." *Security Studies* 18(2): 183–213.

Sjoberg, Laura, and Caron Gentry. 2008. *Mothers, Monsters, Whores: Women's Violence in Global Politics.* London: Zed Books.

Sjoberg, Laura, and Jessica Peet. 2011. "Targeting Women in Wars: Feminist Contributions." In *Feminist International Relations: Conversations about the Past, Present, and Future,* edited by J. Ann Tickner and Laura Sjoberg, 169–87. New York: Routledge.

Sklar, Kathryn Kish, James Brewer Stewart, and Gilder Lehrman. 2007. *Women's Rights and Transatlantic Antislavery in the Era of Emancipation.* New Haven, CT: Yale University Press.

Skoble, Aeon. 2003. "Virtue and Vice in *The Lord of the Rings.*" In *The Lord of the*

Rings and Philosophy, edited by Gregory Bassham and Eric Bronson, 110–20. Peru, IL: Carus Publishing.

Snyder, Richard C., H. W. Bruck, and Burton Sapin, with Valerie Hudson, Derek H. Chollet, and James M. Goldgeier. 2002. *Foreign Policy Decision-Making (Revisited).* New York: Palgrave Macmillan.

Springer, Kimberly. 2002. "Third Wave Black Feminism?" *Signs* 27(4): 1059–82.

Stanton, Elizabeth Cady. 1848. *Declaration of Sentiments.* http://www.fordham.edu/halsall/mod/Senecafalls.html (accessed 1 June 2011).

Steans, Jill. 1998. *Gender and International Relations: An Introduction.* New Brunswick, NJ: Rutgers University Press.

Steans, Jill. 2003. "Engaging from the Margins: Feminist Encounters with the 'Mainstream' of International Relations." *British Journal of Politics and International Relations* 5(3): 428–54.

Steans, Jill, and Lloyd Pettiford, with Thomas Diez. 2005. *Introduction to International Relations: Perspectives and Themes.* 2nd ed. New York: Pearson Prentice Hall.

Stein, Steven J., and Howard E. Book. 2006. *The EQ Edge.* Rev. ed. Missasauga, ON: Jossey-Bass.

Steinberg, Blema S. 2008. *Women in Power: The Personalities and Leadership Styles of Indira Gandhi, Golda Meir, and Margaret Thatcher.* Montreal: McGill-Queens University Press.

Sylvester, Christine. 1994a. "Empathetic Cooperation: A Feminist Method for IR." *Millennium* 23(2): 315–34.

Sylvester, Christine. 1994b. *Feminist Theory and International Relations in a Postmodern Era.* Cambridge: Cambridge University Press.

Sylvester, Christine. 2002a. *Feminist International Relations: An Unfinished Journey.* Cambridge: Cambridge University Press.

Sylvester, Christine. 2002b. "'Progress' as Feminist International Relations." In *Millennial Reflections on International Studies,* edited by Michael Brecher and Frank P. Harvey, 312–20. Ann Arbor: University of Michigan Press.

Tétreault, Mary Ann, and Ronnie D. Lipschutz. 2009. *Global Politics as if People Mattered.* 2nd ed. Lanham, MD: Rowman & Littlefield.

Tessler, Mark, and Ina Warriner. 1997. "Gender, Feminism, and Attitudes toward International Conflict: Exploring Relationships with Survey Data from the Middle East." *World Politics* 49(2): 250–81.

Tickner, J. Ann. 1992. *Gender in International Relations: Feminist Perspectives on Achieving Global Security.* New York: Columbia University Press.

Tickner, J. Ann. 1997. "You Just Don't Understand: Troubled Engagements between Feminists and IR Theorists." *International Studies Quarterly* 41(4): 611–32.

Tickner, J. Ann. 1998. "'Continuing the Conversation . . .': Response to Keohane." *International Studies Quarterly* 42(1): 205–10.

Tickner, J. Ann. 1999. "Why Women Can't Run the World: International Politics According to Francis Fukuyama." *International Studies Review* 1(3): 3–11.

Tickner, J. Ann. 2001. *Gendering World Politics: Issues and Approaches in the Post–Cold War Era.* New York: Columbia University Press.

Tickner, J. Ann. 2005. "What Is Your Research Program? Some Feminist Answers to International Relations Methodological Questions." *International Studies Quarterly* 49(1): 1–21.

Tickner, J. Ann. 2008. "Gender in World Politics." In *The Globalization of World Politics: An Introduction to International Relations,* edited by John Baylis, Steve Smith, and Patricia Owens, 262–77. 4th ed. Oxford: Oxford University Press.

Tickner, J. Ann. 2011. "War and Feminist Lenses: An Engagement." In *Feminist International Relations: Conversations about the Past, Present, and Future,* edited by J. Ann Tickner and Laura Sjoberg, 188–93. New York: Routledge.

Tierney, Michael J. 2007. "Schoolhouse Rock: Pedagogy, Politics, and Pop." *International Studies Perspectives* 8(1): iii–v.

Tinning, R. 1992. "Reading Action Research: Notes on Knowledge and Human Interests." *Quest* 44: 1–14.

Titscher, Stefan, Michael Meyer, Ruth Wodak, and Eva Vetter. 2000. *Methods of Text and Discourse Analysis.* London: Thousand Oaks, CA, Sage.

Tolkien, J. R. R. 1977. *The Silmarillion.* Edited by Christopher Tolkien. Boston: Houghton Mifflin.

Tolkien, J. R. R. 1980. *Unfinished Tales of Númenor and Middle-earth.* Edited by Christopher Tolkien. Boston: Houghton Mifflin.

Tolkien, J. R. R. 1993/1994. *The Lord of the Rings* [I: *The Fellowship of the Ring;* II: *The Two Towers;* III: *The Return of the King*]. Boston: Houghton Mifflin.

Tolkien, J. R. R. 1996. *The Hobbit, or There and Back Again.* Boston: Houghton Mifflin.

Tolkien, J. R. R. 2002a. *The History of Middle-earth I.* Edited by Christopher Tolkien. London: HarperCollins.

Tolkien, J. R. R. 2002b. *The History of Middle-earth II.* Edited by Christopher Tolkien. London: HarperCollins.

Tolkien, J. R. R. 2002c. *The History of Middle-earth III.* Edited by Christopher Tolkien. London: HarperCollins.

Tong, Rosemarie Putnam. 1998. *Feminist Thought: A More Comprehensive Introduction.* 2nd ed. Boulder, CO: Westview Press.

Tyler, J. E. A. 1976. *The Tolkien Companion.* New York: Gramercy Books.

Vasquez, John A. 1999. *The Power of Power Politics: From Classical Realism to Neotraditionalism.* Cambridge: Cambridge University Press.

Viotti, Paul R., and Mark V. Kauppi. 2009. *International Relations and World Politics: Security, Economy, Identity.* 4th ed. Upper Saddle River, NJ: Pearson Prentice Hall.

Waalkes, Scott. 2003. "Using Film Clips as Cases to Teach the Rise and 'Decline' of the State." *International Studies Perspectives* 4(2): 156–74.

Waever, Ole. 1996. "The Rise and Fall of the Inter-paradigm Debate." In *International Theory: Positivism and Beyond,* edited by Steve Smith, Ken Booth, and Marysia Zalewski, 149–85. Cambridge: Cambridge University Press.

Waltz, Kenneth. 1959. *Theory of International Politics.* New York: Columbia University Press.

Waring, Marilyn. 1988. *If Women Counted: A New Feminist Economics.* San Francisco: Harper & Row.

Waylen, Georgina. 1996. *Gender in Third World Politics*. Boulder, CO: Lynne Rienner.

Webber, Julie. 2005. "Independence Day as a Cosmopolitan Moment: Teaching International Relations." *International Studies Perspectives* 6(3): 374–92.

Weber, Cynthia. 2001. "The Highs and Lows of Teaching IR Theory: Using Popular Films for Theoretical Critique." *International Studies Perspectives* 2(3): 281–87.

Weber, Cynthia. 2005. *International Relations Theory: A Critical Introduction*. 2nd ed. London: Routledge.

Weldes, Jutta, ed. 2003. *Confronting Strange Worlds: Exploring Links between Science Fiction and World Politics*. New York: Palgrave Macmillan.

Wendt, Alexander. 1998. "On Constitution and Causation in International Relations." *Review of International Studies* 24: 101–18.

Wendt, Alexander. 1999. *Social Theory of International Politics*. Cambridge: Cambridge University Press.

West, John, Jr. 2002. "The Lord of the Rings as a Defense of Western Civilization." In *Celebrating Middle-earth: The Lord of the Rings as a Defense of Western Civilization*, edited by John G. West Jr, 15–30. Seattle: Inkling Books.

West, Richard C. 1981. *Tolkien Criticism: An Annotated Checklist*. Rev. ed. Kent, OH: Kent State University Press.

Whittick, Arnold. 1979. *Woman into Citizen*. Santa Barbara, CA: ABC Clio.

Wibben, Annick T. R. 2009. "Who Do We Think We Are?" In *Global Politics: A New Introduction*, edited by Jenny Edkins and Maja Zehfuss, 70–96. New York: Routledge.

Wight, Martin. 1992. *International Theory: The Three Traditions*. New York: Holmes & Meier.

Wilcox, Lauren. 2009. "Gendering the Cult of the Offensive." *Security Studies* 18(2): 214–40.

Wodak, Ruth, and Michael Meyer, eds. 2001. *Methods of Critical Discourse Analysis*. London: Sage.

Wollstonecraft, Mary. 1792. *A Vindication of the Rights of Women*. London: T. Fisher Unwin. Available to search at http://books.google.com/ebooks/ (accessed 1 June 2011).

Wood, Molly M. 2005. "Diplomatic Wives: The Politics of Domesticity and the 'Social Game' in the U.S. Foreign Service, 1905–1941." *Journal of Women's History* 17(2): 142–65.

Wood, Ralph. 2003. "Tolkien's Transformation of Justice into Pity in *The Lord of the Rings*." Paper delivered at the American Political Science Association, 29 August. http://bearspace.baylor.edu/Ralph_Wood/www/tolkien/Tolkien MercyJustice.pdf (accessed 4 December 2009).

Wright, J. Lenore. 2003. "Sam and Frodo's Excellent Adventure: Tolkien's Journey Motif." In *The Lord of the Rings and Philosophy*, edited by Gregory Bassham and Eric Bronson, 192–203. Peru, IL: Carus Publishing.

Young, Iris Marion. 2003. "The Logic of Masculinist Protection: Reflections on the Current Security State." *Signs: Journal of Women in Culture and Society* 29: 1–25.

Zehfuss, Maja. 2002. *Constructivism in International Relations: The Politics of Reality*. Cambridge: Cambridge University Press.

Zehfuss, Maja. 2009. "Conclusion: What Can We Do to Change the World?" In *Global Politics: A New Introduction*, edited by Jenny Edkins and Maja Zehfuss, 483–501. New York: Routledge.

Zalewski, Marysia. 2000. *Feminism after Postmodernism: Theorizing through Practice.* London: Routledge.

Zalewski, Marysia. 2010. "Feminist International Relations: Making Sense . . ." In *Gender Matters in Global Politics: A Feminist Introduction to International Relations*, edited by Laura J. Shepherd, 28–43. London: Routledge.

Index